Alison Jasper received her doctorate from the University of Glasgow and lives in Lanarkshire, Scotland.

JOURNAL FOR THE STUDY OF THE NEW TESTAMENT
SUPPLEMENT SERIES
165

Executive Editor
Stanley E. Porter

GENDER, CULTURE, THEORY
6

Editor
J. Cheryl Exum

Sheffield Academic Press

The Shining Garment of the Text

Gendered Readings of John's Prologue

Alison Jasper

Journal for the Study of the New Testament
Supplement Series 165

Gender, Culture, Theory 6

For David, Jean and Maurice, with my love and thanks.

Copyright © 1998 Sheffield Academic Press

Published by Sheffield Academic Press Ltd
Mansion House
19 Kingfield Road
Sheffield S11 9AS
England

Printed on acid-free paper in Great Britain
by Bookcraft Ltd
Midsomer Norton, Bath

British Library Cataloguing in Publication Data

A catalogue record for this book is available
from the British Library

ISBN 1 85075 893 X
ISBN 1 85075 889 1 pbk

CONTENTS

Preface   9
Acknowledgments   11
Abbreviations   12

Chapter 1
INTRODUCTION: READING THE CHRISTIAN SCRIPTURES
AS A WOMAN-CENTRED CRITIC   13
1. Revealing the Truth   13
2. Revealing Which Text?
   What Does the Emperor's Nakedness Signify?   17
3. The Aims of the Present Work   19
4. The Shape of the Study   22
5. Methodological Considerations   25
6. The Shining Garment of the Text   31

PART I

Chapter 2
HAVING HIS CAKE AND EATING IT: THE SYMBOLISM OF
GENDER IN AUGUSTINE'S *TRACTATES* ON THE PROLOGUE
OF JOHN'S GOSPEL   34
1. Introduction   34
2. Female Figures in Augustine's *Tractates*
   on the Prologue of John's Gospel   36
3. The Feminine Identification of Carnality   42
4. The Word Made Flesh?   47
5. Woman and the Feminine and Gender Hierarchy
   in Relation to Dualism and Original Sin   48
6. Conclusions   55

Chapter 3
HILDEGARD OF BINGEN 1098–1179: VISIONARY REFLECTIONS
ON THE PROLOGUE   58
1. Introduction: *Liber divinorum operum*   58
2. The Prologue of John's Gospel   63
3. Hildegard's Reading of Gender in John 1.1-14   73
4. Conclusions   82

Chapter 4
RIDDLES FOR FEMINIST READERS: MARTIN LUTHER'S SERMONS
ON THE PROLOGUE, 1537   87
1. Setting the Scene   87
2. Luther and the Prologue   87
3. The First Riddle: The Absence of Christ's Mother   95
4. The Second Riddle: The Presence of Mary   99
5. Finally, Yet Another Riddle: When Is a Relationship
   not a Relationship?   108
6. Conclusions   111

Chapter 5
DEMYTHOLOGIZING (THE FEMININE) WITHIN RUDOLF BULT-
MANN'S COMMENTARY ON THE PROLOGUE (JOHN 1.1-18)   113
1. A View of Bultmann's Theological and Exegetical Approach 113
2. Feminist Presuppositions   115
3. The Addressing of (Wo)men?   115
4. Selection as a Form of Gendered Interpretation?   119
5. Demythologizing (the Marginalized Mother)   122
6. An Offensive Gospel   127
7. Seductive or Intimidating Otherness?   129
8. Suspicious Conclusions   131

Chapter 6
A SECOND GLANCE AT ADRIENNE VON SPEYR   135
1. Mystic or Masochist?   135
2. A Modern Feminist Reading Context   137
3. Opening Some of the Doors   140
4. Conclusions   159

PART II

Chapter 7
WHICH CAME FIRST: WORD OR THE WORDS? TOWARDS A
FEMINIST TRANSFORMATION 162
1. Some Introductory Remarks to Part II 162
2. Part II—The Possibilities of New Readings? 164
3. A Feminist Critique of the Prologue 165
4. Rhetorical Readings for Women and the Feminine 169
5. A Rhetorical Myth of Feminist Interpretation: God
as Desiring and Inarticulate 177
6. Women Readers? 179
7. Conclusions 180

Chapter 8
FLESH INSIGHTS ON THE PROLOGUE OF JOHN'S GOSPEL 183
1. A Second 'New' Reading of the Prologue 183
2. Word Become Flesh 183
3. 'Σάρξ' and its Evil Associates 193
4. The Prologue 193
5. Eating the Flesh That Is of no Avail (John 6) 198
6. Feminist Suspicions 207
7. Conclusions 209

Chapter 9
IN THE BEGINNING WAS LOVE 210
1. Introduction 210
2. Julia Kristeva and the *Sujet en Procès* 212
3. Reading the Prologue 221
4. Conclusions 232

Chapter 10
CONCLUSION: WRESTLING WITH THE ANGEL 234
1. The Context: Phallogocentricity 234
2. Five Historical Readings 236
3. Challenging the Direction of Traditional Interpretation:
Three Readings 240
4. Should Women Read the Prologue? 242

Bibliography   248
Index of References   255
Index of Authors   258
General Index   260

PREFACE

This book is concerned with the issues facing me as a woman-centred reader of the Christian Scriptures. I am concerned, for example, with the process whereby women's experience has been given or denied value within patriarchal culture. I believe that the patriarchal culture, determined by an approach to human experience which I have described as 'phallogocentric', has used gender difference in a signatory or symbolic sense and that it has employed the *feminine* gender to define an 'otherness' against which it promotes or defends its own identity and value. In consequence, women and, by extension, whatever is associated with their differentiated experiences have suffered a generalized devaluation which, in the most extreme instances, amounts to an attempt to abolish or exclude them altogether. I am also concerned with the sense in which this phallogocentric approach has determined the process of biblical interpretation, demanding singular, exclusive readings of texts whose authority must be guaranteed by the assumption of a transcendent presence or truth.

First of all, my aim is to illustrate this analysis of reading practices within a patriarchal context by examining, in some detail, the interpretative work of five historical readers. In order to contain the project within manageable limits, I have concentrated on a short scriptural text: the Prologue of John's Gospel (Jn 1.1-18). The chosen text is of particular interest because it is linked, thematically, to Christian teaching about Incarnation and yet avoids, in any explicit sense, references to the female character of Mary or to the role of a human woman in bringing the Incarnate Word to birth, leaving the passage open to Docetic or Gnostic interpretations that orthodox Christian teaching always rejects, at least in theory. The five readers represent points of view that are widely separated in experience and historical context, from Augustine, a fifth-century African bishop, to Adrienne von Speyr, a professional woman living in Europe within the latter half of the twentieth century. Yet their interpretations exhibit a common tendency to employ the symbols of woman and the feminine as if they signified the absence or lack of value defined against the absolute validity of masculine-identified divine presence.

The second aim of this book is to propose interpretation of the same passage that resists the interpretative tendencies I have noted in the five historical readings. In order to fulfil this aim, I have given three different readings of the text. These employ both deconstructive and constructive/structuralist forms of criticism. Deconstructive criticism, for example, reveals the ironic potential of this text for affirming the prior necessity of feminine-identified humanity. It uncovers the bloody and satisfying feminine-identified corporeality that lies beneath spiritualized and Eucharistic interpretations of the Word made 'flesh'. A constructive criticism presents the text in terms of the development—an Incarnation—of the human subject, or what Julia Kristeva calls the *sujet en procès*. Taken together, the three readings represent an interpretative multiplicity that, I believe, does justice both to possibilities within the text and also to the necessary multiplicity—in Kristeva's terms, the heterogeneity—of the reader. In this way, I am able to conclude that this particular textual garment may still be 'put on', that is, found significant, by women readers.

ACKNOWLEDGMENTS

Thanks are always due, first of all, to those people who listen sympathetically, wash the dishes, do the shopping, look after the children and help pay the bills so that there is space, time and energy for reading, writing and thinking. For all this and much more, thank you Jean, Maurice and David. Thanks are also due to those people who find it quite difficult to understand why anyone should want to spend five years studying the Bible at all, but still put up with the inconvenience. For this and much more, thank you Hannah, Ruth and May.

While I accept full responsibility for any errors, I believe that a published work is ultimately a joint effort. Whatever is positive and useful in this book must be seen as the result of conversations with thoughtful and generous friends, face to face or through the medium of their books and articles. To all of these very many people I wish to say 'thank you' for your ideas and for your time.

In particular I would like to thank Dorothy Porter Macmillan and Alastair Hunter of Glasgow University for their support and encouragement at an early stage in my postgraduate work. I should also like to acknowledge the kindness and support of all members of the Divinity Faculty and the Centre for the Study of Literature and Theology at Glasgow University. Very special thanks are due to Pamela Sue Anderson of Sunderland University for the many useful comments and suggestions she has made and for her sustaining friendship.

And finally, I should like to thank my supervisor, Professor John Riches. Thank you for your patience. Thank you for helping me, both as a teacher and in other practical ways. I am more grateful than I can possibly say.

ABBREVIATIONS

AB	Anchor Bible
JAAR	*Journal of the American Academy of Religion*
JSNTSup	*Journal for the Study of the New Testament*, Supplement Series
JSOT	*Journal for the Study of the Old Testament*
JSOTSup	*Journal for the Study of the Old Testament*, Supplement Series
JTS	*Journal of Theological Studies*
NCB	New Century Bible
NTS	*New Testament Studies*
RSV	Revised Standard Version
ST	*Studia theologica*

1

Introduction: Reading the Christian Scriptures as a Woman-centred Critic

'Why, he hasn't got anything on!' the whole crowd was shouting at last; and the Emperor's flesh crept, for it seemed to him they were right. 'But all the same,' he thought to himself, 'I must go through with the procession.' So he held himself more proudly than before, and the lords in waiting walked on bearing the train—the train that wasn't there at all.[1]

1. Revealing the Truth

What I want to challenge in the course of this book is the notion that readers can, even theoretically, approach a final, single or definitive understanding of biblical texts. The claim that this is possible concerns me because I believe that it is born out of a culture of univalence and singularity that has been extremely damaging in the past and most particularly to women. Within the West, a logic of identity[2] largely resists

---

1.   Hans Andersen, *Forty-two Stories* (trans. M.R. James; London: Faber & Faber, 1968), p. 107.

2.   French philosopher Jacques Derrida focuses on what he sees as the adherence within Western philosophy to certain logical principles, for example, that everything that is, is, that nothing can both be and not be, and that everything must be either/or. Alternatively, it is expressed in the claim that the spoken word is simpler, clearer and promises a single authoritative interpretation, immune from the interpretative ambiguities of the written word (logocentrism), and should therefore be privileged. This drive towards all-encompassing singularity is also expressed, for example, in the symbol of the phallus as it is used by the French theorist and psychoanalyst Jacques Lacan, representing, as it were, the single and tangible goal of all our desires. The same all-encompassing singularity is expressed in the presence of binary dualisms—a set of oppositions that, between them, claim to 'cover the ground'. In the work of Hélène Cixous these binary dualisms, situated above all in language, exemplify an underlying dualism in terms of gender. See, for example, Hélène Cixous, 'Sorties: Out and Out: Attacks/Ways Out/Forays', in Susan Sellers (ed.), *The Hélène Cixous Reader* (London: Routledge, 1994), pp. 37-46.

polyvalent or multiple interpretations of texts and makes, of woman and the feminine, symbols of whatever the prevailing logic of singularity excludes or rejects. This has had a 'knock-on' effect on the roles of both female readers of the texts and of women or the feminine within the texts, rendering them symbolic of presences that are fundamentally perverse in one way or another.

I hope to demonstrate how the currents of singularity flow in relation both to historical textual interpretations and their presentation of the symbols of woman and the feminine. I attempt to complicate and problematize the apparent singularity of these symbols by presenting multiple readings of both text and symbols. And by doing this, finally, I try to present an example of critically creative reading practice for woman-centred readers, including myself.

During the 1970s and into the 1980s, a number of biblical critics, looking back to earlier traditions of women's interpretation,[3] began to draw attention to the plight of female characters within the Bible, especially what we call the Hebrew Bible and the Christian Old Testament. These characters were, they argued, shamefully mistreated by their fathers and other male relatives within the narratives. Phyllis Trible, for example, wanted us actively to mourn for women like Tamar, Amnon's sister,[4] and the unnamed concubine of Judges 19,[5] setting the drawing of a tombstone at the head of every chapter of her book, *Texts of Terror*.[6] These were, she argued, women who had been reduced to ciphers in struggles that were fundamentally to do with men and treated with quite appalling brutality and indifference as a result. Her work acted upon many readers in a manner rather similar to the way in which the little boy of the children's story about the Emperor's new clothes enabled all the people to 'see' that the Emperor was, in fact, wearing no clothes at all. The abuse, revealed within Scriptures held to be sacred, was shown for what it really was. It was no longer disguised or softened by alle-

---

3.   See particularly, of course, Elizabeth Cady Stanton's edited collection, first published in 1895, *The Woman's Bible* (New York: European Publishing Company). This was a collection of comments and commentaries written by women on a selection of biblical texts and designed to challenge the injustices to women contained there or in their interpretation.

4.   2 Sam. 13.1-22. See Phyllis Trible, *Texts of Terror: Literary-Feminist Readings of Biblical Narratives* (London: SCM Press, 1992), pp. 36-63.

5.   See Trible, *Texts of Terror*, pp. 64-91.

6.   See above, n. 4.

gorizing interpretations or the sort of focus that condoned brutality against women within the larger framework of Israel's salvific relationship with God.

This perception was important. It was particularly important for previously diffident women readers because it encouraged them to exercise a judgment on biblical texts, based on their own experience and feeling, in some cases their *fellow-feeling* with these victims of rape and male arrogance. They were able to articulate a vision of justice based on a *personal* sense of injustice. They were able to express their anger that stories like these had been presented to them as somehow authoritative for their lives as women. But this in itself drew attention to the fact that it was not simply male characters who brutalized female ones within 'sacred' Scripture. The women were being obscured or misrepresented by the sort of interpretation they were given. They were being abused by those who called the narratives 'sacred' in the first place. And it was clear that the majority of those who published or preached on the subject of sacred Scripture were, at that time, men and not women.

One serious implication of the growing view that women within the Bible were largely absent, treated as ciphers or badly used, was that it appeared to compromise the whole status of Scripture as the bearer of 'Good News'. From a more historical critical and faith-committed perspective, the early work of Elisabeth Schüssler Fiorenza sought to address the problem. Fiorenza drew attention to the interpreters. Practices of critical historical scholarship, she argued, were far from objective. They were coloured by largely unacknowledged sexist presuppositions that made it possible to ignore, for example, the evidence of women's significant presence within the earliest historical Christian communities. Moreover, she reminded her readers that history is largely written by the winners[7]—men rather than women in this case. She set to work to *reclaim* the history of those female 'losers', convinced that the New Testament could stand as a memorial to the full and autonomous role of women alongside men within the earliest Christian context.[8] And in this

7. Elisabeth Schüssler Fiorenza, *In Memory of Her: A Feminist Theological Reconstruction of Christian Origins* (London: SCM Press, 1983), p. xix. She is referring here to the words of Alex Haley, the African-American author of *Roots* (Garden City, NY: Doubleday, 1976), an epic retelling of the journey of African Americans from Africa to America.

8. See, for example, 'Remembering the Past in Creating the Future: Historical-critical Scholarship and Feminist Biblical Interpretation', in Adela Yarbro Collins

way she argued that the New Testament could also support the right of women to self-determination within the Christian churches and interpretative communities of the late twentieth century.

Alongside these early works of feminist biblical criticism, contemporary feminist theologians, such as Rosemary Radford Ruether and, more radically, Mary Daly, had drawn attention to the theological and mythological content of a Christian culture. The emphasis remained one of indicating how Christian theology and mythology was implicitly or explicitly hostile to women. Mary Daly eventually moved into a 'post-Christian' phase, concluding that Christian theology is simply the sacralizing of a deeply phallocratic[9] mythology, injurious to any woman's chances of wholeness and happiness. For example, in her 1979 book, *Gyn/Ecology*, she attacks writer Erich Neumann for attempting to mask the necrophiliac tendencies of a phallocracy that places Christ's lingering death by crucifixion at the centre of its mythic structures:

> The bland 'objective' scholarly style dulls the reader's capacity to cut through to a realization of the horror of phallocratic myth. Hags should certainly question *why* such 'fruit' of the tree of death is equated to a pledge of the 'promised land', for the situation hardly looks promising. We should also question how he could be the life at work in the tree since the 'tree' is obviously dead and he is on his way to the same state. As for the 'mysterious... and contradictory nature of the tree'—the confusion here is mind-boggling. For a tree *is* mysterious but it is *not* contradictory. What is contradictory is Reversal Religion's reduction/reversal of the Tree of Life to a torture cross. In this pseudocosmos of ontradictions anything can make 'sense'.[10]

Daly sees the comparison of cross and tree as a ghastly reversal or reading of pre-Christian and pagan mythological associations between women and the tree as a symbol of growing, living, fertile things. Daly's

---

(ed.), *Feminist Perspectives on Biblical Scholarship* (Chico, CA: Scholars Press, 1985), pp. 36-63. For a more specific, textual study see Elisabeth Schüssler Fiorenza, 'Missionaries, Apostles, Co-workers: Romans 16 and the Reconstruction of Women's Early Christian History', in Ann Loades (ed.), *Feminist Theology: A Reader* (London: SPCK, 1990), pp. 57-71.

9.   By this term, Daly refers to the underlying fear of, and aggression towards, women which is present but so disguised within male-constructed moralities that many are deceived. See Mary Daly, *Gyn/Ecology: The Metaethics of Radical Feminism* (London: The Women's Press, 1991), pp. 30-31 (first published in 1978 by Beacon Press, Boston).

10.   Daly, *Gyn/Ecology*, p. 80.

critique, for example, of the 'sado-masochistic' tendencies within Christian mythology implies that Christian texts reflect the hostile intentions of phallocratic writers towards women, and that these are then relayed and amplified by theologians reading them within a patriarchal[11] context where their authority is based upon male power-broking.

2. *Revealing Which Text?*
What Does the Emperor's Nakedness Signify?

I owe a debt to these early readings—and particularly to Daly's book *Gyn/Ecology*[12]—for enabling me to give a name to something I have found troubling within biblical interpretation, and more generally within Christian life and theology. Through these feminist readings, I too saw that the Emperor—in my case this was largely the unyielding corpus (corpse?) of what I was required to read as an undergraduate studying theology 20 years ago—was wearing no clothes. It wasn't simply that I was too dense to understand the subtleties revealed by men more perceptive than myself. The problem was that, in some important respects, their perceptions were different from mine.

But there is a limit to the usefulness of this process of laying bare the Emperor's nakedness. It is my view that the biblical texts, like all texts, are part of a continuing and complex interpretative interplay, such as that described by philosopher Julia Kristeva in terms of 'intertextuality'.[13] Readers must eventually go beyond the admittedly bracing and energizing business of pointing their fingers at the iniquities of patriarchal vanities and power-broking. The early work of Trible, Fiorenza, Daly and Ruether was primarily, and quite understandably, motivated by a concern for women in terms of advocacy that led them to simplify the interpretative interplay with the biblical texts in favour of highlighting the massive evidence of sexist practice—original writers and subsequent readers included. But let me return, for a moment, to the story of the little boy whose words enabled the people to see and name the Emperor's nakedness. In spite of the fact that, in the original version, Hans Andersen makes no reference to the Emperor's physical appearance,

11. By using the term 'patriarchal' or 'patriarchy', I am referring to a model of social and cultural organization which understands all institutions, relationships, roles and activities to be male-defined and to operate in order to protect male privilege.

12. Daly, *Gyn/Ecology*. See above, n. 9.

13. See below, p. 27.

most illustrations make the Emperor's nakedness grotesque, invariably shielding his sex from view. Nakedness, being laid bare, is instantly clothed again in a rich variety of significances. It is being read as a sign of an Emperor's gullibility and vanity, his shame and his common humanity that tells the lie to his imperial pretensions. What is revealed is a great deal more than the fact of his nakedness. Going back to the biblical text, I observe that revealing or laying bare what lies in the biblical text opens the floodgates to further interpretation in much the same way as the nakedness of the Emperor leads us to reflect upon what further story this tells. What further stories does the evidence of biblical 'texts of terror' tell? Perhaps they are stories about the brutal tyranny of men over women. Perhaps they are stories about how the tradition recognizes and notes, rather than obliterates, the brutal tyranny of men over women. Perhaps they are stories that seek to explain why, whatever it is that women represent, this cannot be excised and eradicated because it is troublingly foundational. Perhaps they are stories about the multiplicity of all this.

Mieke Bal's work as a literary critic of biblical texts gives full recognition to this complexity. If she is concerned to illustrate the ways in which the biblical text is interpreted aggressively to control and exclude women—whether readers or characters—she is also concerned to excavate the strength, intelligence and resolve of women buried within the text itself. Using a combination of methodological and conceptual tools —the insights of historical scholarship alongside those of psychoanalysis and modern or postmodern literary theory, she notes, through a process of close reading, the traces within the texts of disruptive, unyielding female presences. Far from simple victims, these presences threaten and trouble male characters and readers alike, challenging the coherence of traditional readings and suggesting new 'counter-coherences'.[14] Fundamentally, Bal continually probes the premises of 'coherent' biblical interpretation to discover where presuppositions are based upon ideological assumptions—for example, about the nature or role of women. She thus clears the ground, allowing other coherences, for example in terms of a psychoanalytic drama, to emerge. But she does not go on to claim that this counter-coherence is itself the only true interpretation but simply that it counters or opposes dangerous and even deadly claims to possess the truth.

14. Mieke Bal defines counter-coherences in *Death and Dissymmetry: The Politics of Coherence in the Book of Judges* (Chicago: University of Chicago Press, 1988), p. 7.

3. *The Aims of the Present Work*

Bal's work is largely focused on female characters within the text—even if they are silent or scarcely more than mentioned—whereas the text I have chosen as an extended 'case study' is the Prologue of John's Gospel (Jn 1.1-18), in which there are no female characters. My aim is to review the relationship between reader and text in a way that reflects both Bal's practice of close reading of the text and her sensitivity to female presences and feminist issues, and to place such reading in the context of specific historical interpretation of the Prologue. By this procedure I hope to draw attention to the characteristic complexities of feminist biblical interpretation.

This Johannine text is, I believe, a particularly appropriate choice. Its historical readers are concerned with the issue of Christ's Incarnation[15] and thus, inevitably, with definitions of 'divine' and 'human' nature[16] and with the relationship between them. And in the light of modern feminist criticism, any discussion of Christ's representative humanity[17] or

---

15. It should be noted that the specifically Johannine concept of 'Logos' clearly introduced a formulative ambiguity into Christian thought at an early stage by, apparently, driving a wedge between the earthly context of Jesus' life and death and the timeless context of divine intervention. Thus, on one interpretation, it forced the early Christian churches to contemplate the ontological status of divine Incarnation. The formulation of orthodox Christology reached at the Fourth Ecumenical Council of Chalcedon (451 CE), that Christ remains dual in respect of 'natures' but still a single 'person', has remained significant for most Christian believers up until the very recent past.

16. Within the Prologue of John's Gospel, the words used for the divine Logos becoming human (Jn 1.14) are the Greek words ἐγένετο (became—the verb may carry the sense of birth) and σάρξ (flesh—distinguished from the expression ἄνθρ-ωπος [human]). There are then strong indications of a connection with that which is symbolically associated with the female.

17. The argument, very recently rehearsed in debates about the ordination of women, that only a man can represent Christ at the altar, suggests that feminist concerns about the extent of Christ's representative function might not be without foundation. There is a strong sense within the Roman Catholic tradition particularly, amounting almost to a substitution of Christ as the new Adam in the parallel devotion to Mary as the new Eve. Jerome indeed wrote, 'Death came through Eve, but life has come through Mary'. See further in Marina Warner, *Alone of All her Sex: The Myth and the Cult of the Virgin Mary* (London: Pan Books, 1990), pp. 50-67 (first published by Weidenfeld & Nicolson, 1976).

of ideal redeemed humanity,[18] or indeed of divinity,[19] must make some reference to gender. It is one of the clearest insights of all feminisms that humanity as a whole has been defined in terms of the normative status of the male and the inferiority or lack of the female.

This text, then, gives feminist commentators scope to refine their understanding of marginality—the manifest absence of woman and the feminine from the visible centre or foundation of modern Western culture. The Prologue of John's Gospel is a text from which, it could be argued, commentators have tried to derive theological justification for this marginalization. In presenting a narrative of creation that harks back to the creation narratives of the Hebrew Bible and the Christian Old Testament, *all* female figures—including the divinely creative Wisdom and Mary, the new Eve—have been omitted.

Reading the biblical texts takes place within an interpretative matrix, operating both in terms of cultural reading practices—who gets to read, when and where—and in terms of the conceptual tools employed. One

---

18. See, for example, the long tradition within the Christian churches of the imitation of Christ, beginning perhaps in the Gospels' vision of Jesus' own mission, but also found more explicitly within the Pauline material in terms of the expected pattern of life within the mystery of 'Christ in you' (2 Cor. 13.35) that might well lead to martyrdom. A more literal interpretation of *Imitatio Christi* is discovered during the mediaeval period in, for example, Bernard of Clairvaux's meditations on the 'states' of the sacred life and also, of course, in the phenomenon known as stigmata, the first reported incident of which was associated with Francis of Assisi. The balance, within the Christian life, as between *imitatio* and, in Luther's expression, *conformitas*, has shifted through the years. But in both cases, differences of gender within a patriarchal culture will have had to have been accounted for. Such is in evidence even within the Pauline material itself where the obedience of a wife to her loving husband, within the conventions of Ephesian society, is upheld, as it were, in imitation of Christ's love for the obedient Church (Eph. 5.25-33).

19. See, for example, Luce Irigaray's essay 'Divine Women', in her *Sexes and Genealogies* (trans. Gillian C. Gill; London: Routledge, 1993), pp. 57-72. Here, Irigaray argues that the absence of woman from Western traditions of the divine is paralysing for women, particularly when accompanied by strong Marian, maternal traditions: 'Our tradition presents and represents the radiant glory of the mother, but rarely shows us a fulfilled woman. And it forces us to make murderous choices: either mother (given that a boy child is what makes us truly mothers) or woman (prostitute and property of the male). We have no female trinity. But as long as a woman lacks a divine made in her image, she cannot establish her subjectivity or achieve a goal of her own. She lacks an ideal that would be her goal or path in becoming' (pp. 63-64).

important feature of this matrix, identified by feminist and postmodern philosophy, is its binary character represented in a classic sense by the difference or distinction between male and female. This distinction is understood not as a purely sexist bias or prejudice that, theoretically, could be eliminated but as a characteristic of the logic within which rational thinking has taken place within the whole patriarchal context of the Christian churches. This perception, characteristic of the work of postmodern philosophers and writers like Jacques Derrida[20] and Hélène Cixous,[21] identifies a logic of identity governing most of Western thought, through whose phallogocentric principles[22] a fundamental conceptual division is opened up. This affects all aspects of human living and is crucially interpreted in hierarchical or exclusive terms. Thus, it supports other cultural and conceptual structures that identify women with that which is different or 'other', shunting them off in the direction of threatening or even diabolical[23] marginality. In the light of

20. On the critical analysis of the 'transcendental signified', that is the presumption of a single being or truth guaranteeing or underpinning all speech and writing, see, for example, Jacques Derrida, *Of Grammatology* (trans. Gayatri Chakravorty Spivak; Baltimore: The Johns Hopkins University Press, 1976), pp. 18-26.

21. See, for example, Sellers (ed.), *The Hélène Cixous Reader*, pp. 37-46.

22. 'Phallocentricity' is a term used by some feminists in arguing that the masculine or male—symbolized by the phallus—is regarded as normative, and the female or feminine—symbolized by the lack of the phallus—is aberration or absence. It is associated particularly with the perception of the 'invisibility' or 'marginality' of the feminine within all forms of cultural expression, and particularly within language seen as a system of male-defined symbols. See, for example, B. du Bois, 'Passionate Scholarship: Notes on Values, Knowing and Method in Feminist Social Science', in G. Bowles and R. Duelli Klein (eds.), *Theories of Women's Studies* (London: Routledge & Kegan Paul, 1983). Phallogocentricity is understood as the centrality, not simply of the masculine symbol (phallus), but of the male voice (logos) in framing the everyday discursive world in which this symbolism of singularity (the phallus) operates. This term is usually attributed to Jacques Derrida, but it is used widely by other commentators. It could be said, perhaps, that the notion of feminine diversity and multiplicity represented by, for example, *jouissance* (female, multiple pleasure) and *écriture féminine* in the work of French feminists such as Hélène Cixous and Luce Irigaray is a specific rejection of and response to this determination.

23. See Irigaray, *Sexes and Genealogies*, p. 64. Irigaray maintains that the 'only diabolical thing about women is their lack of a God and the fact that, deprived of God, they are forced to comply with models that do not match them, that exile, double, mask them, cut them off from themselves and from one another'.

these fundamental presuppositions about a conceptual and logical division, it is perhaps less important to choose texts featuring individual women. Indeed, female characters might reveal considerably less than this pregnant absence within the Prologue.

4. *The Shape of the Study*

In order to explore the intertextualities of reading the Bible as a feminist, I intend to begin with an analysis of five readings, from the fifth to the twentieth century, of the biblical text in question. These interpretations are taken from a variety of theological traditions and include the discourse of (marginalized) women as well as interpretation at the defining centre of patriarchal orthodoxy. The purpose of this initial process of analysis is to lay out more clearly the characteristic patterns of interpretation within a fundamentally pre-feminist, patriarchal context.

Augustine delivered his homilies on John's Gospel some time between 406 and 416, while he was the Bishop of Hippo in North Africa. Augustine, a convert from the dualistic philosophy of the Manichaeans, preached an orthodox view of Christ's full humanity but retains, within these sermons, a symbolic association of body and flesh with the feminine that cannot be separated from his suspicion of sexuality as the site of concupiscence.

Hildegard von Bingen wrote *Liber divinorum operum* during the period from 1163 to 1173 while she was Abbess of a Benedictine convent in the Rhineland. The first part of this work of visionary theology is a meditation on the incarnational theme of the first 14 verses of the Prologue of John's Gospel. Although she writes within a tradition that might be regarded as fundamentally Augustinian, Hildegard's cosmological vision and sapiential themes allowed the bodily and the feminine a far more positive and more integrated significance within this text than Augustine had demonstrated.

Martin Luther began his series of sermons on John 1–4 in July 1537. Within the context of a disputatious and sometimes dangerous age of religious controversy Luther, like Augustine, uses his sermons to address various heretics with the call of reformed orthodoxy. Luther emphasizes, in these sermons, the redemptive humanity of the Word but also wrestles with the implications of such an apparently paradoxical connection with the flesh. A drive in Luther's sermons towards the divine singularity of his theology finds itself hindered by the disturbing flotsam and jetsam, particularly of Marian traditions, dragging along in its wake.

Rudolf Bultmann published his commentary on the Gospel of John in 1941 while war was raging in Europe. Bultmann's work on John is, however, that of a scholar and teacher rather than a pastor or social critic. His approach to the Gospel of John was, nevertheless, in a significant sense innovative, attempting a synthesis between the radical implications of Heideggarian existentialism and the increasing sophistication of 'scientific' historical criticism within the field of biblical studies. While 'Incarnation' within Bultmann's work is demythologized,[24] the demythologized realm of humanity is once again characterized by the 'feminine' features of a typical patriarchal symbolism.

Adrienne von Speyr published her reflections on the Prologue of John's Gospel in 1953. From 1942 she had experienced the stigmata— the visible, sensible marks of crucifixion—each year during Holy Week. Von Speyr's intense meditations on the Prologue envisage a consensual principle of creative obedience within the divinity itself, reminiscent of Hildegard's understanding of God's work of Incarnation in the cosmos and characteristic of Roman Catholic Marian traditions. However, von Speyr's view of obedience and openness to God appears to be bound far more specifically to patriarchal values and to the binary logic of identity. This is illustrated in the way in which she clearly felt herself restricted to a quintessentially 'feminine' form of suffering and silence. In consequence, she seems to have been forced to focus on physical symptoms as her main point of access to the authoritative Word of God.

In all these interpretations it is possible to see the trace of the persistent logic of identity which attempts to escape from the uncomfortably polyvalent implications of Jn 1.14, 'the Word became flesh', by promoting a view of the flesh in terms of a contaminating, perverse otherness, symbolized by woman and the feminine, that is ultimately to be jettisoned without significant loss to either God or man[*sic*]kind.

In the second part of this study of the Prologue, I attempt to read and interpret the text in ways that are explicitly and self-consciously intended to be multiple, in order to unsettle the existing choices of traditional orthodoxy. However, in some sense they could also be characterized as advantageous to women. They are located at the crossroads/point of intersection of text and interpretative need. In other

---

24. Demythologizing is, very broadly, a form of interpretation that attempts to remove the mythic elements of narratives, so that they may be understood in the categories of modern 'scientific' women and men. In theological terms, it is most notably associated with the work of Rudolf Bultmann. See Chapter 5.

words, I am also trying to read this text for myself as a woman. There are undoubtedly other ways to read it.

Against the background of these five historical readings, then, I have written three alternative interpretations of the text that attempt, through their multiplicity, to resist the tendencies of power-broking, singular, monolithic readings and also to challenge or complicate the nature or use of the symbols of woman and the feminine as they are present or absent within the text.

A first reading of the Prologue takes shape from a point of 'focalization'[25] other than that of God or Word or of a narrator whose position could be identified with these. Its 'resistance' is to be found in the proposal that the Prologue be read in an ironic mode whose underlying premise is the feminist challenge to patriarchal culture as a whole. Within the overarching gender symbolism of patriarchal culture, the masculine/feminine relationship is clearly related to the divine/human relationship. The irony is that the human (feminine) term is primary; 'Only the one who is sent can reveal the one who has sent him'.[26] Once again it is suggested that the symbols of woman and the feminine do not have to be read in this text as either perverse or expendable.

The second form of reading the Prologue focuses on how the alternative readings of σάρξ (flesh) within this text reflect an almost thematic instability, which is picked up again in John 6. While contemporary interpretation frequently seeks to smooth away the evidence of such suggestive inconsistencies, σάρξ seems to possess, in terms of this instability, a strong relevance to the very reversal and upheaval of which divine incarnation is the theological expression. Once again the implication is that the symbols of woman and the feminine indicate a highly significant and even potentially positive resonance within this text.

The third alternative 'counter-coherence' is to read this text as a record in mythic terms of a drama of developing human subjectivity. This approach employs the philosopher Julia Kristeva's understanding of subjectivity *'en procès'*—that is to say male and female subjectivity in process and on trial. It focuses on the Prologue as a drama of initial fusion followed by a vital and creative, but always painful, separation. In

---

25. See Mieke Bal, *Narratology: Introduction to the Theory of Narrative* (Toronto: University of Toronto Press, 1985), pp. 100-102.

26. Ernst Käsemann, *The Testament of Jesus: A Study of the Gospel of John in the Light of Chapter 17* (London: SCM Press, 1968), p. 23.

this reading, woman and the feminine appear as fundamentally maternal but they also represent resistance to any form of ultimate exclusion.

5. *Methodological Considerations*

A series of methodological considerations underpins this study. Some of them have to do with handling feminist theory. Feminist theory is a term covering all attempts to describe and articulate a 'woman-centred' perspective. Feminist theory uses certain key organizing concepts such as 'patriarchy', 'phallogocentricity' or 'difference'[27] which deal with the position of women in relation to men. It is also concerned with issues of *female* subjectivity, of the prioritizing of a disciplined attention to sensual pleasures and pains and of intuitive thinking versus an exclusive commitment to logic or intellectual reasoning. It is surely no coincidence, for example, that both Hildegard von Bingen and Adrienne von Speyr were afflicted by forms of physical suffering and debility to which they gave theological significance.[28] It is also notable that Hildegard, who was to a large extent unschooled, gave expression to her devotion in terms of the sensual delights of both music and painting.

One way of introducing feminist or women-centred concerns into reading the biblical text is to employ a hermeneutic of suspicion. The expression 'hermeneutic of suspicion' was first coined by the French critical theorist Paul Ricoeur. In his work, suspicion, such as that cast on

27. Feminists use this term broadly in two ways. First, difference is understood to imply the difference of women's experience of themselves and the world in a potentially positive way that takes systematic social stereotyping of sexual difference head on. This sense of difference can encompass many different aspects of that experience including language (for example in the work of Hélène Cixous and Luce Irigaray), gender identity (for example in the work of Carol Gilligan and Nancy Chodorow), sexual preference (for example, in the work of Adrienne Rich and Mary Daly). Alternatively, difference is related to power, as woman is indexed as, in Simone de Beauvoir's phrase, 'Other to man', and black woman as 'other' to white women (see, for example, Audre Lorde, 'The Uses of the Erotic: The Erotic as Power', in *Sister Outsider: Essays and Speeches by Audre Lorde* (Freedom, CA: The Crossing Press, 1984). Most significant in this study is the sense of difference understood in the work of Julia Kristeva, where difference, defining to all sense of subjectivity, also functions as a guard against a tendency towards monolithic totalitarianism within patriarchal society and culture, particularly as demonstrated in art and literature. This is more specifically enunciated in the concept of heterogeneity. See Chapter 9.

28. See Chapter 3.

the Kantian notion of the will by theorists like Friedrich Nietzsche, Karl Marx or Sigmund Freud, was hermeneutic in the sense that it called for increasing sophistication of the arguments in favour of an ontological position. In the interpretation of religious texts, Ricoeur saw such an 'attitude of suspicion and cautious critical scrutiny' to be necessary in order to reveal more precisely the sense in which their 'peculiar mode of dissimulation' might be defended as positively significant.[29]

The expression was used, analogously, by Elisabeth Schüssler Fiorenza to describe the sharpening of her fundamentally historical critical analysis of the New Testament, in order to defend the possibility of rescuing the autonomous and charismatic women of the early Christian Church.[30] In the context of this study, suspicion is directed at the metanarratives created by readers of the Prologue. The underlying question to be posed is whether the text may indeed be said to possess positive significance for feminist readers.

Another way of giving voice to feminist concerns with voiceless or silenced female voices and presences is through deconstructive analysis. In undertaking a work of feminist biblical criticism, I am clearly, first and foremost, engaging in analysing the biblical text. Of course, one clear trend within feminist theory is to move away from analysis altogether, towards something apparently more creative, such as poetry. Some feminist writers and theologians have wished to move right away from existing texts, especially the classic texts of patriarchy such as the Hebrew Bible or the New Testament. They strive to avoid the very shape of exclusions and the drive towards singularity that seems characteristic of what Hélène Cixous once called 'the spurious Phallocentric Performing Theater'.[31] This they do by, for example, reading and writing on the body, the site of diffuse pleasures and the reverberating

---

29. See Paul Ricoeur's essay in Don Ihde (ed.), *Paul Ricoeur: The Conflict of Interpretations* (Evanston, IL: Northwestern University Press, 1974), p. 442. 'For this reason, religion demands a type of interpretation that is adapted to its own peculiar mode of dissimulation, i.e., an interpretation of illusion as distinct from simple "error" in the epistemological sense of the word, or as distinct from "lying", in the ordinary ethical sense of the word. Illusion is itself a cultural function. Such a fact presupposes that the public meanings of our consciousness conceal true meanings, which can be brought to light only by adopting the attitude of suspicion and cautious critical scrutiny.'

30. See Schüssler Fiorenza, *In Memory of Her*, p. xxiii.

31. See Sellers (ed.), *The Hélène Cixous Reader*, p. 41.

'what-comes-before-language'—in other words the very type of a non-text, so strongly associated with women in the past.

Arguably, however, this *écriture féminine* cannot altogether evade the texts of the past, since these are still determining the overall agenda, by determining which site has been buried or neglected. But it strains towards a poetic that is not mimetic and away from reflecting and imitating existing (male) texts. However, I believe that it can be argued that all forms of mimesis are also poetic.[32] This enables me, critically, to acknowledge the past rather than having to try to dismiss it into oblivion in an attempt to be truly creative. In the words of Luce Irigaray, '[t]he passage from one era to the next cannot be made simply by negating what already exists'.[33] And, as Kirsten Andersen points out, in a recent essay on feminist biblical interpretation, discounting all historical texts and all the insights of their past interpretation leads into mere solipsism and the indefensible claim that 'tradition begins with me'.[34]

The broadly deconstructive mode of analysis undertaken by scholars and critics like Mieke Bal and Julia Kristeva is thus as much ideologically as methodologically suited to my work on the text. It seeks to release the multiplicity of texts, finding another story told in the same words, or to find in the gaps and inconsistencies of any text a clue to the essential heterogeneity[35] of human motivations and desires that may encompass past interpretations as well as encouraging future ones.

My understanding of this process is strongly influenced by Julia Kristeva's notion of intertextuality. In her essay, translated as 'Word, Dialogue and Novel', and published in *The Kristeva Reader*, Kristeva refers to Mikhail Bakhtin's classification of words within a narrative in order to explore the sense in which such words work on different levels.

32. This is a point discussed at some length by Paul Ricoeur in his book, *The Rule of Metaphor* (Toronto: University of Toronto Press, 1977). See especially pp. 36–42.

33. Luce Irigaray, *Je, tu, nous: Toward a Culture of Difference* (New York: Routledge, 1993), p. 23.

34. Kirsten Andersen, 'Mimetic Reflections when Reading a Text in the Image of Gender', in Alison E. Jasper and Alastair G. Hunter (eds.), *Talking It Over: Perspectives on Women and Religion 1993–5* (Glasgow: Trinity St Mungo Press, 1996), pp. 1-21 (19).

35. Fundamentally, Kristeva uses this term to describe, in the journey of the subject, a sort of functional inability entirely to heal the wound of separation or close completely the boundaries between the semiotic and the symbolic. Moving between the two is a restless, painful process but also a creative one.

Possessing varying degrees of ambivalence, they appear to contest the notion that narrative can be regarded as monologic, or univocal. Narrative is

> an *intersection of textual surfaces* rather than a *point* (a fixed meaning), as a dialogue among several writings: that of the writer, the addressee (or the character) and the contemporary or earlier cultural context.[36]

From Bakhtin, Kristeva adopts the notion of dialogism that becomes the basis for her own view of the text as a mosaic of quotations in which any text is 'the absorption and transformation of another'.[37] What she wants to make clear, however, is that there is also a pressure within language itself that continually frustrates and, indeed, mocks analytical effort from within homogenous static systems.[38] She is, so to speak, always aware that the universe cannot be entirely reduced to literature any more than literature can be entirely reduced to the work of literary criticism or theoretical analysis.[39] For Kristeva, all elements involved within interpretation do not belong on the same level. She indicates that the semiotic, pre-linguistic drives and energies of the human body are also implicated in any process of reading and interpretation, signalling their presences through slips and logical inconsistencies, and sounding in the linguistic miming of bodily rhythms. This is the point at which her interests dovetail with those of other feminist philosophers since she endeavours in this way to uncover the presence of the female-identified

---

36. Julia Kristeva, 'Word, Dialogue and Novel', in Toril Moi (ed.), *The Kristeva Reader* (Oxford: Basil Blackwell, 1986), p. 36.

37. Moi (ed.), *The Kristeva Reader*, p. 37.

38. See, for example, Kristeva's essay, 'Word, Dialogue and Novel' and Toril Moi's introduction to *The Kristeva Reader*, p. 34.

39. See Gérard Genette, 'Structuralism and Literary Criticism', in David Lodge (ed.), *Modern Criticism and Theory: A Reader* (London: Longmans, 1988), p. 64. In Julia Kristeva, *Revolution in Poetic Language* (trans. Margaret Waller; New York: Columbia University Press, 1984), pp. 59-60 (first published as *La révolution du langage poétique: L'avant-garde à la fin du XIXe siècle: Lautréamont et mallarmé* [Paris: Seuil, 1974]), Kristeva speaks about intertextuality as the passage of one sign system to another: 'The term *inter-textuality* denotes this transposition of one (or several) sign system(s) into another; but since this term has often been understood in the banal sense of "study of sources", we prefer the term *transposition* because it specifies that the passage from one signifying system to another demands a new articulation of the thetic'.

body in the arena of conceptual rational analysis and creative writing.[40]

One important presupposition of this book, then, is that the text has no 'meaning', in so far as that implies a single, fixed or 'correct' interpretation, but neither is it 'meaningless'. I do not dispense with the idea of a text altogether but argue that any question or project has to be directed at, or formulated from, the face of intersection between text and interpreting or reading subjectivity—whether unified or fragmented, mine or someone else's.

It is for this reason that the book is divided into two sections. In the first section, the primary intertextuality is between myself as reader and a series of historical readers of the Prologue. In the second section, the primary intertextuality is between myself as reader and the text of the Prologue. Illustrating the complexity of the reading process, there are subsidiary intersections in both cases; every text is itself a reading, an interpretation of some further text or oral narrative and every reader is reading with an eye upon any number of other interpretative dialogues or conversations. These may be with other readers of the text or even with the unconscious within their own 'subjectivity'.[41]

In this study, I am not concerned with what the 'original meaning' of the text might have been, if, for example, that is defined in terms of the intentionality[42] of its author or the notion of an original 'intended reader'.[43] This does not mean that I absolutely abandon any concept of authorial intention. Naturally enough, an author's view of what he or she is doing presents one obvious interpretative framework! But such

40. See Chapter 9, in which I attempt an analysis of the Prologue based on the principles of Kristeva's 'semanalysis'. This aspect of her theoretical work is treated in greater detail at this point.

41. I use this term in the sense understood by Kristeva in speaking of the *sujet en procès*. See Chapter 9.

42. The issue of authorial intention and the limitations of such a concept in the analysis of any text was most notably raised by W.K. Wimsatt, Jr, and Monroe C. Beardsley in 'The Intentional Fallacy', in *The Verbal Icon* (Lexington, KY: University of Kentucky Press, 1954).

43. The idea of John's 'intended readership' plays a structural part within the analysis proposed by John Ashton in his book, *Understanding the Fourth Gospel* (Oxford: Oxford University Press, 1991), p. 113: 'the intended impact on the readers is the only kind of aim or purpose which is really integral to a full understanding of the work as such. *Pace* Bultmann, it must be included in any complete account of *das erste Rätsel*, the problem of locating the Fourth Gospel within the history of early Christianity.'

perceived intentions cannot be exclusively authoritative. In the first place, an author's conscious intentions very rapidly become—in an ultimate sense—a matter of speculation once they are no longer on hand to explain. Some authors never explain. And even intentions stated publicly by authors may be, or may be accounted, lies or self-deceptions, or unsatisfactory and insubstantial, particularly by later commentators in search of the 'truth'.

Texts may function quite satisfactorily for readers without explanatory notes. Moreover, of course, the writers of explanatory notes always have their own agendas. So I assume that the significance of any text transcends the conscious intentions of its author as every new moment of reading and interpretation inevitably creates its own intertextualities. In as far, then, as I make reference to the work of biblical critics, Church historians or historians of Western culture, these are seen as individual readers or, possibly, as representatives of a certain *genre* of interpretation. Undoubtedly they have much to contribute and have already contributed much in terms of critique or corroborative evidence but I believe that they must still be seen to operate their own sets of presuppositions and relations of power within a patriarchal reading context. As, indeed, must I.

The text becomes 'significant'[44] in interaction with readers. By 'readers', this study—unless otherwise indicated—implies real readers and not the literary concept of an 'implied reader'. The concept of the 'implied reader', which is taken originally from the work of Wolfgang Iser, was introduced to readers of the secondary Johannine literature through Alan Culpepper's ground-breaking study *Anatomy of the Fourth Gospel*.[45] Culpepper, in trying to get away from approaches to the text that focused

---

44. The term 'significant', used in preference to 'meaning' for example, refers the reader to conclusions drawn originally from the work of the linguist Ferdinand Saussure, who proposed that signifiers (that is the word or acoustic image, 'ox' for example) were related to the signified (that is the concept, ox) only by convention, within a system of such conventional relations. Julia Kristeva understands 'significance' as incorporating within such a linguistic system an encoding of archaic and fluidly pervasive (feminine?) forces that are not given open expression, but which nevertheless may produce disruption within the patriarchal context. See, for example, Julia Kristeva, *Desire in Language: A Semiotic Approach to Literature and Art* (Oxford: Basil Blackwell, 1984), of which a section is reprinted within Moi (ed.), *The Kristeva Reader*, pp. 34-61.

45. R. Alan Culpepper, *Anatomy of the Fourth Gospel: A Study in Literary Design* (Philadelphia: Fortress Press, 1983), p. 6.

exclusively on sources and origins, used a communicational model of narrative derived from the work of Seymour Chatman to support his reading of the Gospel as a unified narrative.[46] This model suggests that an 'implied' author and an 'implied' reader are constructed by the selection and organization of the material and by the literary choices involved in such processes as characterization, narrative settings, the movement of the plot and by the implicit commentary of a particular symbolism or the use of irony or the role of the narrator. This author and reader are part of the—rhetorical—project of the Gospel, seen as the communication of a series of vital theological insights into the events they purport to report.

While this is suggestive work, it does not speak in any substantial sense to the needs of feminist interpretation, since it is once again situated within the interpretative model that sees texts as related primarily to the intentionality of authors, understood in a fundamentally redactive sense.

6. *The Shining Garment of the Text*

The title I have chosen for this work is an attempt to indicate something of the multiplicity of themes that have emerged for me, as a result of making this study. One of these themes is that of the *text*. Texts are interpreted, or 'put on', by every new reader, according to her desires or anxieties and according to his desires and anxieties. But text, like the material of the Emperor's new clothes, is an intangible substance. What the story reveals is always ambivalent. And in particular, readers of texts, like the Emperor of the story, must reckon with the danger of any attempt to make use of texts either to clothe themselves with authority or to cloak their most profound intentions from view. In other words, by trying to use texts, they run a real risk of revealing themselves. I am concerned here to challenge those who would similarly use texts rather than read them.

Secondly, the title refers to a figure of the *flesh* as a garment. This fleshly garment is strongly associated, in the Christian West, with Woman as the site or cause of sensual desire, physical changeability and decay. It becomes something of a text in its own right because, illuminated through this sort of association, are the outrageous pretensions

---

46. Seymour Chatman, *Story and Discourse: Narrative Structure in Fiction and Film* (Ithaca, NY: Cornell University Press, 1978).

of readers who try to reduce all the multiplicity of human living to such a symbol of the flesh, and then go on to declare that this is simply a veil, a container or an adornment for the divine *Word*, without any intrinsic value. Less frequently, however, the fleshly garment is also seen as the manifestation of the divine, an expression of that divine love in itself. In other words I am concerned by the fact that it is still incredibly difficult for readers of biblical texts to accredit something positive to the realm of body and bodily desires.

Thirdly, the implication of a shining garment draws attention to an image that has intrigued many modern feminists—that of *the mirror*. Virginia Woolf,[47] Mary Daly[48] and Luce Irigaray,[49] among others no doubt, see the ironies, the dangers and the opportunities of mirrors for women, as, in the past, the mirrors of men and now to be used in order to reflect long and carefully upon themselves. Here is an attempt to look and see what, in the context of a self-conscious feminism, is now being mirrored in the Word(s) of the Prologue. One vision I look for, of course, is my own feminine face.

---

47. See, for example, Virginia Woolf, *A Room of One's Own* (London: Grafton, 1977), p. 41 (first published in 1928).

48. See, for example, Mary Daly, *Beyond God the Father: Towards a Philosophy of Women's Liberation* (London: The Women's Press, 1986), pp. 195-98 (first published in 1973 by Beacon Press, Boston).

49. See, for example, Irigaray, *Sexes and Genealogies*, p. 65, and, of course, Irigaray, *Speculum de l'autre femme* (Paris: Minuit, 1974; ET *Speculum of the Other Woman* [trans. Gillian C. Gill; New York: Cornell University Press, 1985]), in which Irigaray adapts Lacan's image of the mirror.

PART I

2

Having his Cake and Eating It:
The Symbolism of Gender in Augustine's
Tractates on the Prologue of John's Gospel

...drive carnal thought from your hearts that you may truly be under grace.[1]

1. *Introduction*

The term 'tractates' refers in a technical sense in Latin Christian writings to a form of homily, specifically that of a bishop to his congregation.[2] Seemingly, the *Tractates* on John's Gospel were originally delivered extemporaneously within a liturgical setting and taken down in some sort of shorthand.[3] In origin, therefore, they were designed for a mixed congregation that Augustine was teaching against the background of a number of other persuasive philosophical and theological alternatives.[4]

---

1. *Tractate* 3.19.1.
2. See John Rettig (ed. and trans.), *St. Augustine: Tractates on the Gospel of John 1–10* (Washington: Catholic University of America Press, 1988), pp. 31-32.
3. Rettig (ed. and trans.), *St. Augustine: Tractates 1–10*, pp. 8-9.
4. Although the Emperor Constantine (274 or 288–337 CE), ending persecution of the Church, had embraced Christianity and worked to unite the Christian Church with the secular state, pagan philosophy and religions continued to flourish during Augustine's formative years. Among the most important influences and alternatives open to Augustine, born to a pagan father and a Catholic mother, were Neoplatonist philosophy—a reinterpretation and expansion of Platonic ideas, particularly as found in the work of Plotinus and his pupil Porphyry, and Manichaeism. Manichaeism was a form of heterodox Christianity with an ultra-ascetic code of morality, derived from a fundamentally dualistic cosmology. In later years, as a Catholic bishop, Augustine remained preoccupied with theological debates, engaging particularly with the work of Pelagius—declared heretical in 418 CE. Pelagius, a British lay monk, took issue with Augustine on the grounds of the freedom of the will. He contested Augustine's conviction that humankind is entirely dependent, for

These are not texts written simply for the sophisticated or for wholly committed Catholics. There is no final consensus about when the first three *Tractates*, usually considered within a somewhat larger grouping, were written.[5] Various dates have been suggested during the 10 years from 406[6] to 416 CE.[7] All, at least, place the work during the period when Augustine was settled as Bishop of Hippo in North Africa.

In the course of the first three *Tractates* on the Prologue of John's Gospel, Augustine defends Catholic orthodoxy against Arians,[8] Manichaeans[9] or Neoplatonists[10] for the benefit of doubters and the faithful alike. He interprets the Prologue as saying that everything has been created by God the Word: the world, the sky and the earth and also the spiritual powers of angels and archangels.[11] He says that God created all things and is not—like a craftsman who constructs a chest which is then separate from him—somehow detached from the world.[12] But although

whatever they do or are that is good, upon the grace of God. He believed that such an attitude was incompatible with any sense of human responsibility and would lead to lawlessness and sinful indulgence. Augustine was also preoccupied with the Donatists, a schismatic Christian group that looked with great suspicion on the, as they saw it, secularizing activities of Catholic bishops. Those who cooperated with the civil authorities and were prepared to live at peace with their pagan neighbours were thought to have destroyed the authentic holiness and ritual purity of the Church.

5.   To set these *Tractates* in the historical context of Augustine's better known writings: the *Confessions* have been commonly dated as belonging to the last years of the fourth century (397–398 CE according to R.S. Pine-Coffin [ed. and trans.], *St. Augustine: Confessions* [Harmondsworth: Penguin Books, 1961]), while the *City of God* undoubtedly belongs to the period after the sacking of Rome by Alaric and his Goths in 410 CE (413–426 according to David Knowles (ed.), *Augustine: City of God* [trans. H. Bettenson; Harmondsworth: Penguin Books, 1972]).

6.   See A.-M. La Bonnardière, *Recherches de chronologie augustinienne* (Paris: Etudes augustiniennes, 1965) and, for different reasons, M.-F. Berrouard, 'La date des Tractatus I–LIV In Iohannis Evangelium de saint Augustin', *Recherches Augustiniennes* 7 (1971), pp. 105-68.

7.   See S. Zarb, 'Chronologia Tractatuum S. Augustini in Euangelium primamque Epistolam Ionannie Apostoli', *Angelicum* 10 (1933), pp. 50-110. A summary of scholarship concerned with the dating of these tractates is to be found in Rettig (ed. and trans.), *St. Augustine: Tractates 1–10*, pp. 23-31.

8.   See, for example, *Tractate* 1.11.1.

9.   See, for example, *Tractate* 1.14.2.

10.   See, for example, *Tractate* 2.4.1.

11.   *Tractate* 1.9.3.

12.   *Tractate* 2.10.1.

God, infused in the world, may be seen in the world,[13] it is not enough. For humankind is blinded by pride and swollen with sin. And the true light came precisely to 'weak minds, to wounded hearts, to the vision of bleary-eyed souls'.[14] John the Baptist, a man of 'immense merit, great grace, great eminence'[15] but not himself the light, comes first as a witness to the true light who will shed his rays even on those who have injured eyes.[16] The true light, shed by the cross of Christ, is a boat or ship which holds the faithful up as they struggle to cross the sea of the world.[17] The faithful, though born of the will of the flesh, are, through Christ's birth from a woman, 'remade' through grace and born of God. And this astonishing grace,[18] administered by Christ the physician,[19] cures the damaged sight. But, with the cured sight, the faithful do not see with the 'eyes of the flesh'.[20] The physician's medicines are still 'rather bitter and sharp'[21] and in order to be truly under grace rather than under the law that simply points out the sickness without offering a cure, there must still be a struggle and an enduring. Finally Augustine urges his people: 'drive carnal thoughts from your hearts that you may truly be under grace, that you may belong to the New Testament'.[22]

2. *Female Figures in Augustine's* Tractates *on the Prologue of John's Gospel*

Augustine's rhetoric has a persuasive rather than coercive tone. He ac-knowledges that the truth of the matter is ineffable and yet listeners and speakers, even the apostle and evangelist John himself, must persist in trying to speak as they are capable, inspired by God:

> Ultimately, God's mercy will be present so that there will perhaps be ben-efit enough for all, and each person will grasp what he can. In fact, the speaker, too, says what he is capable of saying. For who can say it as it is?[23]

13. *Tractate* 2.4.1.
14. *Tractate* 2.7.1.
15. *Tractate* 2.5.1.
16. *Tractate* 2.7.2.
17. *Tractate* 2.2.4.
18. *Tractate* 2.15.2.
19. *Tractate* 3.3.1.
20. *Tractate* 3.18.1.
21. *Tractate* 3.14.2.
22. *Tractate* 3.19.1.
23. *Tractate* 1.1.1.

Something of the appeal of Augustine's writing is contained in this preliminary remark. While it is quite clear that the matters with which he deals are of overwhelming importance to him, he does not harangue his listeners. In this sense his commitment to reason and to the logic of the mind seems eirenic in an exemplary way. It excludes, theoretically at least, the mere imposition of views based upon his power as teacher or bishop.[24] It accepts the need for conviction to grow as the gradual accumulation of arguments, individually acknowledged. His understanding of faith does not preclude the assent of the rational mind.

And yet a certain pre-eminence of reason and the rational mind within the patriarchal context is something that feminists have found disturbing. Within this patriarchal context the symbols of woman and the feminine typically represent the absence or antithesis of reason or rationality. Admittedly, there is little indication in Augustine's work of the virulent misogynism to be found, for example, in the earlier writings of Tertullian (c. 160–220 CE).[25] Neither does he assume that individual women are essentially less rational than men, as is suggested, for example, in the work of Philo (c. 20 BCE to 50 CE) in his synthesis of Genesis with Greek philosophy.[26] Augustine was quite clear that women as well as men were made in God's image and that they were possessed of reason in equal measure. However, given that the account of Genesis proposed some divine reason for creating men and women differently, he justified the subordination of women on the grounds that that subordination represented a subordination of corporeal, fleshly or practical concerns to a higher spiritual form of reason:

> But because she differs from man by her bodily sex, that part of the reason which is turned aside to regulate temporal things could be properly symbolised by her corporeal veil; so that the image of God does not

24. However, it does have to be said that, as a bishop, Augustine was prepared to endorse the imperial government's forcible interventions against the Donatist extremists of Numidia. Moreover, he devoted some time and energy to providing a rationalization for this policy which, while bringing an end to implacable antagonisms and sporadic violence, particularly against Catholic clergy, also had the consequence of strengthening the hand of the Catholic Church in North Africa. See, for example, Henry Chadwick, *Augustine* (Oxford: Oxford University Press, 1986), p. 75.

25. See, for example, *De cultu feminarum* 1.1. Here, it is Eve who is deemed 'the Devil's Gateway'.

26. See Genevieve Lloyd, 'Augustine and Aquinas', in Ann Loades (ed.), *Feminist Theology: A Reader* (London: SPCK, 1990), pp. 90-99.

remain except in that part of the mind of man in which it clings to the contemplation and consideration of the eternal reasons, which, as is evident, not only men but also women possess.[27]

The superiority of reason and the rational mind in Augustine's work, then, was bound to compound and concentrate reflection on woman and the feminine as natural symbols of a *devalued* realm of human experience.

If Augustine's attitude towards women and the feminine does not seem essentially misogynistic within his theological work in general, there is a clear sense in which feminine images and roles in the tractates on the Prologue are seen as submissive, ancillary or preliminary.

One feminine image that he might have used within his exegesis of this text is certainly absent. In his first *Tractate on the Gospel of John*—on Jn 1.1-5—Augustine comments on the Wisdom of God by which all things were made:

> For he himself is the wisdom of God and in the Psalm it is said, 'You have made all things in wisdom'. If, then, Christ is the wisdom of God and the Psalm says, 'You have made all things in wisdom', as all things were made through him, so they were made in him.[28] The earth was made; but the earth itself which was made is not life. There is, however, in wisdom itself, in a spiritual way, a certain reason by which the earth was made: this is life.[29]

Augustine's principal scriptural quotation at this point is Ps. 104.24. The psalm plays richly, in a meditation on the greatness of God, on the themes of creating and giving life. And this creative, sustaining function—which Augustine uses here to describe Christ and the work of the Word—is frequently associated with the *female* figure of Wisdom in the Wisdom literature.[30] But of the specifically female hypostasis or personification so characteristic of the Wisdom literature of the Old Testament and the Apocrypha, there is no sign within Augustine's discussion at this point.

As symbols, woman and the feminine appear to belong to a discourse of sovereignty and subordination in Augustine's work that makes values

27. *De Trinitate* 12.7.
28. *Tractate* 1.16.1.
29. *Tractate* 1.16.3.
30. See, for example, Prov. 8.22-31—Wisdom as the master-builder, Sir. 24—Wisdom as agent of creation and giver of life, Wis. 9—Wisdom creates, saves and reveals.

or qualities identified as masculine normative or superior to the feminine. It may be simply for this reason that the female figure of Wisdom from the Wisdom literature of the Apocrypha and the Old Testament appears to hold no particular attraction for Augustine. Or there may be more complex reasons. Wisdom features as an aspect of the divine: the beauty and power of God's creative and sustaining word or the attraction of the Law. In Proverbs 9, for example, Wisdom is presented as strong and positively feminine. But then she is contrasted with Folly—a deceptive and seductive woman. The very contrast itself draws attention to a strongly negative cultural paradigm of woman. Wisdom's own probity is subtly undermined.[31] It is perhaps this very 'pitch', drawing attention to a view of woman as potentially deceptive and seductive, appealing to some irrational and dangerous passion in men, that makes Wisdom's gender problematic and, for Augustine, renders her feminine persona unhelpful in this exegetical context.

Of course, it could also be argued that in the earliest Christian centuries, very little significance was attached generally to the gender of Wisdom in its connection with the Word of the Prologue. Thus, Augustine's omission might be merely 'circumstantial'. Some modern biblical scholars are beginning to argue, however, that the relationship between Wisdom and the Word of the Prologue is a good deal more significant than earlier commentators have allowed. The implication of this might be that earlier commentators such as Augustine have actually contributed to the *suppression* of a connection between the two. Adela Yarbro Collins, for example, writing in the early 1980s, argues that the presentation of the Logos in the Prologue is parallel with the typical presentations of Wisdom in the Wisdom literature, and she argues that Wisdom and Logos are virtually interchangeable in the Wisdom literature of Solomon and Philo.[32] She is the more convinced of this argument in the context of the Prologue, because she believes that a very female personification of Wisdom is called to mind at various other key moments in the Gospel—for example she points to the motif of Jesus offering food and drink as symbols of instruction and revelation,[33] that is

31. See Judith McKinlay, *Gendering Wisdom the Host: Biblical Invitations to Eat and Drink* (JSOTSup, 216; Gender, Culture, Theory, 4; Sheffield: Sheffield Academic Press, 1996), p. 62.

32. See Adela Yarbro Collins, 'New Testament Perspectives: The Gospel of John', *JSOT* 22 (1982), pp. 47-53 (50).

33. See indirectly Jn 2.8; 4.10; 6.11-14, 35.

both characteristic of Wisdom personified[34] and of activities culturally associated with women and with the nurturing that they represent.[35]

Martin Scott, making similar connections, builds a convincing case for saying that these Wisdom traditions offered, within the history of the Jewish religion, a means of accommodating feminine aspects of God while retaining the heavily masculinized monotheism that distinguished it so clearly from the cults and religions alongside which it developed. Scott argues strongly that the gender of Wisdom was *always* of central significance and that for precisely this reason her position did not remain unchallenged. He traces in Sirach, for example, both a development and elevation of her role as creatrix[36] and also an identification with Torah, seeing in this identification an attempt to suppress the significance of the gender of Wisdom. When it comes to John's Gospel, Scott argues that it is precisely the awkwardness of gender that prevents a closer identification of Jesus with Wisdom, although he also argues at length that the Gospel presents a fully developed 'Sophia-Christology'.

Whereas Collins suggests that references to Wisdom in John cannot generally be said to belong to the conscious intentionality of its author(s), Scott believes that Jesus-Sophia is an essential key to the whole Gospel. But this hypostasis or personification is undeniably veiled. Even Scott recognizes that she cannot be named directly and that she cannot be named as feminine, suggesting that, in the light of the developed theory of pre-existence in this Gospel, it may be precisely Jesus' masculinity that is constitutive of what or who is pre-existent. But whatever Scott or Collins, for example, argue about the resources available for more inclusive ways of interpreting the Gospel of John, references to the female identity of the Wisdom figure depend on a series of inferences.[37] The explicitly masculine images of Logos and Son of God within the Prologue have acquired a certain unassailable predominance. And Augustine shows no interest in challenging this by reference to a female figure of Wisdom.

34. See, for example, Prov. 9.1-5.

35. Yarbro Collins, 'New Testament Perspectives', p. 51.

36. Martin Scott, *Sophia and the Johannine Jesus* (JSNTSup, 71; Sheffield: JSOT Press, 1992), p. 78.

37. The strongest arguments relate to the connection between the creative, sustaining work of Word (Jn 1.3-4), and the close textual relationship between the Prologue and such passages from Wisdom literature in, for example, Prov. 9.1 and Sir. 24.8.

Augustine's tractates employ a number of structural metaphors or in-terpretative symbols. In the first tractate which is concerned with under-standing the relationship of God and Word, he employs the metaphor of the nursing mother and her milk. This is the development of a scriptural metaphor taken especially from the writings of Paul where a mother's milk sometimes represents the first and most easily digested spiritual sus-tenance; a necessary prelude for Christian believers not ready for 'strong-er meat', because they are yet 'of the flesh'.[38] The evangelist John himself—identified with the 'beloved disciple'—is seen by Augustine to have been first nursed at the Lord's breast but, ultimately, to have replaced that milk with words:

> that John, my brothers, who reclined upon the breast of the Lord and who drank from the breast of the Lord that which he might give us to drink. But he has given you words to drink.[39]

Later on Augustine uses the same image to give encouragement to those who might find the discussion hard going:

> 'If, therefore, the Word was in the beginning, and the Word was with God, and the Word was God,' if you cannot imagine what it is, put it off so that you may grow up. That is solid food; take milk that you may be nourished, that you may be strong enough to take solid food.[40]

And the same image takes another turn when those who find the argu-ment hard to follow are encouraged to 'nurse' what they can follow like a child who is eventually to grow up. Significantly, this child is asso-ciated with Christ, born of the flesh, and the whole metaphorical cluster is tied into a reference to something necessary but necessarily to be superseded:

> Let each person grasp as he can, as far as he can; and he who cannot grasp, let him nourish it in his heart that he may be able to. With what is he to nourish it? Let him nourish it with milk so that he may arrive at solid food. Let him not withdraw from Christ, born through flesh, until he arrives at Christ, born from the one Father, the Word, God with God, through whom all things were made.[41]

It seems that Augustine sees the female figure of the nursing mother and the milk she produces from her body as an appropriate configuration of

38. 1 Cor. 3.1-2. See also Heb. 5.12, 13; 1 Pet. 2.2.
39. *Tractate* 1.7.2.
40. *Tractate* 1.12.2.
41. *Tractate* 1.17.3.

the person and activity of the Lord himself. But the figure and the substance she produces are associated, as in the New Testament sources of the metaphor, simply with spiritual infancy. Milk and presumably also mother are to be left behind by the spiritually mature. Of course, in terms of his reflections on the text of the Prologue, Augustine is using this image rhetorically to encourage his listeners to persist in trying to make sense of such a profound passage of Scripture rather than as an interpretative model for something within the passage itself. The metaphor of milk still functions, however, to support and strengthen the hierarchical pattern of bodily subordination, since it represents a lower level of spiritual development. The spiritualized category of 'milk' is to be superseded by that of 'word'.

3. *The Feminine Identification of Carnality*

Explicitly feminine images within Augustine's sermons on the Prologue seem to be something of a blind alley for the feminist reader. Wisdom is absent and the nursing mother (Mary—Mother of the Word/Mother of the Church of believers?), while present, seems definitively subordinate.[42] Could anything be said to escape from or challenge the hierarchical pattern of gender-identified values and roles within Augustine's sermons on the Prologue?

'Flesh' figures in the *Tractates 1–3* very largely, as it does in the Pauline literature. It is related hierarchically to a masculine-identified 'spirit'. The pattern of the subjugation of flesh to spirit is very clearly drawn, and explicitly related to a standard cultural model of gender hierarchy:

> and the Apostle says 'he who loves his wife loves himself. For no one ever hates his own flesh.' Therefore 'flesh' is put for 'wife', just as also sometimes 'spirit' is put for 'husband'. Why? Because the latter governs,

---

42. It is interesting to note, however, the way in which Augustine describes his mother's behaviour towards him in the *Confessions*. While he is critical of her possessiveness and certainly does not exempt her from the inheritance of sorrow which is 'Eve's legacy' (*Confessions* 5.8), he dwells on her suffering in language that evokes both Christic and Marian themes. 'Night and day my mother poured out her tears to you and offered her heart-blood in sacrifice for me' (*Confessions* 5.7). He speaks of her anxiety for his spiritual birth in terms of the pain of childbirth (*Confessions* 5.9). He comes close to giving her the credit, through her perseverance and prayer, for his reconversion to Catholic Christianity (*Confessions* 5.9).

the former is governed; the latter ought to rule, the former to serve. For when the flesh commands and the spirit serves, the house is awry. What is worse than a house where the woman has absolute authority over the man? But upright is the house where the man commands, the woman obeys. Upright, therefore, is mankind itself when the sprit commands, the flesh serves.[43]

Once spirit and flesh are identified in this gendered way, of course, the justification for making the relationships between actual men and women relate more closely to the symbolic pattern is all the stronger. The symbolic masculinity of the spirit is, in this quotation, used to justify the argument that men ought to control women and to support the stereotyping of women as incapable of controlling a household properly. Arguably Augustine's view that defects of the soul are passed on through physical conception[44] is itself an illustration of the same dynamic at work. After all, humankind's (spiritual, masculine) contamination through irrational (fleshly, feminine) desire is perfectly illustrated in sexual intercourse between unequal partners (male and female, or female substitute).

Augustine, accounting the natural man '*ex anima et carne*' as 'fleshly' in body *and* mind, would submit them both to a spiritual scrutiny and control. Woman and the feminine, within this system, belong to a symbolic realm *doubly* to be distrusted. They signify powerfully the essential bodily, material elements of all human experience, which are suspect because characterized by the change and decay that is not shared by the things of God, and they also represent a perniciously irrational carnality that affects both body and mind[45] and needs to be controlled by the masculinity of the spiritual. And I believe that one may read here, in the description of concupiscence, the imprint of a phallogocentricity that characterizes the whole of *human* experience in terms of a drive towards a singular *male* identity and an anxiety about its loss or confusion.

And yet, of course, within this text, Augustine recognizes that, within the divine scheme of Incarnation, whatever is represented by 'flesh' is divinely necessary. Augustine reads this necessity in terms of human need of course. In order that humankind can be born of God, God must first be born in the 'flesh'. The intertwining of human birth from God

43. *Tractate* 2.14.3.
44. *Tractate* 3.12.1.
45. *De Trinitate* 12.8.

and the birth of the divine as human is the main theme of the second
Tractate (Jn 1.6-24):

> Why then are you astonished that men are born of God? Notice that
> God himself was born of men: 'And the Word was made flesh, and dwelt
> among us'.[46]

And yet it is questionable whether Augustine's reading of Incarnation in
this Johannine text ever seriously challenges the prevailing hierarchy of
spirit over flesh, or recognizes its autonomous validity.

Augustine, like most other commentators, apparently feels the *necessity* of introducing Jesus' mother[47] into interpretation of the Prologue,
although she is not mentioned in the text. To include the human mother of the Word is, of course, in one sense, to make a very clear suggestion about the necessity of the 'flesh'. Without the human mother, the
Word could not be born as human child. However the tendency is,
somehow, to try to dissociate the Word from the contaminating 'otherness' or disturbing confusion of which woman and the feminine have
become such rich and disturbing symbols within patriarchal culture.
Thus the mother is typically described as a virgin and thus utterly separated from sexual knowledge, that highly evocative symbol of human
heterogeneity.

But although he appears to take them for granted,[48] Augustine does
not lay great stress on the mother's virginity or innocence of the carnal
passions. In fact, rather to the contrary, the fleshliness of Christ and his
dwelling alongside humankind is stressed as the necessary means whereby individuals can be born safely[49] of God. But the necessity of the
'flesh' attested within this Johannine narrative of Incarnation is, for
Augustine, largely carried by a very different metaphor in these tractates.
This image is one of blindness and its cure, which focuses on the
description of carnality, not in terms of flesh, but of earth or dust or
mud. And it is arguable that Augustine must here plead guilty to the
charge that he is performing theological conjuring tricks by sleight of
hand, since his use of earthy indices of carnality in this context, which
is in any case very largely given a spiritualized interpretation, distracts

---

46. *Tractate* 2.15.2.
47. *Tractate* 2.15.1.
48. *Tractate* 2.15.1: 'For Christ is God, and Christ was born from among men.
Indeed, he sought on earth only a mother since he already had a father in heaven.'
49. *Tractate* 2.15.1.

attention from the tricky area of just how carnal and fleshly the Incarnation must be to produce its effect.

> Indeed, because 'the Word was made flesh, and dwelt among us,' by the nativity itself he made a salve by which the eyes of our heart may be wiped clean and we may be able to see his majesty through his lowliness.[50]

Augustine constructs a powerful image of the Incarnation as a remedy that will enable man, blinded by lack of faith, to see the glory of God (Jn 1.14):

> His glory no one could see unless he were healed by the lowliness of his flesh. Why could we not see? Concentrate, my beloved people, and see what I am saying. Dust, so to speak, had forcibly entered man's eye; earth had entered it, had injured the eye, and it could not see the light. That injured eye is anointed; it was injured by earth, and earth is put there that it may be healed. For all salves and medicines are nothing but [compounds] of earth. You have been blinded by dust, you are healed by dust; thus the flesh had blinded you, flesh heals you. For the soul had become carnal by assenting to carnal passions; from that the eye of the heart had been blinded. 'The Word was made flesh'. That physician made a salve for you. And because he came in such a way that by his flesh he might extinguish the faults of the flesh and by his death he might kill death, it was therefore effected in you that, because 'the Word was made flesh' you could say, 'And we saw his glory'.[51]

Incarnation within these tractates stands as a recognition of the efficacy, the value, the central *necessity* of 'flesh'/carnality. The analogy with the remedy is strange but suggestive since the healing salve is composed from the same source as the dust which caused the injury. And the potential of 'dust'—of carnality—to both harm and heal displaces it momentarily from hierarchies of value, from the discourse of subjugation. It is removed temporarily from the prevailing hierarchical view of the subjection of flesh to spirit.

But of course the action of healing is performed by the physician. The motif of the physician as an image of Christ was used widely by the Christian Fathers as by Augustine[52] himself and there is thus little real potential for reading a deconstructive challenge to spiritual values which exclude the flesh within Augustine's interpretation. The re-inscription

---

50. *Tractate* 2.16.1.
51. *Tractate* 2.16.2.
52. See Rettig (ed. and trans.), *St. Augustine: Tractates 1–10*, p. 73 n. 42.

of Incarnation as healing refers specifically to the healing of spiritual blindness caused by carnality. Restored sight enables us to see the glory 'as of the only begotten of the Father, full of grace and truth'.[53] New birth is cure. The sovereignty of sight, transcendent reason, is quickly restored:

> Now because he did this, he cured [us]; because he cured [us], we see. For this, namely that 'the Word was made flesh, and dwelt among us,' became a medicine for us, so that since we were blinded by earth, we might be healed by earth.[54]

In reading Augustine's tractates on the Prologue, and particularly the representation of divine Incarnation as the cure for an inherited spiritual blindness, some connection with the text of John 9 naturally suggests itself. Here indeed is the physician, Jesus, curing blindness with a salve of earth and spittle in defiance of the (Sabbath) law that can only diagnose the weakness and not provide the remedy (Jn 1.17).[55] Here too is an insistent if uneasy discussion of the relationship of birth and sin. The mother hovers in the background, signifying—in her cooperation with/corruption of her husband—body and carnality, the cause of spiritual blindness she is impotent to cure (Jn 9.1-2, 18-22). For here birth that is related to human conception is clearly read by Augustine as having to do with inherited sinfulness:

> this blind man is the human race, for this blindness happened through sin in the first man from whom we all have taken the origin not only of death, but also of wickedness.[56]

There is thus a parallel between the metaphor of the remedy and the physician in the second and third *Tractates* and Augustine's reading of the story of the blind man in John 9 in *Tractate* 44. Physical birth is again related to spiritual blindness. Thus physical birth is unavoidably presented as an indication of spiritual sickness. Yet, in reading these two passages, Augustine interprets defilement as the cure, the story linking blindness with lack of faith as an inherited flaw.[57] And once again there

---

53. *Tractate* 3.6.3.
54. *Tractate* 3.6.2.
55. *Tractate* 3.14.1.
56. *Tractate* 44.1.2.
57. In Latin, *vitium*. See John W. Rettig (ed. and trans.), *St. Augustine: Tractates on the Gospel of John 28–54* (Washington: Catholic University of America Press, 1993), pp. 175-76.

is an echo both of *necessary* carnality and sleight of hand. Linking Word
and spittle and flesh and mud,[58] Augustine declares this as a symbol of
the mystery: the Word become flesh. And the resulting salve or oint-
ment of mud and spittle is besmeared on the blind man's eyes. To be
healed, released from the inherited defilement, requires the man to
become 'besmeared', that is, defiled again. But just as before, in Augustine's description of divine Incarnation in the earlier tractates, the
suggestion of a more radical cure for carnality through carnality is
modified by the image of the physician. Here the cure seems performed
in two modes: besmearing and then washing—a washing clearly associated with baptism:

> What did I say about the spittle and the mud? That the Word was made
> flesh. The catechumens also hear this; but for the purpose for which they
> have been besmeared this does not suffice for them. Let them hurry to
> the baptismal font if they seek light.[59]

Once again, the Incarnation figures as dust, as the defiling and defining 'otherness'. But it is identified here with the proper subjugation of
the female to the male. This dust is accounted the cure of spiritual
blindness. But ultimately, the salvific role of carnality is undercut within
Augustine's writing on John 1 and John 9 by his unwillingness to abandon the fundamental discourse of subjection and the sovereignty of
(masculine) reason. However necessary 'flesh' might be in divine Incarnation, it is always configured as the lower term in a hierarchy of values
that accounts spiritual values higher. Thus references to the 'flesh' in
these tractates are already largely metaphors for Augustine's spiritual
concerns.

4. *The Word Made Flesh?*

If the reader then looks for the feminine within Augustine's exegetical
sermons on the Prologue she is to be found, explicitly and positively, as
the nursing mother, configuring both the Lord, and Augustine himself
as exegete, even though she and her milk remain associated with imma-
turity and—spiritualized—dependence. But she is also present implicitly
and, perhaps more ambivalently, in Augustine's treatment of the 'flesh'.
In itself, 'flesh' is an image of something injurious to the soul, something

58. *Tractate* 44.2.1.
59. *Tractate* 44.2.2.

whose effects are damaging or disruptive. Defined within a discourse of male sovereignty and female subjugation, I believe that 'flesh' presents Augustine with something of a problem. I think that he gets around the difficulty largely by treating the disruptive 'flesh' as merely the sign of the ultimate divine (masculine/singular) imperialism. Contained within the hierarchical definition of values that Augustine adopts, whatever of difference or of 'otherness' is represented by reference to 'flesh' is simply absorbed without remainder by the divine, becoming part of his divine and spiritual splendour. Safely spiritualized or, so to speak, transposed into a divine key, 'flesh' may be recognized as necessary. Spiritually speaking Christ's Incarnation was necessary to restore spiritual sight and wholeness.

What is clear is that Augustine himself was comfortable with the hierarchical implications of a gendered dualism, moving from 'masculine' to 'feminine' positions depending upon the context. If he advocated the feminine role vis-à-vis God for human believers[60] or made a clear association between woman and the disturbing forces of sexuality, his preference for an authoritative masculine divinity remained etched into his theological position, but—self-consciously—largely unexplored.

5. *Woman and the Feminine and Gender Hierarchy in Relation to Dualism and Original Sin*

Augustine's attitude towards and use of the symbolism of gender may be further explored in an examination of how, in these three short tractates on the incarnational text of the Prologue to John's Gospel, he draws together the characteristic outlines of his teaching on original sin and against any fully Manichaean dualism. In both cases woman and the feminine play a very particular role.

---

60. See William E. Connolly, *The Augustinian Imperative: A Reflection on the Politics of Morality* (Newberry Park, CA: Sage Publications, 1993), pp. 55-61. Connolly argues that Augustine adopted, in relationship to God, the model he believed had been given to him by his mother, Monica, in coping with and influencing the men in her life. That is to say, Connolly argues, that she maximized the potential of her subject position and prevailed through patience, obedience but also gentle persistence. Or, putting it another way, he rationalized his mother's sufferings and the injustice of her treatment by regarding it as an effective way of dealing with a tempestuous tyrant.

Augustine's interpretation of Jn 1.17, which brings together, in the same verse, both the gifts of the law and of grace and truth, makes of this juxtaposition a comparison in an explicitly Pauline sense. He quotes 'the Apostle': 'The Law entered in that sin might abound'[61] (Rom. 5.20), and he designates Moses, through whom the Law was given, as a servant incapable of granting release from guilt:

'The Law was given through Moses; grace and truth came through Jesus Christ.' Through a servant the Law was given; it made men guilty. Through an emperor pardon was given; it set free the guilty. 'The Law was given through Moses.' Let the servant not consign to himself anything greater than what was done through him. Chosen for a great ministry as a faithful man in the house, but still a servant, he can act according to the Law; he cannot release from the guilt of the Law.[62]

The reference to the Law draws Augustine into a discussion of the concupiscence of the flesh, and of the solidarity of all men as sinners, with Adam:

It was not because they willed it that men have been born from Adam; nonetheless all who are from Adam are sinners with sin.[63]

Augustine, in formulating his understanding of an inherited propensity to sin—to break God's law and will evil rather than good—seems to have been attempting to project a vision of God that would do justice to a spectrum of deeply felt emotions, including his longing both to love and be satisfied[64] and his aesthetic and sensual sensitivity as well as a strong sense of human helplessness and anxiety. At the same time, for him, any such vision needed to be intellectually rigorous and in accordance with his rational understanding. His approach, formed by the rhetorical training of his youth, was defined in intellectual terms. While Augustine saw that there was often an intellectual arrogance in the solutions proposed by thinkers he met along his long journey to faith in the Catholic Church, he was not anti-intellectual. A proposal to suit all these requirements proved, for a long time, beyond his grasp.

61. *Tractate* 3.11.1.
62. *Tractate* 3.16.1.
63. *Tractate* 3.12.2.
64. *Confessions* 2.2, 5: 'The eye is attracted by beautiful objects, by gold and silver and all such things. There is great pleasure too, in feeling something agreeable to the touch and material things have various qualities to please each of the other senses. Again, it is gratifying to be held in esteem by other men and to have the power of giving them orders and gaining the mastery over them.'

The solution he proposed eventually had the result of focusing attention upon sexual desire as a form of punishment—and it is quite clear within the *Confessions* that this is precisely how he is both reconstructing and indeed *experiencing* his own youthful—and considerable—desire for sexual satisfaction. But in fact, of course, he understands the first sin, as recounted in Genesis, to be disobedience—or perhaps more exactly the *wilfulness* of going against God's prohibition. And this wilfulness is distressing largely because it seems inexplicable to Augustine in any rational sense, even that sense that would see disobedience as a means to achieving some wicked end. In the *Confessions*, Augustine dwells at length on what he sees as a particularly shameful incident in his youth, when he, along with a group of other boys or young men, stole pears from a tree:

> I was willing to steal, and steal I did, although I was not compelled by any lack, unless it were the lack of a sense of justice or a distaste for what was right and a greedy love of doing wrong. For of what I stole I already had plenty, and much better at that, and I had no wish to enjoy the things I coveted by stealing, but only to enjoy the theft itself and the sin ... We took away an enormous quantity of pears, not to eat them ourselves, but simply to throw them to the pigs. Perhaps we ate some of them, but our real pleasure consisted in doing something that was forbidden.[65]

According to Augustine this will to evil had no cause or was its own cause, a sort of convention for the category of nothingness—outwith God; the futile gesture of the convicted prisoner, pointing to an alternative that was no alternative; a defiance against any sort of rationality; the result of a fundamental *misconception* of the founding relationship between God and humankind. Essentially, it was something defective and not effective at all.

> The truth is that one should not try to find an efficient cause for a wrong choice. It is not a matter of efficiency, but of deficiency; the evil will itself is not effective but defective. For to defect from him who is the Supreme Existence, to something of less reality, this is to begin to have an evil will. To try to discover the causes of such defection—deficient, not efficient causes—is like trying to see darkness or to hear silence. Yet we are familiar with darkness and silence, and we can only be aware of them by means of eyes and ears, but this is not by perception but by absence of perception.[66]

---

65. *Confessions* 2.4.
66. *City of God* 12.7.

It thus becomes clearer how such ideas might be reconnected with his commentary on the Prologue, where Augustine appears to see the Law and the lawgiver, Moses—in contradistinction perhaps to many modern commentators[67]—as something essentially to be delivered from, by God's grace. The law against stealing and against fornication and adultery was, in terms of Augustine's tormented understanding of wilfulness, a scourge, revealing, at least to him, the essential helplessness of the will, without God, to avoid willing what is evil. And, of course, there is a perfectly clear line of inference from such a conviction to the belief that this irrational defect was passed on through the act that itself carried the rational soul—particularly as Augustine understands this in the *Confessions* in relation to his own life—so close to the chaotic waters of irrational, inexplicable motivation; the formation of the new soul through the spiritual and creative generation of man and woman in sexual intercourse.[68]

A late-twentieth-century feminist perspective suggests that part at least of his problem with sexuality seems to have been caused by the overvaluation of reason and rationality within patriarchal society as a whole and in his intellectual circles in particular. He was clearly deeply sensitive to the sense in which the urgency of his own sexual demand challenged that rationality, that intellect within him by which, and only by which, he came to account himself better than the animals and made in the image of God:

> If therefore you are better than an animal precisely because you have a mind with which you may understand what the animal cannot understand, and, in fact, therein a man because you are better than a cow, the light of men is the light of minds. The light of minds is above minds and transcends all minds.[69]

---

67. See, for example, Raymond E. Brown, *The Gospel According to John I–XII: A New Translation with Introduction and Commentary* (AB, 29; New York: Doubleday, 1966). Brown sees the reference to Moses in honorific terms, relating Jn 1.17 to Jn 1.45; 3.14; 5.46.

68. Augustine favoured a 'generationist' position on the origin of souls. That is to say he rejected the idea that human souls were created either individually or *en masse*, before their bodies were produced by their parents' sexual relationship. Equally, of course, he rejected the idea that souls were simply and solely the product of human intercourse.

69. *Tractate* 3.4.3.

In the *Confessions*, his confusion is revealed in the suggestion that the institute of marriage, defined simply in relation to procreation as God's purpose, and the making of himself a eunuch for love of the kingdom of heaven, represent some sort of realistic alternatives. As he himself attests, he desperately needed some solution to the problem of relating those powerful elements within him of sexuality, affective emotion and intellect:

> I was tossed and spilled, floundering in the broiling sea of my forni-
> cation, and you said no word. How long it was before I learned that you
> were my true joy.[70]

Eventually, he seems to have resolved the difficulty by cutting the sexual urge and the joyousness of its satisfaction loose, and redefining them as aberrant. Desire and its satisfaction are spiritualized and re-routed through the forms of a fundamentally feminine compliance[71] in obedient, joyous devotion to the God of grace. If it worked for Augustine it undoubtedly left Western Christendom with something of a legacy. For at least the next ten centuries, and probably much longer, orthodox Christianity was deeply influenced by this Augustinian anxiety about the body and its non-rational motivations and modalities that bore witness to a fundamental drive towards masculine singularity and away from the claims of humankind to express a positively evaluated heterogeneity.

As a convert from the Manichee philosophy, Augustine was more conscious than many, of course, of its potential attractions. He drew up a comparison between Catholic and Manichee positions, most explicitly in a series of books (c. 421 CE), *Against Two Letters of the Pelagians*, which were fundamentally addressed to the position of Julian of Eclanum, who led a movement of bishops against the condemnation of Pelagianism.[72]

70. *Confessions* 2.2.

71. See Connolly, *The Augustinian Imperative*, p. 58. 'After her death, Monica continues to live within Augustine as a set of tactical dispositions through which to relate to the (masculine) god who stands above him. Augustine internalizes the voice of Monica with respect to his god. Specifically, I want to suggest, Augustine enacts the traditional code of a devout woman with respect to this god and the traditional code of an authoritative male with respect to human believers and non believers below him.'

72. Julian of Eclanum was an adherent of the Pelagians' teaching on free will and the essential goodness of humankind. Fundamentally, Pelagius believed that to account humankind too damaged and too weak to help itself was to discourage individual effort to improve and do good. Eventually, Pelagius's teaching was

Julian accused the Catholics, and particularly Augustine, of being covert Manichees. Augustine therefore felt that it was important to make distinctions between all three positions—Catholic, Manichee and Pelagian—in order properly to answer Julian's criticisms.

The dispute between Augustine and Julian, however, became somewhat of a slanging match, terms such as 'Pelagian' and 'Manichee' being bandied about rather as abusive slogans. But, in substance, Julian accused Augustine of slipping back into modes of thought that belonged to an earlier Manichaean period before his conversion to Catholic Christianity.[73] One general issue of contention between the two men concerned marriage and the role of sexual intercourse within that. The religion of Mani simply relegated genital sexuality to the realm of the devil, though for the lower grade of adherents or 'Hearers', sexual partners were tolerated.[74] Against those of Julian's opinion, who complained that Augustine, favouring celibacy, condemned marriage, Augustine also wrote *De bono conjugali* and *De nuptiis et concupiscentia* in which he attempted to defend both the state of marriage and his own distinctive approach. The key to Augustine's position was that although marriage was good, sexual union was not, except in so far as there was a very specific purpose to it:

> It lay beyond the control of reason, and that, to Augustine, and to the mind of any contemporary Platonist, showed it to be, not a good but intrinsically an evil thing, sanctified only within marriage and for the procreation of children... The desire to have children and care for them and educate them is surely, says Augustine, an appetite not of the lust (libido), but of the reason... It is the mode of begetting which has been infiltrated by evil, as a result of the sin of Adam. If Adam had not sinned, he would have begotten his children not by lust but by rational decision (*De nupt*; II. vii. 18).[75]

It does seem that once again, Augustine is trying to have his cake and eat it too. The reason why the Catholics were accused by Julian and his

condemned by the Catholic Church but Julian refused to accept the ruling, gathering together a group of sympathetic Italian bishops. Eventually in 419 CE he was forced into exile, from where he continued to write letters and books, some of them directed specifically at Augustine.

73. Augustine describes this event, understood to have occurred during 386 CE, in great detail in *Confessions* 8.

74. See Chadwick, *Augustine*, p. 11.

75. Gillian R. Evans, *Augustine on Evil* (Cambridge: Cambridge University Press, 2nd edn, 1990), p. 144.

like of being covert Manichees was not so much that they favoured celibacy over marriage—although the Manichaeans certainly did this—but, surely, that the *reasons* for this preference, as expounded by Augustine and other Catholics, were based upon an association of marriage with sexuality and sexuality with the material realm understood as evil. The dualistic tenets of the Manichee philosophy therefore were seen as the underlying explanation for their unwillingness to accord marriage a greater status. Jovinian, for example, had accused the Catholics of being Manichaean on account of their teaching about the virginity of Mary even after the birth of Jesus. Such a teaching perhaps offended against the perception that procreation and sexuality are intrinsically physical and bodily and that these are also definitively human. Thus for Christ to become 'human' without the physical, bodily, material point of reference—conception by sexual intercourse—shared (at that time) by all other human individuals, is to draw an absolute distinction between the humanity of Christ and the humanity of every other human being. And this is a distinction that lends itself to the definition, so characteristic of the Manichee point of view, of materiality as evil.

Certainly, Augustine distinguishes the notion of an evil will very clearly from the notion of materiality as intrinsically evil. But one senses that in his writing about marriage and sexual intercourse within marriage, the distinction dilutes the sacramental solemnity of marriage that was taken up in later mediaeval spirituality, for example, in its understanding of the relationship between Christ and his Church which is centrally concerned with the admixture of divinity and materiality in the Incarnation. It is as if, repeatedly, Augustine cannot quite face the logical inference from the very form of Incarnation which he teaches, that it represents some ultimate reversal, some absolute status for what he would regard as lying beyond the realm of positively divine (masculine) value and within the realm of the carnal, in its very irrational (feminine) desires.

In *De bono conjugali*, Augustine speaks of marriage in terms of Roman law, as constituted by the consent of the couple rather than having to do with sexual consummation. In the same work he praises three good constituents of marriage—the purpose of procreation and the benefits of mutual fidelity and 'sacramental' indissolubility. While he certainly makes mention of sexual pleasure, this is not accounted as especially good, but as an impulse which has a right use but also a tendency to be 'misused'.[76] In sum, Augustine's attitude towards sexual intercourse within marriage could be justifiably described as marked by suspicion, mistrust and anxiety. By the letter of what Augustine writes, it is accounted positive and God-given, but his approval is circumscribed and guarded.

Of course, one might argue that Augustine here presents a view of marriage that attempts to see it as more than the mere context of sexual satisfaction. This is a point of view that might find favour with modern feminists by contesting the view of woman, within patriarchal forms of marriage, as merely a receptacle for semen and babies.[77] But the impression remains that, as a Christian, Augustine accepted divine authorization of the dangerous delights of sexual involvement as an exercise in humility. In one sense it required humility since the impulse towards sexual satisfaction and sexual ecstasy swamps the mind[78] and literally motivates the body without conscious control, obliterating the icon of rationality that, for Augustine, clearly represented God himself. In another sense, as he relates in the *Confessions*, the account of his own life revealed how far this particular impulse had, in the past, ruled his own life.

6. *Conclusions*

I believe that the process whereby Augustine reached his definition of a damaged or tainted will is illuminated by the conclusions of modern theoretical feminism which would explain this process in terms of an anxiety produced by the unavoidable evidence of 'otherness' within the singular phallogocentric structures of patriarchal culture. I also believe that Augustine's efforts to make sense of and to articulate his perceptions of that which was strictly beyond the control of his conscious will be centred upon a common cultural hierarchy of values which had a gendered character. Thus the sort of incomprehensible desire for something apparently valueless is aptly symbolized in terms of sexual desire leading to intercourse with a woman (or female substitute), the very symbol of valuelessness. However, the Prologue of John's Gospel, an important source for orthodox Christian teaching about divine Incarnation, forces

76. See, Chadwick, *Augustine*, pp. 114-15.
77. See Margaret Atwood's treatment of the notion in her dystopic novel, *The Handmaid's Tale* (London: Virago, 1987).
78. See *Contra Julianum Pelagianum* 4.7.

the reader to address the question of how exactly God might engage with this incomprehensible desire or 'otherness' in becoming 'flesh'.

The solution Augustine offers here is ultimately, through grace, to make that 'flesh' disappear. By means of the 'flesh' that disturbs him because of its invocation of all that lies beyond the control of singular masculine rationality, 'flesh' is finally banished. 'Fleshly' birth, by the end of Augustine's commentary on the Prologue, is irrelevant, inessential and absent. And yet he is able to retain the appearance of commitment to the necessity of the 'flesh' by claiming that it has had an essential role in making possible our birth 'in Christ' without the concupiscence of the flesh.[79] In other words it has become itself the means of severing its own connections with inarticulate and desiring human experience. It has become the means to spiritualize humankind. And of course by this means, all references to woman and the feminine, their roles and modalities, become metaphorical, related to the lower term in a hierarchy of entirely spiritual values. Woman as a sexual, gendered being is eradicated because the will, damaged by a hereditary taint, is healed by the Incarnation so that the carnality, the materiality and the irrationality of sexuality are no longer necessary. Christian believers may continue to reproduce, but they will do so rationally, performing their parts in order to fulfil God's plan and not to satisfy any turbulent desire. Christian readers are urged, 'drive carnal thought from your hearts that you may truly be under grace, that you may belong to the New Testament',[80] seeing not with the eyes of the flesh[81] and in no need of carnal promises like the Israelites in the Wilderness.[82]

For individual women, Augustine appears to have had as much affection or respect as any other elitist male of the fourth or fifth century CE.[83] But it is also very apparent that he read this incarnational text

79. *Tractate* 3.12.1.
80. *Tractate* 3.19.1.
81. *Tractate* 3.21.1.
82. *Tractate* 3.19.3.
83. The *Confessions* attest movingly, for example, both to his love for his concubine (see 6.15 for example) and his spiritual companionship with his mother (see 9.10 for example). But, equally, the *Confessions* reveal that he saw no overriding reason against marrying, as an adult, a girl who had only just reached sexual maturity (see 6.13), for casting off a woman who had, on his own admission, been a loyal and loving companion (6.15), or for counselling anything more than prudence and compliance in the case of the flagrant physical abuse of women by their husbands (see 9.9).

within a phallogocentric context and that he therefore sought to articulate his experience according to its view of (masculine) singularity. Nevertheless, he clearly found that Christian orthodoxy ultimately suited him better than a more extreme dualism. And in conclusion, it seems to me that this may well have been because it enabled him to have his cake and eat it too. In other words, while he took the Prologue of John's Gospel, for example, to be saying that everything was created by God—thereby denying that there could be an autonomous demiurge or multiple principle of creation—he found that he could also effectively obliterate the troublesome aspects of material creation including those aspects of humankind related to desire. He could do this by defining the essentials of humanity simply in terms of its rationality, that is, the sense in which it was made in the image of God.[84] And by effectively redefining 'flesh' in fundamentally spiritual terms—as the bottom end of a gendered hierarchy of spiritual values—all aspects of human existence not included under the heading of the intellect could safely be relegated, ignored or excluded altogether from consideration. The material, feminine and physical nature of much of Augustine's imagery seems then, to me, to be deceptive. It does not recognize the positive value of the 'flesh' in itself, which might challenge God's divinely and masculine spiritual singularity, as try to tame and control it by rendering it merely metaphorical.

84. *Tractate* 3.4.

3

Hildegard of Bingen 1098–1179:
Visionary Reflections on the Prologue

At a later time I saw a mysterious and wonderful vision so that my inmost core was convulsed and I lost all bodily sensation, as my knowledge was altered to another mode, unknown to myself. And by the inspiration of God, drops, as it were, of sweet rain were sprinkled on my soul's understanding as the Holy Spirit filled John the Evangelist when he sucked the most profound revelations from the breast of Jesus... Thus the vision taught me and allowed me to explain all the words and teachings of the Evangelist which concern the beginning of God's works.[1]

1. *Introduction:* Liber divinorum operum

Hildegard von Bingen wrote *Liber divinorum operum* (Book of Divine Works) during the years 1163–1173.[2] It is a description of ten visions

---

1.   From *Vita Sanctae Hildegardis.* See Sabina Flanagan, *Hildegard of Bingen, 1098–1179: A Visionary Life* (London: Routledge, 1989), p. 141. The passage is a description of the experience that resulted in the writing of *Liber divinorum operum* which, in her own judgment, was Hildegard's most important work.

2.   The English version of Hildegard's Latin text referred to here, 'The Book of Divine Works: Ten Visions of God's Deeds in the World and Humanity', in Matthew Fox (ed.), *Hildegard of Bingen's Book of Divine Works with Letters and Songs* (trans. Robert Cunningham; Santa Fe, NM: Bear and Company, 1987), is an edited version, based on Heinrich Schipperge's German translation, entitled *Welt und Mensch: Das Buch 'De operatione Dei'* (Salzburg: Muller Verlag, 1965). Schipperge's version—also edited—is, in turn, based largely upon Codex 241, a manuscript in the library of the University of Ghent with the title *De operatione Dei* (On God's Work). It is believed that this Codex was prepared, under Hildegard's supervision, at Rupertsberg between 1170 and 1173. Schipperge also uses three other copies of the work, all entitled *Liber divinorum operum*: a thirteenth-century copy of Codex 241 found in the Wiesbadener Riesencodex (giant codex at Wiesbaden); Codex 683 of the Bibliothèque Municipale at Troyes (previously at the Abbey of Clairvaux); and Codex 1942 of the Biblioteca Governativa/Statale di Lucca. The first printed

and interpretations. Visionary experience was part of Hildegard's life from an early age. By her own account, she experienced her first vision before she was four years old.[3] However, it was not until she was in her forties that she came to understand these visions as something she had to communicate publicly. As she recalls in the preface to her first visionary work, *Scivias*,[4] the dramatic revelation, directing her unambiguously to write down what she saw, had begun quite suddenly during her forty-second year. And such voices then continued to instruct her:

> Transmit for the benefit of humanity an accurate account of what you see with your inner eye and what you hear with the inner ear of your soul.[5]

Hildegard admits she was at first extremely hesitant about complying with her heavenly orders. At first the anxiety and uncertainty made her ill. Ultimately however, she interpreted this sickness as God's punishment for her inactivity and silence and she confided in her male colleagues and superiors at Disibodenburg—the Benedictine monastery

edition appeared in 1761 under the name of Archbishop Giovanni Domenico Mansi. Although there are some doubts about its reliability, this edition contains the entire work and, in the nineteenth century, Jacques-Paul Migne used Mansi's complete edition in volume 197 of his monumental 221-volume *Patrologia Latina* (Paris: J.-P. Migne, 1844–65). Migne's work is now being replaced by *Corpus Christianorum Continuatio Mediaevalis* (CCCM) (Belgium: Brepols).

3.   Fragments of autobiographical material are included in the earliest biographical work, *Vita Sanctae Hildegardis* (Life of St Hildegard), begun by Godfrey, a monk from Disibodenburg who acted as Hildegard's secretary but died in 1176, leaving his biographical work unfinished. It was completed by Theodoric of Echternach in 1186. See quotation translated by the author in Peter Dronke, *Women Writers of the Middle Ages: A Critical Study of Texts from Perpetua (d. 203) to Marguerite Porete (d. 1310)* (Cambridge: Cambridge University Press, 1984), p. 145: 'And in the third year of my life I saw so great a brightness that my soul trembled; yet because of my infant condition could express nothing of it.'

4.   *Scivias*, 1151. The two further works in the trilogy of Hildegard's major works are *Liber vitae meritorum, per simplicem hominem a vivente luce revelatorum*, 1163 and, of course, *Liber divinorum operum (or De operatione Dei)*, 1173. See Barbara Newman, *Sister of Wisdom: St. Hildegard's Theology of the Feminine* (Aldershot: Scolar, 1987), p. 11 n. 29. Also see Flanagan, *Hildegard of Bingen*, p. 57: 'Hildegard's three major visionary works ... stand apart from her other writings because of their length, their shared visionary form, and their similar theological concerns.'

5.   See Hildegard's foreword to the first part of the work 'The World of Humanity', in Fox (ed.), *Hildegard of Bingen's Book*, p. 5.

where she had lived from the age of seven or eight.[6] They appear to have been supportive, affirming the particular charism she disclosed to them,[7] but it is clear that, initially, she still felt considerable disquiet about drawing attention to herself, a woman, in this way.[8]

Hildegard's responsibilities, reputation and assurance had grown substantially by the time she came to write *Liber divinorum operum*. She was then over 60, having an established reputation as a writer and spiritual advisor. From 1136,[9] she had been acknowledged as the leading figure among those nuns who lived within the environs of the monastery in Disibodenburg. Already, against strong opposition,[10] she had negotiated

6. Hildegard, the daughter of a minor nobleman in the area of Alzey (about 20 km south-west of Mainz), was enclosed by her parents as a child of seven or eight years, in the cell of Jutta, an anchoress of noble birth. Jutta's cell was attached to the Benedictine monastery at Disibodenburg. Although they were strictly and literally enclosed within the anchorage, other noble parents and daughters were undoubtedly attracted by the combination of respectable birth and notable spirituality they came to represent. Thus by 1113, when Hildegard was old enough to make her profession as a nun, Jutta and Hildegard had been joined by a number of other women, forming something more akin to a small convent community. See Flanagan, *Hildegard of Bingen*, pp. 2-3.

7. See Caroline Walker Bynum, *Holy Feast and Holy Fast: The Religious Significance of Food to Medieval Women* (Berkeley: University of California Press, 1987), pp. 229-30. Bynum draws attention to the sense in which the piety of women of the mediaeval period was sometimes welcomed by men. In their very displacement from the centre of mainstream ecclesiastical and theological structures, they were able to focus areas of ambivalence, for example to do with wealth and power, and their role as implicit or explicit critics of clerical corruption was widely recognized.

8. See, for example, a passage translated from Hildegard's *Vita* in Dronke, *Women Writers*, p. 145: '...in that vision I was forced by a great pressure (*pressura*) of pains to manifest what I had seen and heard. But I was very much afraid, and blushed to utter what I had so long kept silent.'

9. Jutta, Hildegard's teacher and mentor for more than 30 years, died in this year. Hildegard was her natural successor.

10. Hildegard proposed a move from the established monastic community at Disibodenburg to a largely undeveloped site about 30 km away. Objections were raised on the grounds that Hildegard was suffering from delusions. The authorities at Disibodenburg were probably also distressed at the prospect of losing both the prestige of Hildegard's presence and, also, the financial gains accruing as a result of dowries and endowments given to the monastery by the families of wealthy novices and sisters. See extract from the *Vita*, translated in Dronke, *Women Writers*, pp. 150-51.

a move for these sisters (c. 1150) to a separate establishment at Rupertsberg and she was, by this time, in the process of founding a second
convent.

Sabina Flanagan notes the sense in which Hildegard appears, increasingly after the revelatory experiences of 1143, to use her accounts and
interpretation of visions in a systematic way to develop certain key theological themes. Flanagan admits that it would be an oversimplification to
say the visions were a deliberate fiction, designed to give weight and
authority to theological speculation that might otherwise have been dismissed because of its author's gender and lack of formal education.[11] But
she argues that Hildegard's freedom to publish and preach was intimately bound up with her perceived divine gift of visionary prophecy.[12]
Certainly, in whatever Hildegard's visionary experience actually con-
sisted,[13] once it had been discussed at the synod at Trier in 1147–48 and
Pope Eugenius III had issued a letter of greeting to her with an apostolic
licence to continue writing, Hildegard's fame was assured among her
contemporaries at least. One indication of this is the increasing weight
and significance of her correspondence after this time.[14]

---

11. It seems clear that Hildegard always needed some secretarial assistance to
write her works. Barbara Newman notes 'Hildegard, despite her encyclopaedic
knowledge, never mastered Latin grammar well enough to write without a secretary
to correct her cases and tenses. Even with such assistance, her style suffers from
redundancies, awkward constructions, and baffling neologisms; and her ideas often
stretched her limited vocabulary to the breaking point' (Newman, *Sister of Wisdom*,
pp. 22-23).

12. See, for example, Newman, *Sister of Wisdom*, Chapter 1, '"A poor little
female"'.

13. The suggestion that Hildegard's visionary experiences were consistent with
the symptoms of both common and classical migraine has been referred to frequently since it was first made by Charles Singer (ed.), in *Studies in the History and
Method of Science* (2 vols.; Oxford: Clarendon Press, 1917–21). There is some
discussion of the idea in both Dronke, *Women Writers*, p. 147, and in Flanagan,
Hildegard of Bingen, pp. 199-209. Peter Dronke also offers a definition of the nature
of Hildegard's visions, based upon the analysis by a contemporary Scottish mystic,
Richard of St Victor, of four types of visionary experience. Dronke accounts
Hildegard's visions as belonging to the third type described by Richard, that is to say
a form of spiritual rather than purely physical vision in which 'the human spirit,
illuminated by the Holy Ghost, is led through the likenesses of visible things, and
through images presented as figures and signs, to the knowledge of invisible ones'
(Dronke, *Women Writers*, p. 146).

14. Correspondents after 1147 included three popes (Anastasius IV, Hadrian IV,

In attempting to distinguish the major philosophical and theological influences on Hildegard's work, readers are given a more difficult task than usual. Even a woman from a branch of the minor nobility could not expect to follow, systematically, the study of those subjects and techniques that were the basis of all secular and sacred learning during the mediaeval period.[15] But Hildegard was more fortunate than most girls of her time. She was taught to read—from the Bible—and, as Sabina Flanagan suggests, there may have been some cultural interchange between the monastery at Disibodenburg and the anchorage within its precincts. In her *Vita*, Hildegard notes, for example, that she had chosen, as a *magister*, one of the monks. He may well have provided her with ideas or even theological works to read for the purpose of spiritual development if for no more than this.[16]

Hildegard was living at a time during which the principles of mediaeval scholasticism were being put together by men like Anselm of Canterbury (1033–1109) and Peter Abelard (1079–1142).[17] But it seems that she looked beyond the theological mainstream and, perhaps, a little deeper into the Church's more popular traditions for inspiration. Her work is characterized by a great familiarity with Scripture, often interpreted mystically and allegorically and particularly by the figure or attributes of Wisdom, associated with a Platonizing cosmology that saw the divine as all-pervading, all-knowing and life-creating.[18] In 1 Corinthians, Paul refers to Christ as 'the wisdom of God' (1 Cor. 1.24) and

Eugenius III) and a number of European monarchs (Conrad III, Frederick Barbarossa, Henry II of England, Eleanor of Aquitaine, and the Byzantine Empress, Irene). See Dronke, *Women Writers*, p. 149, and Newman, *Sister of Wisdom*, p. 9.

15.   Somewhat ironically, such subjects were sometimes personified as female figures. See, for example, the Lady Philosophy of Boethius's *De consolatione philosophiae*. Boethius died in about 524 CE, but his work was important throughout the mediaeval period.

16.   See Flanagan, *Hildegard of Bingen*, pp. 36-37.

17.   It should perhaps be noted, however, that she pre-dated what many consider the ultimate formulation of the scholastic project, the *Summa theologica* (c. 1272–74) of St Thomas Aquinas (d. 1274), by almost a century.

18.   One or two contemporary theologians, such as William of Conches and Peter Abelard, argued for an explicit identification of this all-knowing Platonic world soul with the Holy Spirit. Abelard's teaching on this was condemned. Hildegard never mentions the term but arguably the vision of Caritas or divine Love in the first vision of *Liber divinorum operum* is itself a revelation of a comparable '*anima mundi*'. See Newman, *Sister of Wisdom*, p. 69.

many of the Greek Fathers of the Church use 'Wisdom' as a synonym for the Incarnate Word or Logos of John's Prologue. In so many ways influenced by the theological presuppositions of Augustine, the Western mediaeval Church seems not to have been inhibited by his lack of interest in this female figure. She figures widely in mediaeval thought, both learned and popular.[19] Hildegard's use of this theme of divine Wisdom supports the development of powerful feminine paradigms such as *Ecclesia*/Mother Church and Mary which set the feminine divine on centre stage in the cosmic dramas of creation and Incarnation.

In *Liber divinorum operum*, Hildegard presents her readers with a vision of the whole of God's works. It comprises three books: 'The World of Humanity', 'The Kingdom of the Hereafter' and 'The History of Salvation'. The scope of the visions is vastly ambitious and attempts to delineate the divine work in all its aspects: its ultimate Incarnation in the shaping of the cosmos—earth, heaven and hell—on the divinely ethical principles of love and justice; its characteristic salvation history from the Word's creation of Adam in the world through to the projection of a final conclusive apocalypse; and its particular indexing in the very structure of the human form. In its own right, *Liber divinorum operum* is a complex and considered work of theology.

2. The Prologue of John's Gospel

A phrase-by-phrase commentary on Jn 1.1-14 comes at the end of the first part of *Liber divinorum operum*, 'The World of Humanity'. Robert Cunningham gives the fourth and final vision described within that part of the work the title 'On the Articulation of the Body'. Unlike Augustine the Bishop, of course, Hildegard had no automatic or regular access

---

19. See Newman, *Sister of Wisdom*, p. 42. Newman notes that the Carolinian period (Charlemagne c. 742–814 CE) saw the development of something like a cult of *Sapientia*. She draws attention particularly to the dedications of York Minster and the palace chapel in Soissons to the Holy Wisdom, after the example of the Cathedral of Santa Sophia, Constantinople, in 538 CE. Alcuin (c. 735–804 CE) composed a votive *Mass of the Holy Wisdom*, which was still in use in 1570. See Marina Warner, *Alone of All her Sex: The Myth and the Cult of the Virgin Mary* (London: Pan Books, 1990), pp. 197-98. Warner writes about the 'complex of symbolism that associated the Virgin with Wisdom'. Particularly she notes a legend of St Bernard of Clairvaux, who saw a vision of the Virgin, and was fed by her with the milk of her breast. Such feeding and such milk—symbols of the sustenance of the Christian soul—are powerfully connected to the iconography of Wisdom.

to a public platform for scriptural exegesis. Why then did Hildegard make a special reference to *this* scriptural passage and why is it included at this point?

All four visionary texts within this first book are linked in one way or another to the human form. By 'human form', I refer first to Hildegard's understanding of the essential nature of humanity as composed of both body and soul.[20] Secondly I would argue that in her visions and theological reflections on them, she sees the shape or appearance of human figures as representing, besides the essentially composite—microcosmic—human entity, a yet larger composite—macrocosmic—entity. That is to say, such figures frequently symbolize aspects of the creation and workings of the whole divine cosmos. In the first three visions, Hildegard describes a form that is either human or like a human as the vision's central feature.[21] In the fourth vision, along with an extended discussion of the relationship of the human soul and body, the *parts* of the human body, separately described, form the basis for a discourse on the scope of God's cosmological economy.

I believe that the scriptural passage Jn 1.1-14 is presented as both summary and conclusion in this reflection on the human form as *model and essence of divine Incarnation*. The four preceding visions are, so to speak, extended illustrations or illuminations of the central incarnational theme of that passage. This is a hymn to the splendour and loving vital-

20. Vision 4.104. See Migne (ed.), *Patrologia Latina*, CXCVII, p. 888: 'Itaque ...talis est forma hominis cum corpore et anima opus etiam Dei cum omni creatura existens' (Such is the human form...made up of body and soul and we exist as God's work together with all creation).

21. One of the aspects of Hildegard's work that has particularly appealed to more recent admirers is undoubtedly the series of beautiful illustrations associated with her visions. These illustrations are fairly faithful renderings of central images within her written accounts. Illustrations from the *Liber divinorum operum,* reproduced in Newman, *Sister of Wisdom*, Flanagan, *Hildegard of Bingen*, Matthew Fox (ed.), *Illuminations of Hildegard of Bingen* (Santa Fe, NM: Bear and Company, 1985), are all taken from Lucca, Biblioteca Statale, Codex 1942. Illustrations in Fox (ed.), *Hildegard of Bingen's Book*, have been copied by Angela Werneke from the same manuscript. These illustrations date from 1200, after Hildegard's death, but still contain her 'signature' in the left-hand corner of each page, indicating a close reliance on the written texts. Reliable information is available, however, about the illustrations in Hildegard's earlier work, *Scivias*. It is at least clear, in this case, that Hildegard personally supervised the preparation of an illuminated manuscript edition of this earlier work in about 1165, and that therefore she must have regarded such illustrations as appropriate illustrations of her visionary theology, alongside her written descriptions.

ity of God and a vision of that love and vitality envisaged in the human form—body and soul together. It is indeed a vision that accords well with the view of women as more in tune with the pleasures and rhythms of the body and the relationship of both soul and body to the divine address, calling on humankind to respond, 'look at God in faith and acknowledge [its] Creator'.[22]

First of all, the descriptions of these visions contain reflections on divine creativity and Incarnation that explore the 'intertextuality' between the Prologue of John's Gospel and, in particular, the book of Genesis.[23] The first 14 verses of John's Gospel evoke for Hildegard the story in Genesis of the creation of all creatures, including man and woman in God's image. She understands the Word of Jn 1.1 in this sense of biblical creativity and records the interpretation of God's creative speech in the form of heavenly words:

> I spoke within myself my small deed, which is humanity. I formed this deed according to my own image and likeness so that it would be realized with respect to myself because my Son intended to adopt the garment of flesh as a human being.[24]

Hildegard combines these reflections with certain theories about the actual workings of the human body and soul that effectively increase the scope of the theological into what strikes the modern reader as a more purely medical or scientific writing.[25] But the interconnectedness of the two is one more illustration of her theme, emphasizing the interconnectedness and symbolic interdependence between all aspects of creation

---

22. *Liber divinorum operum*, Vision 4.105.

23. See, for example, *Liber divinorum operum*, Vision 1.2: 'For I am life. I am also Reason, which bears within itself the breath of the resounding Word, through which the whole of creation is made. I breathe life into everything… I am life, whole and entire (vita integra)—not struck from stones, not blooming out of twigs, not rooted in a man's power to beget children. Rather all life has its roots in me. Reason is the root, the resounding Word blooms out of it.' See also *Liber divinorum operum*, Vision 1.13: 'The figure treads upon both a frightful monster of a poisonously dark hue and a serpent' and references to Eve ('the woman'), *Liber divinorum operum*, Vision 1.17, and to Mary as, for example, the descendant of faithful Abraham, rather than of a deceived woman, Eve, *Liber divinorum operum*, Vision 1.20.

24. *Liber divinorum operum*, Vision 4.105.

25. See, for example, *Liber divinorum operum*, Vision 3: 'On Human Nature'. Here, Hildegard develops a theory of the humours of the human body. See also Newman, *Sister of Wisdom*, p. 126, on the mediaeval doctrine of elements.

so characteristic of her anthropology in general. Both health and disposition are linked to wider cosmic forces.

But is it possible to be more precise about the way in which Hildegard's visions of the human form can be related to her understanding of this Johannine passage? In the first place, the human form, placed centrally in Hildegard's visionary experience, is a structural element in her theological reflections on the Incarnation. The human form, understood as body and soul, interdependent and in relation both to each other and, together, to the whole cosmos, appears in these four visions as a key to unlock the mysteries of divine creation and especially the mystery of Incarnation powerfully and traditionally represented in the words of the Prologue to John's Gospel and understood by Hildegard as determining both the order and the purpose of the cosmos *from the beginning*:[26]

> We are an essence made up of body and soul, and we exist as God's work together with all of creation (*opus Dei cum omni creatura*). This is what is meant by the words John set down under my inspiration: IN PRINCIPIO ERAT VERBUM.[27]

26. Hildegard understood the Incarnation as the divine purpose for which the world was made. This absolutist or predestinarianist position stood in contrast to the mainstream view, as expressed, for example, in Anselm's *Cur Deus Homo?*, that God became man because it was the only way the evil of Adam's fall could be righted. Hildegard's visionary theology saw the Incarnation as the divine purpose set from the very beginning. Her position on this may have been influenced by reading the work of her contemporary Honorius of Regensberg, who popularized the work of the ninth-century Irish scholar Erigena (c. 810–877), who was, in turn, influenced by the Fathers of the Eastern Church. Erigenian teaching of absolute predestination regarded the Incarnation of the Word as predestined by God from the beginning, independently and without reference to Adam's fall from grace. The purpose of Incarnation according to this doctrine, which is strongly influenced by Neoplatonic themes, is the reuniting of the primordial causes with their created effects—wisdom, reason, power, justice. The divine Wisdom of the biblical and apocryphal Wisdom literature is thus brought together, within Hildegard's work, with the notion of the virtues, including wisdom, as causes or ideas within a mythological framework of emanation and return. The fulfilment of God's plan, whose completion is the reuniting of creation with divine Creator, is not placed in doubt, even by the fall into sin.

27. *Liber divinorum operum*, Vision 4.104.

Hildegard writes that 'God has inscribed the entire divine deed on the human form'.[28] And it is perhaps for this reason that she then makes no emphatic distinction here between the human form in a general sense, and the specific Incarnation of the Word in the person of Jesus. In other words the human body is already the pattern of divine Incarnation. And if the creation of the human body is seen to be in this way so significant, Hildegard's reading of verses Jn 1.3-4 similarly emphasizes the significance of creation as a whole as against a narrower framing of divine enlightenment, concentrated on the Incarnate Word in a more restricted and largely spiritual sense. She then appears to read these verses as if they suggested that 'the created universe was life in him, and that this life was the light of men'.[29] In other words, she expands the definition of the Word's enlightening Incarnation explicitly to include 'all things'.[30] For

28. *Liber divinorum operum*, Vision 4.105.

29. This is an alternative reading of Jn 1.3-4 rejected in C.K. Barrett, *The Gospel According to St John: An Introduction with Commentary and Notes on the Greek Text* (London: SPCK, 2nd edn, 1978 [1955]), p. 156. Some disagreements about interpretation of the earliest Greek texts of the New Testament have undoubtedly been caused by the fact that these texts were not punctuated and this is clearly the problem here at Jn 1.3-4. Barrett distinguishes two alternatives, with historical precedent, for dividing up Jn 1.3-4: (a) 'χωρὶς αὐτοῦ ἐγένετο οὐδὲ ἕν ὃ γέγονεν. ἐν αὐτῷ ζωὴ ἦν' ('without him was not anything made that was made. In him was life' (see RSV, 1971), and (b) 'χ. αὐ. ἐγ. οὐδὲ ἕν. ὃ γέγονεν ἐν αὐτῷ ζωὴ ἦν' ('apart from him not a thing came to be. That which had come to be in him was life'), see Raymond E. Brown, *The Gospel According to John I–XII: A New Translation with Introduction and Commentary* (AB, 29; New York: Doubleday, 1966), p. 3. Barrett notes that reading (b) was favoured by the earliest Fathers and some heretics. However he rejects it—and the interpretation quoted above which is related to it—on the grounds that it does not make as much 'Johannine sense' as the alternative interpretation that reads 'in him (the Word) was life'.

30. A number of modern biblical commentators who reject the interpretation of Jn 1.3-4 that Hildegard's theology seems to favour make a distinction between the life of 'all things' and a definition of life that is strictly tied to Word, and interpreted in a much more spiritual sense. Thus, for example, both Barrett, *The Gospel According to St John*, p. 157, and Brown, *The Gospel According to John*, p. 7, argue that the association of 'life' (Jn 1.4) with the life of the greater creation, or 'natural' life, is uncharacteristic of the evangelist's work as a whole. Brown argues, for example, that in the Johannine literature, life (ζωὴ—Jn 1.4) never implies 'natural' life (ψυχή; see Jn 13.37 and Jn 15.13; see also Brown, *The Gospel According to John*, p. 506), having to do with sin (see Brown, *The Gospel According to John*, p. 507) and 'to which death is a terminus' (Brown, *The Gospel According to John*, p. 506), but rather eternal life (ζωὴ αἰώνιος) to which, presumably, these things are unconnected.

Hildegard, the life of creation is *indeed* the light of humankind (Jn 1.4) and the very manifestation of God's Word.

> The life that awakened the creatures is also the life of our own life, which becomes alive as a result. Through understanding and knowledge it gave us light. In the light we should look at God in faith and acknowledge our Creator. We are flooded with light itself in the same way as the light of day illuminates the world. For we imagine our conscience's ability to soar to be like the heaven that gives rise to the sun and moon.[31]

To return to the human figure within Hildegard's view of the divine scheme of things, it is as if the particular redemptive act or mode of the Word has been, for Hildegard, already recorded in the providential 'articulation' of both the symbolic human figure of her visions, and of each human individual. And in all this, what is significant is the *human form* rather than its quality of 'fleshliness' or its tendency towards concupiscence, its Augustinian misdirected will, its fallenness or its purpose as the garment of the soul. God's creative act, from the beginning, can be seen as Incarnation—embodied and also illustrated and displayed in the very minutest workings of the human body as projected by its Creator from the beginning.

This use of the human form as a *living model* of Incarnation within Hildegard's commentary on the Prologue is striking. It resembles a theological or even a divine 'artificial memory'[32] for the benefit of

However Hildegard appears to effect a blend of the two ideas. It is through the created cosmos that the discerning believer sees God.

31. *Liber divinorum operum*, Vision 4.105.

32. Techniques for improving the power of memory had been commonly studied in antiquity as an element of the standard training all students received in rhetoric. The art of 'artificial memory', a form of mnemonic of places and images, is dealt with by Cicero, for example, in his *De oratore* and by Quintillian in his *Institutio oratoria*. An unknown teacher in Rome compiled a textbook on the subject (c. 86–82 BCE) called *Ad Herennium*, which was probably the most familiar text on the subject during the mediaeval period. During the mediaeval period, however, the rhetorical techniques of artificial memory were put to use as a much more virtuous and indeed mystical activity, Paradise and Hell in particular becoming memory places—sometimes with diagrams—connected with virtues and vices, made vivid in order to aid the faithful in reaching Heaven. Albertus Magnus (c. 1200–80) and his pupil Thomas Aquinas (c. 1225–74) advocated the exercise of 'artificial memory' as a part of Prudence. See on the subject in general, Frances A. Yates, *The Art of Memory* (Harmondsworth: Penguin Books, 1969).

humankind. The 'accurate account'[33] she gives of her vision appears to this reader as the presentation of a map, a plan, a guide, whose purpose is not simply to employ some rhetorical device. The human form in its actual wholeness and composite essence is a means whereby 'human beings should learn how to know their Creator and should no longer refuse to adore God worthily and reverently'.[34]

There are many delightful examples of the way in which the human form is seen within this part of Hildegard's work, as an imprint of the divine deed:

> The sphere of the *skull* indicated the dominant power of humanity... God reveals through our *eyes* the knowledge by which God foresees and knows everything in advance ... God opens up to us through our *ability to hear* all the sounds of glory about the hidden mysteries ... by our *nose* God displays the wisdom that lies like a fragrant sense of order in all works of art... by our *mouth* God indicates God's Word the Word by whom God has created everything.[35]

The body becomes almost playfully representative, like a child's action song by which to remember a whole catechism of both human and divine features, from the eyebrows that remind us of wings and thus of God's wings which we may hear in the wind's blowing,[36] to our mouth that indicates God's Word, by whom God has created everything.

There are other ways too in which Hildegard uses the human form instructively. Within her exegetical text, John the Baptist, for example, is compared to the stomach, transforming food into nourishment.[37] John is also related through the unusual sexual circumstances of his conception ('the fire of God's Word has caused the dry flesh of his parent to turn green again')[38] to the thighs of the human figure of Incarnation[39] as a witness to the corporeality of humanity and God's 'wondrous work'.[40] In this way humanity exemplified by the human individual

33. See n. 2 above.
34. *Liber divinorum operum*, Foreword.
35. *Liber divinorum operum*, Vision 4.105.
36. *Liber divinorum operum*, Vision 4.105.
37. *Liber divinorum operum*, Vision 4.105.
38. *Liber divinorum operum*, Vision 4.105.
39. *Liber divinorum operum*, Vision 4.105.
40. *Liber divinorum operum*, Vision 4.105.

John, becomes 'both a significant achievement and a light from God (*designatum opus et lumen a Deo*)'.[41]

The failure of the world to acknowledge or recognize the coming or achievement of holy Godhead in Jn 1.10 is compared, somewhat curiously, to our knees and, once more, to the thighs. The rather peculiar analogy appears to compare such ignorance to the feebleness or perhaps softness of an infant's legs. In such a way, the failure to recognize is seen as a childish aspect of the human species, that prevents us walking along the path of justice.[42]

In yet another sense, Hildegard regards the relationship of soul to body as illustrative of the relation of Word to a world in which the human symbol is central. It is also within God's providence for humankind that the rest of creation is imprinted with reminders of God's nature and of our proper disposition towards him as human creatures. Thus the sun and the moon by giving light indicate the knowledge of good, and night serves the purpose of reminding us of the infinite darkness that rejected the light, and which 'our knowledge of the good, on the basis of reason, holds back'.[43] This is Hildegard's interpretation of the light, or lights, that shine in the darkness (Jn 1.5).[44] It is to see a moral and theological import in every feature of the natural world and, perhaps, to give a yet deeper resonance to the divine words of the second vision, that state:

> All nature ought to be at the service of human beings so that they can work with nature since, in fact, human beings can neither live nor survive without it.[45]

Finally, in determining why Hildegard chose to use exegesis of this Johannine passage as the summary and conclusion to the first part of her visionary text, 'The World Of Humanity', it is vital to consider the figure of Sapientia/Wisdom. This figure, found originally of course within biblical and apocryphal literature,[46] became important in mediaeval theology and within the work of Hildegard the sapiential themes are implicit throughout.[47] Hildegard's theology as a whole may be de-

---

41. *Liber divinorum operum*, Vision 4.105.
42. *Liber divinorum operum*, Vision 4.105.
43. *Liber divinorum operum*, Vision 4.105.
44. *Liber divinorum operum*, Vision 4.105.
45. *Liber divinorum operum*, Vision 2.2.
46. See for example Prov. 8; Sir. 24; Wis. 7–9.
47. Among the more obvious and explicit examples, see *Scivias* 3.9.25. Here

scribed as 'sapiential'. And, in particular, the themes of cosmic creation and Incarnation with which Wisdom/Sapientia is particularly associated, in both biblical and apocryphal literature and also in mediaeval theology, are absolutely crucial for undersanding the whole of this first part of *Liber divinorum operum*, 'The World of Humanity'.

Certainly, Wisdom/Sapientia is not referred to directly in the commentary on the Prologue within the fourth vision, but this must surely be because Hildegard reads the words of Scripture concerning Logos as simply the reiteration of the same vision. In other words Wisdom is replaced here by Word in the words of Scripture, but is fully explored within the preceding visions. Thus, the figure of Sapientia in the guise of Caritas or divine Love, decked in the iconography of the Trinitarian God—the bearded head of God the Father, the winged figure of the Holy Spirit, carrying the lamb, the Son—opens *Liber divinorum operum* with her stirring declaration of creative power:

> I, the highest and fiery power, have kindled every spark of life, and I emit nothing that is deadly. I decide on all reality. With lofty wings I fly above the globe: With wisdom I have rightly put the universe in order. I, the fiery life of divine essence, am aflame beyond the beauty of the meadows.[48]

Implicitly, of course, Sapientia/Wisdom is present throughout since the Incarnation in the human form—Hildegard speaks of the 'flesh' here

---

Wisdom/Sapientia is featured richly dressed with the regalia of royalty. She also appears on several occasions in *Liber divinorum operum*, most notably in the first, the eighth and ninth visions. In the account of the ninth vision, Wisdom/Sapientia is described as a dazzling female figure in white silk with a green mantle, richly decorated. Characteristic associations are with the created world of humanity, with the Incarnation of God's Son, and with what lies beyond human reason: 'The figure in the northern corner indicates the Wisdom of true rapture, a Wisdom whose beginning and end are beyond human reason. The silken garment indicates the virgin birth of the Son of God; the green cloak indicates the world of creation along with the human species associated with it; the adornment too, is a symbol of the order of creation that is subordinate to humanity' (*Liber divinorum operum*, Vision 9.2). In the eighth vision described within the *Liber divinorum operum*, the resonances between the figure of Wisdom and Word in the Johannine Prologue are more pronounced: 'Out of her own being and by herself she has formed all things in love and tenderness. Nor was it possible any more for anything to be destroyed by an enemy. For she oversaw completely and fully the beginning and end of her deeds because she formed everything completely, just as everything was under her guidance...' (*Liber divinorum operum*, Vision 8.2).

48. *Liber divinorum operum*, Vision 1.2.

without prejudice— is the very revelation of the hidden Word.

> The Word is concealed in the flesh… the Word remained Word and the
> flesh remained flesh. Yet they became one because the Word, which was
> within God without time and before all time and which does not change,
> concealed itself within the flesh.[49]

In other words, this flesh is viewed as the visible revelation of the invisible divine and as such is revered, even celebrated. It is, as belonging to
the human form, the soul's beautiful and delightful adornment. It is, as
belonging to the divine cosmos, the revelation of the Word. Once
again, such revelation belongs to the traditional remit of Sapientia/
Wisdom, the feminine divine.

Sapientia/Wisdom also by tradition represents the synergetic relationship existing between Creator and creature—the mystery of Incarnation
and creaturely response in faith and virtuous living.[50] Wisdom is the gift of
the Holy Spirit by means of which humankind may see and then
respond in love to the initiatives of God. This sapiential theme is
undoubtedly present for Hildegard in the Johannine passage that speaks

49. *Liber divinorum operum*, Vision 4.105.

50. Thus the few direct references to Wisdom in this first part of the work and
outside the more specific commentary of Vision 4.105 consistently emphasize the
sense in which humanity is empowered to respond to God in both faith and
virtuous living: 'The power of human virtue is fulfilled in the fire of the Holy Spirit
and the moisture of humility within the vessel of the Holy Spirit, where Wisdom
has made her abode' (*Liber divinorum operum*, Vision 4.36). Again, Hildegard refers in
Vision 2 to a strengthening, guiding Wisdom, who pours into us a faith that pro-
tects: 'Wisdom, however, pours into the chambers, that is, into the spirit of human
beings, the justice of true faith through which alone God is known. There this faith
presses out all the chill and dampness of vice in such a way that such things cannot
germinate and grow again' (*Liber divinorum operum*, Vision 2.19). Significantly
perhaps, it is at this point that Hildegard goes on to characterize response to
Wisdom's gift of faith in terms of an image of the (feminine) divine as a nursing
mother: 'believers should rejoice and be glad in true faith… Thirsting for God's
justice, they should now suckle the holy element from God's breast and never have
enough of it, so that they will be forever refreshed by the vision of God.' This is
a relatively conventional image within the mediaeval period. See, for example,
Caroline Walker Bynum's discussion of female images of God in *Fragmentation and
Redemption: Essays on Gender and the Human Body in Medieval Religion* (New York:
Zone Books, 1991), pp. 157-65. In this way, Wisdom's concern with creaturely
response to all the initiatives of divine Incarnation is once more located within the
model of the human form; the affective but also nourishing, protective activity of a
nursing mother and her infant.

of a light that enables all to believe (Jn 1.7) and that rewards those who receive him with the kiss of the faithful[51] with a parental, and perhaps above all, a maternal embrace (Jn 1.12).

The commentary on Jn 1.1-14 is translated in its entirety by Robert Cunningham. Only the first 14 verses interest her in this context.[52] She concludes with our perception of God's glory *in the world*. The particular redemptive work of the Incarnate Son of God through his crucifixion and the final conclusion of his peculiar mission is dealt with elsewhere.

3. *Hildegard's Reading of Gender in John 1.1-14*

What then of the question of gender in this text? In what sense could it be said to find expression here? Are there perceptible indications of woman's identification with bodily materiality, sexuality, sin and death?[53] Is gender simply employed as an metaphor for the familiar hierarchical dualism as between the glory of the divine Word and the humility of his Incarnation in human flesh[54] or between soul and body, God and material world? And what of the figure of the mother, absent from the Johannine text?

Hildegard works with a definition of humanity which in *theological* terms does not take a very positive view of sexuality (a sense of a sexual self, an *embracing* of sexual desire or action independent of mere reproduction).[55] This makes her commentary on the first 14 verses of John's

---

51. *Liber divinorum operum*, Vision 4.105.

52. Hildegard does not offer any specific commentary on Jn 1.15-18, treated by most modern biblical scholars as if it belonged within the literary unit of Jn 1.1-18, in its final form. See below, Chapter 7, for Sjef van Tilborg's discussion of a possibly different arrangement of the material in Jn 1. See Brown, *The Gospel According to John*, pp. 18-23, for a brief summary of more recent scholarly conjecture about the balance of borrowed versus original material within Jn 1.1-18. All the scholars he mentions (pre-1966) appear to accept the division of Jn 1.1-18 from the rest of the chapter as a given.

53. In Vision 1.17, Hildegard combines an identification between woman and the earth with the untouched purity of the Virgin Mary: 'God chose from Abraham's stock the dormant Earth that had within itself not a jot of the taste whereby the old serpent had deceived the first woman. And the Earth, which was foreshadowed by Aaron's staff, was the Virgin Mary.'

54. In Vision 4.101, Hildegard notes that 'Man is in this connection an indication of the Godhead while woman is an indication of the humanity of God's Son.'

55. She does, in Vision 3, speak of reason coming to flower within the sex

Gospel appear conservative and conventional, although its tone is not marked by the sort of excesses that would lead one to think her unusual within the context of mediaeval theology in general. It maintains the Augustinian view of inherited guilt through sexual intercourse[56] that is based upon an interpretation of Genesis 2–3.[57] Hildegard writes:

> God created Adam to live forever without any change. But he fell because of his disobedience and as a result of heeding the serpent's advice. Hence, the serpent believed Adam to be lost once and forever. But that was not God's wish. He granted the world as a place of exile for us, and in the world thereafter we humans conceived and bore our children in sin. Thus we as well as our descendants, became subject to death. Indeed, when we are conceived, the sinful foam of human seed is transformed into an inferior material. And this situation will continue until the Last Day.[58]

In her commentary, what distinguishes new birth as children of God (Jn 1.12-13) is, as one would expect within this Augustinian framework, the absence of fleshly desires or the exchange of blood between parents.[59] What significance this metaphor of birth retains, is, of course, its implicit denial of death hedged about by the explicit denial of an evil, death-related sexuality. New birth as a child of God comes about as the result of good works and from the 'gift of divine revelation in the purification of baptism and through the ardent effusion of the Holy Spirit'.[60] In other words, Hildegard follows Augustine making the 'fleshly' sometimes merely a reference to spiritual evil or failure.

Similarly Hildegard's understanding of the Word made flesh is based on the familiar (and, for modern readers at any rate, perplexing) assumption that it is possible to affirm the humanity of the Word while aborting his sexuality and making his mother a virgin.

> he was conceived by the Virgin through the fire of the Holy Spirit. To that end there was no need of the sex act of a man in the same way as

---

organs, 'so that we can know what to do and what to leave off. On this account we enjoy what we do'. See *Liber divinorum operum* 3.12.

56. Note, however, Hildegard's frequent reference to the fall of Lucifer in this work as the first act, so to speak, of the drama of the Fall. In other words, the weight of the cause of sin does not rest simply on the reading of Genesis.

57. *Liber divinorum operum* 4.105.

58. *Liber divinorum operum* 4.105.

59. *Liber divinorum operum* 4.105.

60. *Liber divinorum operum* 4.105.

every other human being is begotten in sin by the man who is that person's father.[61]

Within this scheme of things, 'fleshly desires' do not belong to the constitution of the first human beings,[62] nor, it is suggested, to those that are finally restored to wholeness. It is therefore unnecessary for the Word to take part in 'sinful' conception in order to be concealed within the flesh. Reiterating, Hildegard's visions occur within a fundamentally Augustinian framework with an understanding of 'flesh' as a subjection to concupiscence or to uncontrolled desires that are absent from the state of childlike simplicity and innocence to which we should aspire. She could, with some justification, be said to use a concept of body that excludes sexuality, and a concept of Word made simply human, that is soul within body in a fundamentally asexual sense:

> our body is the concealing garment of our soul, and the soul offers services to the flesh through its actions. Our body would be nothing without the soul, and our soul could do nothing without the body... But the Word of God adopted flesh from the unfurrowed flesh of the Virgin without any flame of passion. As a result, the Word remained Word and the flesh remained flesh. Yet they became one because the Word, which was within God without time and before all time and which does not change, concealed itself within the flesh.[63]

It is hardly surprising then, that the illustrations commonly associated with this text portray a naked human figure that is short-haired, flat-chested and yet without any indication of male sex-organs, which is to see the notion of 'normative masculinity' in a new light.

But, of course, it is just not that simple. Hildegard's use of 'flesh' (as opposed to 'body' or 'human form'),[64] is close on occasions to an

---

61. *Liber divinorum operum* 4.105.
62. *Liber divinorum operum* 10.9.
63. *Liber divinorum operum* 4.105.
64. It is not always clear precisely what distinction Hildegard makes between body and flesh. At times the two terms appear to be used interchangeably. However, as a rough rule of thumb, it might be said that 'flesh' is associated with an Augustinian sense of original sin and inherited guilt, related to different experiences of lust or loss of control. '[W]hatever frisks about wildly with indecent actions' (*Liber divinorum operum* 2.27) seems to refer especially to sexual passion (see also 2.12, 47), but probably includes all forms of undisciplined activity, such as gluttony or pride (4.80). 'Body', on the other hand, implies an essential element of that which is called the human form and which belongs inseparably to humanity.

understanding of humankind driven by uncontrolled sexual lust. But it is difficult for Hildegard (as for many others) to maintain consistency in interpreting the word 'flesh' in this passage. The problem of adhering rigorously to Augustinian orthodoxy is that it simply does not do justice either to the complexity of the text or to Hildegard's obviously profound common sense. While rampant sexual energy clearly troubles her, she knows that it is intimately related to a vital fertility whose signature is to be found within the articulation of the Incarnate body:

> The fertile Earth is symbolized by the sex organs, which display the power of generation as well as an indecent boldness. Just as unruly forces at times rise from these organs, the recurring fertility of the Earth brings about a luxuriant growth and an immense overabundance of fruits.[65]

And, of course, she knows—whether or not from personal experience it is impossible to say!—that the sexual body may give delight.[66] Here there is undoubtedly some interesting confusion. If the human body is full of significance, 'flesh' lacks the power of life and is not of itself sufficient to be called human, even in the case of the Incarnate Word. But conversely, without 'flesh' we could not be called human:

> The spirit does not become flesh, nor does the flesh become spirit. But by the flesh and the spirit we are completed. If it were otherwise, we could not be human beings or be called human beings.[67]

Hildegard's *theological* construction of humanity does not, as I have already said, allow for much in the sense of positive sexuality. What Adam and Eve fell into, indeed, was sexuality. However, if it is correct to identify such a complicated construction of sexuality—combined of desire and prohibition[68]—with the cultural symbols of woman and the feminine, then this may very well be one reason why Hildegard looked

---

65. *Liber divinorum operum* 4.79

66. See, for example, Dronke, *Women Writers*, pp. 175-76. From a 'medical passage': 'When a woman is making love with a man, a sense of heat in her brain, which brings with it sensual delight, communicates the taste of that delight during the act and summons forth the emission of the man's seed. And when the seed has fallen into its place, that vehement heat descending from her brain draws the seed to itself and holds it, and soon the woman's sexual organs contract and all the parts that are ready to open up during the time of menstruation now close, in the same way as a strong man can hold something enclosed in his fist.'

67. *Liber divinorum operum* 1.17. Eve is the one who has been deceived. She desires something she should not possess.

68. See *Liber divinorum operum* 1.17.

particularly to images of the feminine divine. She was profoundly committed to a vision of the Church, accepting its authority and its right to impose prohibitions. But she was also profoundly and, above all, realistically aware of the springs of human energy—the modern psycho-analytical concept of *libido* or *jouissance* seems useful and illustrative here. The gloriously divine feminine Sapientia/Wisdom, which was also and equally Mary and Mother Church through its gendered symbolism, un-doubtedly finds a place for both these elements but, within the pre-vailing patriarchal framework, it is an inherently unstable dialectic.

Another rather more conventional solution to the conundrum of divine Incarnation, proposed within this work, is the construction of humanity as soul and body linked together in a loving but hierarchical relationship. As an essence made up of body and soul,[69] soul has to overcome the body and be in charge.[70] Hildegard's account of the fourth vision strives to prevent the first or higher term of soul becoming merely exclusive of the secondary or lower term, and from toppling over into a rejection of the body:

> And thus the soul says after every victory: 'O my flesh and you my limbs, in which I have my dwelling, how much do I rejoice that I have been sent to you who are in agreement with me and who send me out to my eternal reward'.[71]

For Hildegard, as indeed for Augustine, orthodox Christian beliefs about the Incarnation of Christ discourage dualistic descriptions of the relationship between body and soul. If Christ became human in the same way in which we are human, then this is a factor in favour of our whole humanity, whatever its physical vulnerability or apparently irra-tional motivations. In Hildegard's work, there is a perception of the human soul and body belonging to each other in potentially joyous and even comfortable cooperation, mirroring the joyous relationship of Word to the flesh of the Incarnation:

> The Word is concealed in the flesh in the following way: The Word and the flesh formed a unified life. But they did not do so as if one of them had been transformed into the other; but rather they are one with unity

69. *Liber divinorum operum* 4.104.

70. *Liber divinorum operum* 4.78. See *Liber divinorum operum* 9.3: 'For no one—so long as he or she is burdened by a mortal body—can gaze upon the transcendent Godhead that illuminates everything'.

71. *Liber divinorum operum* 4.19.

> of a person. Thus it is that our body is the concealing garment of our
> soul, and the soul offers services to the flesh through its actions. Our
> body would be nothing without the soul, and our soul could do nothing
> without the body. And thus they are one within us, and we accept this
> arrangement. And thus God's work, humanity, has been created in the
> image and likeness of God.[72]

She defends the orthodox position in this work, against, for example,
the views of the Cathars, which were first introduced into the Rhineland at about this time.[73] Catharism was a form of dualism, which saw
the world and particularly procreation as the devil's work. Hildegard
rejected this position. And she views the first verses of the Prologue cul-
minating in Jn 1.14 as a forthright rejection of any dualistic or christological position that denigrates the material or bodily elements of
God's creation:

> God formed us out of clay and breathed into us the spirit of life. Hence,
> God's Word also adopted in his humanity a royal garment along with a
> soul endowed with reason. He took the garment totally and completely
> to himself, and remained in it. For the spirit in a human being, which is
> called the soul, penetrates completely and fully the flesh and considers it
> to be a delightful garment and a beautiful adornment.[74]

On occasions in *Liber divinorum operum*, Hildegard makes the conventional association between the feminine and what is weaker or lesser,
speaking of the 'feminine' or 'womanish' weakness of the last days.[75]
Equally, what is masculine represents that which is—in theory—stronger
and comparable with the dimension of soul within the body/soul continuum or the distinction between divinity and humanity:

> Thus woman is the work of man, while man is a sight full of consolation
> for woman. Neither of them could henceforth live without the other.
> Man is in this connection an indication of the Godhead while woman is
> an indication of the humanity of God's Son.[76]

What is certainly lacking in her writing is the indication that what is
lesser and humbler has no part in God's plan. Hildegard saw nothing
intrinsically evil in the material of the divine cosmos or in the human

---

72. *Liber divinorum operum* 4.105.

73. At the request of a religious community in Mainz, Hildegard wrote a tract
against them, *De Catharis*. See Newman, *Sister of Wisdom*, p. 12.

74. *Liber divinorum operum* 4.105.

75. See, for example, *Liber divinorum operum* 10.8, 20.

76. *Liber divinorum operum* 4.100.

form. And, in fact, her work on the Prologue manifests a much greater confidence in the potential of the lower, feminine and bodily element to cooperate fruitfully with its controlling partner than Augustine's commentary on the same passage. However, the sense of an important distinction remains. In other words, in a writer so absorbed by the notion of macrocosmic/microcosmic correspondences, the deference owed to the male by the female appears, essentially, and within the creative wisdom of the divine, the eternal illustration of divine/human relations.

Finally, it is interesting to note here that Hildegard makes relatively little use, explicitly, of Eucharistic themes within this passage. Hildegard was living and working at a time when, as Caroline Walker Bynum has indicated, many women, through irregular and sometimes dramatic Eucharistic devotion and practice, were increasingly drawing attention to the corporeality of the Word as Eucharistic food and drink. Some of these women saw the Eucharistic elements as a symbol of Christ's bodily suffering. Such Christlike actions could be imitated and entered into through the ascetic practice of fasting, often combined with the frequent preparation of food for others.[77] Summarizing the main thrust of Bynum's argument, women of the mediaeval period sought to give meaning to their existence as women by moulding the bodily and nurturing element with which they were particularly associated in both domestic and religious culture. Sometimes this resulted in quite, to modern opinion, gruesome feats of self-starvation and torture. Nevertheless, it was an effective, visible and even *permissible* form of expression and religious ministry for women. Moreover, such practices succeeded to some degree in challenging the logic of separation,[78] compromising

77. See Walker Bynum, *Holy Feast and Holy Fast*, pp. 76-93. Bynum draws attention particularly to the phenomenon of fasting accompanied by Eucharistic fervour, which she argues was a particularly female food practice around this period, as opposed to gluttony, held to be more characteristic of men. 'Stories of people levitating, experiencing ecstasy during the mass, or racing from church to church to attend as many eucharistic services as possible are usually told of women—for example, of Hedwig of Silesia (d. 1241), Douceline of Marseilles (d. 1274).'

78. See Julia Kristeva, *Powers of Horror: An Essay on Abjection* (trans. Leon Roudiez; New York: Columbia University Press, 1982), p. 103. Kristeva is particularly concerned, in this book, with the concept of difference, including, of course, the key difference between male and female. She uses this expression in the context of describing attempts made by religious practices to maintain definitive separations,

or breaching the barrier represented by the distinction between both divine and human, and between the Word and the flesh, that seemed to have been erected by theology that focused upon flesh as a sign of a troubling and woman–identified 'otherness' threatening a divine and masculine singularity. For example, the mediaeval period saw many examples of the phenomenon of *inedia*, in which it was alleged that (usually) women survived for long periods, simply on Eucharistic bread and wine. Here God viewed as food,[79] in the most literal sense, dramatically illustrates the powerful heterogeneity of the Eucharistic symbols, crossing or transgressing the divide between divinity and humankind.

Hildegard's Eucharistic theology is present here in the *Liber divinorum operum*, implicitly in the incarnational themes of the whole work. In *Scivias*, Hildegard describes the daily consecration of the Eucharist in terms of a daily Incarnation, a repeated process brought about by the Holy Spirit descending like a mother bird and hatching the chick with its warmth.[80] This much gentler vision of a sacramental rather than a sacrificial Eucharist accords much better with the sapiential themes of *Liber divinorum operum* as a whole, in which Sapientia/Wisdom creates and then sustains through the mystical human form of Word Incarnate. The conundrum remains however. Sustaining flesh is accounted for. The excess of its disturbing associations with sin and death and unconsecrated heterogeneous, unseparated materiality is not.

In the first of Hildegard's three major visionary works, *Scivias*, there occurs an account and an illustration of a vision which encapsulates something central both to Hildegard as a mediaeval woman and as a theologian. God the Trinity, symbolized by fire, flame and a blast of wind, offers Adam a shining white flower[81]

and defend the 'clean and proper' boundaries of both individuals and communities.

79. See Walker Bynum, *Holy Feast and Holy Fast*, p. 116. Bynum notes, for example, the experience of a thirteenth-century woman, Ida of Louvain. She 'experienced bizarre sensations of eating when no food was present. She received the "food of spiritual reading" into her stomach, felt the eucharist slip down her throat like a fish, said to the other nuns before communion, "Let us go devour God", and found her mouth filled with honeycomb whenever she recited Jn 1.14: "Verbum caro factum est" '.

80. *Scivias* 2.6.36.

81. *Scivias* 2.1, Eibingen MS. See Newman, *Sister of Wisdom*, p. 169.

hanging upon the flame like a dew drop upon a blade of grass. The man
scented its fragrance with his nostrils, but did not taste it with his mouth
or touch it with his hands. So, turning away, he fell into thick darkness
from which he was unable to rise.[82]

As Barbara Newman has remarked, Hildegard has, effectively, 'altered
the legend to replace the sin of taking a forbidden fruit with the failure
to take a mandatory flower'.[83] It is suggestive in its refusal to blame the
woman (Eve) for the man (Adam)'s failure. And of course, as Newman
also notes, it is undoubtedly a prefiguration of the annunciation to the
Virgin Mary. Adam refuses the sensual pleasures of the lily of obedience.
Mary—and Hildegard—grasps them and holds on tight.

Among the various significant female figures in Hildegard's work as
a whole, the Virgin Mary frequently represents the crucial importance
of obedience—perhaps more illuminatingly seen, in this case, as in a
sapiential sense, as the positively creative cooperation brought about
through the gift of and through Sapientia/Wisdom as the Holy Spirit. In
Liber divinorum operum, the Virgin Mary speaks 'of herself as God's
handmaid'. She 'believed the messenger of God and wished matters to
be as he had stated'.[84] And, for Hildegard, her agreement was crucial.
The Word Incarnate, through the creative cooperation of divine Love,
Wisdom, Church and Virgin, encompasses the whole of creation, Christ
himself and his Church. And yet, the burden of Hildegard's sapiential,
synergetic theology is, over and over again, that nothing is done or
created without a cooperative obedience or agreement, identified with
one or other of the female figures within Hildegard's works. It becomes,
as it were, an aspect of the divine itself—divine Wisdom, divine Love,
the Mother of God, the divine Mother of all souls.

It is, then, slightly surprising to discover within the short commentary
on Jn 1.1-14 that the Virgin Mary, introduced to 'flesh out' the Johannine vision of Incarnation, appears rather conventionally, as the guarantor of the Word's exceptional purity, in unmistakably Augustinian tones:

> Thus he became in an unusual way a human being who was not like any
> other...[85] the Word of God adopted flesh from the unfurrowed flesh

---

82. *Scivias* 2.1, Eibingen MS. See Newman, *Sister of Wisdom*, p. 168.
83. Newman, *Sister of Wisdom*, p. 168.
84. *Liber divinorum operum* 1.17.
85. *Liber divinorum operum* 4.105.

of the Virgin without any flame of passion...[86] he was conceived by he Virgin through the fire of the Holy Spirit. To that end there was no need of the sex act of a man in the same way as every other human being is begotten in sin.[87]

Here creative obedience is subordinate to a more cultural notion of purity or to the need to prove a miraculous divine power that overrides the natural order. Once again, the Augustinian sleight of hand is in evidence: Mary, through the richness of her associations with what is material, earthly and belonging with the created world,[88] guarantees the humanity of the Incarnate Word. Yet that which lies beyond the margins of divine masculine reason, the uncontrolled, anarchic over-abundance of fleshly desires, and the inexplicable horrors of death and decay, are excluded in this specific context beyond and outside reason's virginal purity. So that the Word, 'born of the Virgin Mary and without sin',[89] may shore up the boundaries against these abominations.

And yet, and at the same time within this short commentary, Hildegard's understanding of cooperative obedience as an aspect of the feminine divine itself is perhaps still reflected in her understanding of the very first verse of the Gospel:

> In the beginning of things, God's will opened itself up to the creation of nature. Without such a beginning God would have remained within God without revealing God. For the Word had no beginning at all.[90]

4. Conclusions

Some of the reasons for the recent revival of interest in Hildegard's work are fairly straightforward. Here is a woman who is not submerged or silenced within a patriarchal culture. In an age when even women from wealthy and influential families were rarely educated, and were certainly discouraged from speaking openly on religious matters, Hildegard published and preached. In an age when it was unusual for a woman to participate in public life, Hildegard maintained a correspondence with popes, bishops and secular rulers. Her writings and correspondence reveal a rich complexity of orthodox theology and vividly

86. *Liber divinorum operum* 4.105.
87. *Liber divinorum operum* 4.105.
88. *Liber divinorum operum* 1.17.
89. *Liber divinorum operum* 4.105.
90. *Liber divinorum operum* 4.105.

creative metaphor and images including female figures of divine authority. In an age of some misogynism,[91] Hildegard maintained her independence and apparently got what she wanted, by a mixture of tough
realism and the astute, if genuinely pious, management of what she saw
as her gift from God—her visionary experiences.

When readers focus attention on the specifics of her biblical interpretation within *Liber divinorum operum*, a more complicated picture
emerges in which there is a detectable fault-line running through her
whole theological approach. On the one hand there is an orthodox
commitment to the sovereignty of (masculine) Word as divine reason,
holding the excesses of human (body and soul) irrationalities and lusts at
bay, excluding the troubling differences and heterogeneity suggested by
gender and generation. Hildegard expresses a fundamentally Augustinian
preference for virginity and sensual delight is said to lead to disgust and
death.[92] It could be said that within this work, Hildegard expresses a
distrust of what lies beyond the definitions of patriarchal Christian
orthodoxy. Within the first part of *Liber divinorum operum*, there is
expressed a need to maintain order and balance within the human form
of the cosmos. Reason banishes all disorder, even within the seductive,
dangerous human sex organs.[93] On the other hand there is a vision of
(feminine) Wisdom as the substance of creation and Incarnation and as
its very energy.

Julia Kristeva's late-twentieth-century critique of Christian theology
sets out to identify, among other things, those procedures that she
believes subjugate all definitions of pleasure to its own and then prohibit

---

91. By 'misogynism' I understand the sense in which attitudes towards women
are derived from a form of dualism found in antique as well as mediaeval philosophical and scientific traditions, whereby woman functions as an incomplete male
or as an inferior partner in reproduction. Such attitudes reinforced a theological—
fundamentally Augustinian—understanding of woman as inferior because she is symbolically associated with flesh and with the roots of sin in rebellious physical and
bodily appetite. Undoubtedly such attitudes were evident in arguments against
allowing women a place in Church leadership or in the evangelical activities of
mendicant orders, in the work of, for example, Aquinas and Bonaventure. See
Walker Bynum, *Holy Feast and Holy Fast*, p. 216.

92. See for example, *Liber divinorum operum* 4.19: 'if at times the body succumbs
to the desires of the flesh, disgust will usually ensue…delight drives me onto a
treadmill. I do the deeds of death'.

93. *Liber divinorum operum* 3.12.

it. She uses the term '*jouissance*' to refer to a total joy or ecstasy that includes but is not exhausted by a definition of genital sexual orgasm that serves the symbolic order structured according to the needs and self-understanding of men rather than women. Hildegard's work is full of references to joy and the expression of apparently blameless sensual pleasures. Within the first part of *Liber divinorum operum*, for example, she claims that the Incarnation is the cause of sheer joy,[94] and that the Word considers the flesh—an ambiguous term within the work—to be a 'delightful garment and a beautiful adornment'.[95] An interesting question then to ask of the theology of Hildegard, focused on this significant text, is whether these expressions of material and bodily joy and pleasure within her work represent a different key, a more truly feminine *jouissance*, in which the humanity of the Incarnate Word has become something in which we may recognize the full challenge of heterogeneity represented by symbols of woman and the feminine to the logic of identity or separation. Does Hildegard's sapiential theology go some way towards articulating a heterogeneous *jouissance* that may deconstruct a divine economy constructed within the (masculine) symbolic order of the Christian churches simply to serve the needs and anxieties of men?

One of the central convictions of Kristeva's philosophy is that women have a need to enter into the (masculine) symbolic order somehow, and will seek to do this, even if it means compromising their own joys and pleasures. She sees that historically, and particularly within the history of the Christian churches of the West, women have chosen the paths of martyrdom, publicly adopted virginity and, more usually, motherhood as ways to enter this symbolic domain and achieve some degree of *jouissance*. She believes that none of these paths is wholly satisfactory for women.[96] Nevertheless she points out that these paths towards joy and pleasure were much more clearly laid out and integrated into our culture during the period of the Christian past in which the cult of the virgin in all its variety flourished, and that the loss of these traditions of the feminine divine has been a great one.

The joys and also the sensual pleasures—Kristeva's *jouissance*—expressed within this mediaeval work are still largely associated with the

---

94. *Liber divinorum operum* 3.19.

95. *Liber divinorum operum* 4.105.

96. See, for example, Julia Kristeva, 'About Chinese Women', in Toril Moi (ed.), *The Kristeva Reader* (Oxford: Basil Blackwell, 1986), p. 146.

modes of self-sacrifice or motherhood. It has to be said that Hildegard's use of the notion of 'greenness', often given expression in highly sensuous terms, does clearly have some relationship with fertility and growth. And here of course the earth itself takes on some fairly obviously maternal characteristics as fertile and nourishing:

> From the gentle layer of air moisture effervesces over the Earth. This awakens the Earth's greenness and causes all fruits to appear through germination, and it also bears aloft certain clouds containing all that is superior, just as they, in turn, are strengthened from on high... In the warmth of the rising sun, this air causes to descend upon the Earth a dew that the Earth exudes like honey in a comb. And this honey at times melts away in the east wind's gentleness to a rain that brings refreshment.[97]

But it can at least be said that in interpreting the first 14 verses of John's Gospel in the light of strongly sapiential themes, Hildegard taps into an extremely rich incarnational tradition that has the potential, at some points, to challenge the inherent tendency of interpretation to adopt a view of humanity that marginalizes women and the feminine and refuses to engage with the forces and energies of which culture has made them the symbol, in terms of exclusion or prohibition. And, of course, Hildegard is herself still somewhat troubled and ambivalent in this respect, unwilling altogether, and certainly within her theological work, to shake off this logic of separation represented by the dangerous lusts of the flesh. At the same time, she has attempted to define the human nature of Incarnation in terms of a cooperative dependence between elements that, while preserving the hierarchical and culturally gendered cast, become even the shape and model of the inner economy of the divine. In other words, she recognizes this cooperative duality as a characteristic of God's work in Incarnation. Thus Hildegard is not drawn towards a rejection of body in favour of soul, because body and soul working together in agreement are the type of God's activity, the opening up of God's will to the creation of nature.[98]

The essentially hierarchical nature of this duality is of considerable importance to Hildegard herself, since on the basis of her own symbolic identification as a woman within the inferior term—as she said of herself '*ego paupercula feminea forma*'[99]—rested the basis of her paradoxical au-

---

97. *Liber divinorum operum* 4.7.

98. *Liber divinorum operum* 4.105.

99. J.-B. Pitra (ed.), *Analecta Sanctae Hildegardis* (Analecta Sacra, 8; Monte Cassino: 1882), Epistola 2.

thority and freedom within mediaeval society. It is perhaps above all this paradoxical freedom that deconstructs, for her, the myth of virginal obedience, elevating her rather to the position of Wisdom, the principle of active generation within the divine itself.

4

Riddles for Feminist Readers:
Martin Luther's Sermons on the Prologue, 1537

1. *Setting the Scene*

In the *German Mass* of 1526, Martin Luther (1483–1546) suggested that the Gospel of John should be the text expounded at preaching services held on Saturdays and it is from his own sermons on the Gospel of John, preached in Wittenberg on Saturdays from 7 July 1537,[1] that we have a text of his commentary on the Prologue of John's Gospel.[2] He was at this time 'filling in' for Dr Johannes Bugenhagen Pomeranus, the pastor in Wittenberg, who was temporarily engaged on a mission to the Church in Denmark.

2. *Luther and the Prologue*

In the 11 exegetical sermons on the Prologue of John's Gospel,[3] preached during 1537, Luther's key preoccupations quickly emerge. The Johannine text is first and foremost for Luther a statement of Trinitarian orthodoxy:

---

1.   See Jaroslav Pelikan (ed.), *Luther's Works*. XXII. *Sermons on the Gospel of St. John, Chapters 1–4* (trans. Martin H. Bertram; 55 vols.; St Louis, MO: Concordia, 1957), pp. ix-x.

2.   It should be noted, of course, that the commentary referred to throughout—unless otherwise noted—is the result of a long process of collection and editing by those who respected and valued Luther's insights and therefore wanted to preserve them. In between Luther's sermons on Jn 1–4 and a modern reader of the St Louis edition of Luther's words in English (1957) stand the original transcribers of his sermons, a sixteenth-century German editor, John Aurifaber (d. 1575), a nineteenth-century German edition (*D. Martin Luthers Werke: Kritische Gesamtausgabe* [Weimar: Bohlau, 1883–]), and translator Martin Bertram.

3.   Sermons 1–11 cover the text of Jn 1.1-18.

From the very beginning the evangelist teaches and documents most convincingly the sublime article of our holy Christian faith according to which we believe and confess the one true, almighty, and eternal God. But he states expressly that three distinct Persons dwell in that same single divine essence, namely, God the Father, God the Son, and God the Holy Spirit. The Father begets the Son from eternity, the Holy Spirit proceeds from the Father and the Son, etc. Therefore there are three distinct Persons, equal in glory and majesty; yet there is only one divine essence.[4]

Luther tries to show how God's creative activity, his Word, is related to the historical person of Christ,[5] without suggesting that this person is merely God's creation;[6] how Christ can be both fully divine and yet also participate fully in creaturely humanity;[7] and how these truths may be understood only by the faithful and believing and not by any exercise of human reason.[8]

Luther's sermons certainly attend to the scriptural themes of this passage. But the reader has to reckon with these sermons as a form of defensive polemic—against the heretics of the Christian past,[9] against

4.   See Pelikan (ed.), *Sermons on the Gospel of John*, pp. 5-6.

5.   See, for example, Pelikan (ed.), *Sermons on the Gospel of John*, p. 14: 'This is the text that establishes the divinity of Christ... He is not to be counted among the angels; but He is the Lord and Creator of the angels and of all creatures.'

6.   Note Luther's challenge to the christology of Arius, recounted in Pelikan (ed.), *Sermons on the Gospel of John*, pp. 18-19: 'And in order to dupe the people and deceive them with cunning speech, to blind them to his blasphemous lie, he declared that Christ was the best and the most glorious of all creatures...'

7.   See Pelikan (ed.), *Sermons on the Gospel of John*, p. 22: 'if Christ is divested of His divinity, there remains no help against God' s wrath... If He is deprived of His humanity, we are lost again. This is what the heretical Manichaeans did. In high-sounding phrases they declared: "God is so holy, pure, and immaculate that it is impossible for Him to assume the nature of a creature, even that of an angel"?'

8.   See Pelikan (ed.), *Sermons on the Gospel of John*, p. 21: 'We can never grasp and comprehend this article of our salvation and eternal welfare with our human reason. But we must believe it, steadfastly adhering to what Scripture says about it, namely that Christ, our Lord, is true and natural God and man, coequal with the Father in His divine essence and nature.'

9.   See Pelikan (ed.), *Sermons on the Gospel of John*, p. 7—Cerinthus; p. 17—the Jews and Moslems; p. 18—Arius; p. 21—Manichaeans; p. 67—a whole list: 'Marcion, Ebion, Novatus, Manes, Arius, Pelagius, Mohammed and finally numberless sects and factions in the papacy'.

the traditions of scholasticism in which Luther was educated as a student[10] and as an Augustinian monk,[11] against the contemporary Church

10. Luther was educated at the Cathedral School at Magdeburg, at Eisenach, and later at Erfurt University (1501–1505). At Erfurt, in common with students throughout Europe, he studied the work of Aristotle and the scholarly disciplines of the quadrivium—music, arithmetic, geometry and astronomy. The Arts Faculty at Erfurt University was committed to a form of scholastic scholarship called the *via moderna*, associated with nominalism. Nominalism was a movement within late mediaeval thought which questioned assumptions, widespread in the earlier mediaeval period, of a Platonist nature, about the separate existence of abstract universals, apart from the individuals in which they were identified. Nominalism relied largely on the critique provided by Aristotle, whose work had been reintroduced into Europe through the commentaries of Thomas Aquinas (c. 1225–74). Nominalists, such as William of Occam (d. 1349), Gregory of Rimini (d. 1358) and Pierre d'Ailly (1350–1420) took the view that it is the human intellect that produces abstractions, based on the sensory perceptions of unique entities. In other words, sensory perception of reality does not lead directly to the cognition of universal realities. This view they formulated in response to what they saw as a dangerous tendency in scholasticism to argue for the objective reality of certain mental constructs—a failure to understand mental constructs as models. The danger they perceived was that highly speculative and ideological patterns of thought were too easily reified, stifling intellectual freedom. But such ideas naturally enough also problematized Neoplatonic visions of God as a pre-existent reality. Aquinas had integrated his understanding of Aristotle into his vision of Christian faith, arguing that Aristotelian reasoning and faith could be genuinely partners. For Luther, however, nominalism simply formed the background to his own reliance on faith in God's word *rather than* reason. Luther was soon applying to the works of Aristotle the critique of reason that nominalism legitimated or even required. In 1518 he broke with Jodokus Trutfetter, his professor at Erfurt, because Trutfetter saw Luther's attacks on Aristotle as fundamentally misguided. Luther's response was along the lines—much in keeping with the principles of nominalism—of a later (1520) statement: 'I demand arguments not authorities. That is why I contradict even my own school of Occamists, which I have absorbed completely' (*D. Martin Luthers Werke: Kritische Gesamtausgabe*, VI, pp. 4-5, 195).

11. Having gained his degree as Master of Arts, Luther's original intention was to enter the higher Faculty of Jurisprudence at Erfurt, and prepare for a career in the law. Instead, on 17 July 1505 he entered the monastery of the Augustinian Hermits at Erfurt, apparently after making a vow during a terrifying thunderstorm near Stotternheim to become a monk should his life be spared. As a monk, Luther caught the attention of Johann von Staupitz, vicar general of the Augustinian Observant congregation. Luther was encouraged to continue his academic studies in Theology and was ordained priest in 1507. Staupitz also required him to take on lecturing at both Erfurt and Wittenberg Universities, while he prepared for his doctoral degree.

of Rome,[12] or, as Luther would have it, 'the blasphemous Roman see',[13] and even against those fanatical 'schismatic spirits' who carried their opposition to Roman Catholic practices so far that they thought faith could survive without any structures at all.[14]

It has to be said that Luther is not preoccupied in his sermons on the Prologue with arguments about Christology in the technical or intellectual sense of how exactly divinity and humanity may be 'held together'.[15] Rather, he is concerned with what the saving consequences of this union are for human individuals and, more importantly, how human beings have *access* to the Word in this saving way. Luther explains in the Prologue that the means to saving grace is revealed as the Word. The Word, in Luther's sermons, is defined as the thoughts of God's heart, the internal divine conversation or dialogue. And this is further elaborated by analogy with powerful emotions, particularly love or anger,[16] such that a person may be entirely taken up and filled with such thoughts.

---

12. See, for example, Pelikan (ed.), *Sermons on the Gospel of John*, p. 65: 'St Francis, St Dominic, all the popes with their monks and nuns and priests should hide their face and extinguish their light. For if they make themselves the true Light, and not Christ then they shed no more light than manure in a lantern. This may give off a stench, but it does not give off light.'

13. Pelikan (ed.), *Sermons on the Gospel of John*, p. 58.

14. Pelikan (ed.), *Sermons on the Gospel of John*, p. 48: 'It takes toil and trouble to engender faith in people by the God-ordained means of the preaching ministry, absolution, and the Sacrament.'

15. See Marc Lienhard, *Luther: Witness to Jesus Christ* (trans. Edwin H. Robertson; Minneapolis: Augsburg, 1982), pp. 29-30. Lienhard argues that Luther's earlier Christology was significantly influenced by 'Occamists' such as William Occam, Jean le Charlier de Gerson, Pierre d'Ailly and Gabriel Biel. In what was perhaps an attempt most of all to preserve the true humanity of Christ, these theologians strove to make a radical distinction between the uncreated being of the Logos and the created being—between the two natures. It is a union in which the human existence subsists in the divine persona, but this human existence of Christ also has its own characteristic way of being—as, for example, in being able to die on the cross. Lienhard goes on to argue that Luther's Christology changes significantly in later life, the divine nature significantly overwhelming the human. Thus, for example, in the later controversies over the Eucharist, Luther attributed the principle of ubiquity—a property of the divine—to the human nature. (See particularly the *Disputations* of 1539 for a Christology consciously opposed to Occamist ideas.)

16. See, for example, Pelikan (ed.), *Sermons on the Gospel of John*, p. 10.

The same picture may be applied to God. God too, in His majesty and nature, is pregnant with a Word or a conversation in which He engages with Himself in His divine essence and which reflects the thoughts of His heart. This is as complete and excellent and perfect as God Himself. No one but God alone sees, hears, or comprehends this conversation. It is an invisible and incomprehensible conversation... He brought all creatures into being by means of this Word and conversation. God is so absorbed in this Word, thought, or conversation that He pays no attention to anything else.[17]

This 'Word' is God's Word and the Word of Scripture and entirely unrelated to human reason. Human reason[18]—'blind and mad'—can comprehend that there is one God, but the Trinity is 'a sublime article of faith beyond the grasp of reason'. Similarly, to understand the meaning of the text, it is faith and not reason that is needed since 'we know that nothing is too sublime or impossible for faith'[19] and faith is guided by God's Word:

Therefore we should leave our reason at home, and we should not fall into the snares of idle speculation. Rather we must believe the Holy Spirit, who has declared through Moses and John that God had a Word all by Himself, apart from any creature.[20]

Of course, according to much modern feminist writing, reason is a privileged category within the patriarchal context. But it is not, apparently, understood in this way by Luther.[21] On the other hand, 'flesh' remains an important concept that Luther clearly finds disturbing in its shadowy and tangled relationship to sin, death, and invariably also to woman and the feminine.[22]

17. Pelikan (ed.), *Sermons on the Gospel of John*, p. 10.

18. Luther's disposition towards human reason seems here to diverge from that of Augustine. See Rettig (ed. and trans.), *St. Augustine: Tractates 1–10*, Tractate 3.4.2-3. Note that Augustine regards human reason, mind or intellect as the only grounds on which humankind may boast, because it is made in the image of God. It is the only thing that distinguishes human beings from beasts.

19. Pelikan (ed.), *Sermons on the Gospel of John*, p. 76.

20. Pelikan (ed.), *Sermons on the Gospel of John*, p. 13.

21. See, for example Pelikan (ed.), *Sermons on the Gospel of John*, p. 12: 'You often say: "Didn't I have a presentiment of this? Didn't my heart tell me this? Didn't I sense this?" But when God speaks a Word to Himself or carries on a conversation with Himself, we find that people refuse to grasp this; much less will they believe it, for it runs counter to reason.'

22. Although Luther's attitudes towards women were not in a straightforward

Luther's attitude to 'the flesh' within these sermons is not hostile in any straightforward way. In fact, the implication of Luther's words is that the Word cannot act or guide the faith of any individual unless it is first spoken—that is, so to speak, 'incarnate' or 'made flesh':

> And now mark well the words of our text, which are intended to honor the external Word...it was necessary for John to come with his external

way misogynistic they did tend to be stereotypical. See, for example, his description of Eve in Jaroslav Pelikan (ed.), *Luther's Works*. I. *Lectures on Genesis Chapters 1–5* (St Louis, MO: Concordia, 1958), p. 147. Eve's sin is here described in terms of her disobedience to God's word. It should be noted that Luther, predictably, takes the line that Eve was tempted first because she was reckoned the easier target by Satan. 'And I, too believe that if he had tempted Adam first, the victory would have been Adam's. He would have crushed the serpent with his foot and would have said: "Shut up! The Lord's command was different".' Luther explicitly brushes aside scholastic allegorizing interpretations of Adam and Eve as the upper and lower parts of reason here. He substitutes a rather more general assumption of male superiority, p. 151: 'Although both were created equally righteous, nevertheless Adam had some advantage over Eve. Just as in all the rest of nature the strength of the male surpasses that of the other sex, so also in the perfect nature the male somewhat excelled the female.' There is little sense or consistency behind Luther's analysis on this point, though his exegesis of the conversation between the serpent and Eve is subtle and compelling. Luther nowhere explains, for example, why Adam is unable to treat his wife as, he suggests, he would have treated the serpent. Why could not Adam have told Eve, similarly, to 'Shut up!'? The answer is perhaps to be found in Luther's words on this text elsewhere. For example, Luther presents Eve's fault, in an 'off the cuff' moment, not so much as disobedience to God's commandment, as in reversing the proper order of things by proving the stronger partner: 'Never any good came out of female domination'. God created Adam master and lord of living creatures, but Eve spoilt it all when she persuaded him to set himself above God's will. 'Tis you women, with your tricks and artifices, that lead men into error', *Table Talk* (trans. William Hazlitt; London: Fount Paperbacks, 1995), p. 335, number 727.

Nevertheless, Luther avoids misogynistic excess: see Theodore G. Tappert (trans. and ed.), *Luther's Works*. LIV. *Table Talk* (Philadelphia: Fortress Press, 1967), p. 171. He waxes hot and strong against the suggestion that priests should not marry because of some objection to the 'stinking putrid, private parts of a woman'. This opinion, credited to the Cardinal Archbishop of Mainz, Luther describes as blasphemous: 'That godless knave, forgetful of his mother and his sister, dares to blaspheme God's creature through whom he was himself born'. (He rather spoils the effect by adding 'It would be tolerable if he were to find fault with the behavior of women, but to defile their creation and nature is most godless'.)

Word or testimony, to point at Christ with his finger, and to say: 'That is He'. There was no other means or method.[23]

In this sense, Luther firmly links the saving effect of the christological mystery to the 'incarnate' Word—the preaching, the external, oral 'fleshly' business of speech and action within some sort of earthly and physical community, the 'God-ordained means' of engendering faith.[24]

Thus there is no other means of attaining faith than by hearing, learning, and pondering the Gospel.[25]

And yet, in so far as 'fleshly' relates to human consequence or autonomy, Luther cuts the ground from under the feet of critics and adversaries who take this necessary Incarnation as the basis for elevating the significance of any human, 'fleshly' agency. The condition of humanity is dire.[26] 'Flesh'—understood as the condition of being human, body and soul together, weak and mortal—is under the judgment of God because of the sins of the human race.[27] Human reason is little more than idle speculation. Human rank, although ordained by God, affords us no ultimate comfort or advantage.[28] And human saints have only one purpose—that of drawing attention to Christ. Thus, for example, John is not worthy of special honour since his only job is to draw attention to the light.[29] Mary needs no special mention since her one concern was the Incarnation.[30] Moses, and the laws he delivered too, must direct us to Christ.[31]

Luther's sermons on the Prologue reflect a tremendous and passionate conviction against any form of reliance on what is human, any 'fleshly' pride. He makes his listeners aware of just how radical is their degradation and helplessness as inheritors from human parents and how inexpressibly glorious is their inheritance as children through faith.[32] And he

23. Pelikan (ed.), *Sermons on the Gospel of John*, p. 48.
24. See n. 14 above.
25. Pelikan (ed.), *Sermons on the Gospel of John*, p. 55.
26. Pelikan (ed.), *Sermons on the Gospel of John*, p. 133.
27. Pelikan (ed.), *Sermons on the Gospel of John*, p. 111.
28. Pelikan (ed.), *Sermons on the Gospel of John*, p. 101.
29. Pelikan (ed.), *Sermons on the Gospel of John*, p. 49.
30. Pelikan (ed.), *Sermons on the Gospel of John*, p. 109.
31. Pelikan (ed.), *Sermons on the Gospel of John*, p. 147.
32. Pelikan (ed.), *Sermons on the Gospel of John*, pp. 87-102. See, for example: 'Indeed, we would regard the world's riches, treasures, glories, splendor, and might—compared with the dignity and honor due us as the children and heirs, not

insists that the means to this faith is not through any human accom-
plishment but through the Word of the Gospel:

> Therefore we should feel impelled gladly to give ear to this blessed proc-
> lamation; and if it were not so close at hand, we should even be willing
> to crawl on our knees more than a hundred miles to get it, and then
> engrave it deeply in our hearts for our assurance ... This is the procla-
> mation of the Gospel. It is decidedly different from that found in the
> books of the philosophers, of the sages of the world, of the asinine pope,
> and of his scribblers.[33]

Luther believes that God created the world within the cosmos.[34] And to
this extent, of course, the created world cannot be 'vile slime', as he says
the Manichaeans think it.[35] But, significantly perhaps, he expresses little
warmth for that creation in these sermons. There is here no trace of
Hildegard's regard for the sensual beauty and complex wonder of the
created world or for the tremendous significance of the human form—
Incarnation within the cosmic scheme as a whole. He does not, like her,
present the reader or listener with any sort of map that could make her
feel 'at home' in this cosmos. What he perceives is more like a shining
clue in some deep, dark and terrifying maze. And it is as if, beyond the
acknowledgment in faith of God's creative goodness, Luther is sometimes overwhelmed by perceptions of human baseness and stupid self-
complacency and visions of degeneration and physical decay that go
beyond any simple Manichaean dualism.[36] The Incarnation of the Word

of a mortal emperor but of the eternal and almighty God—as trifling, paltry, vile,
leprous, yes, as stinking filth and poison. For this glory, no matter how great and
magnificent it may be, is, in the end, consumed by maggots and snakes in the grave.'

33. Pelikan (ed.), *Sermons on the Gospel of John*, p. 101.

34. Pelikan (ed.), *Sermons on the Gospel of John*, p. 20.

35. Pelikan (ed.), *Sermons on the Gospel of John*, p. 112.

36. In the Weimar edition of Luther's works (*D. Martin Luthers Werke: Kritische
Gesamtausgabe*, I, p. 47), Luther admits that, even as a young man, it was not sexual
appetite that caused him the greatest torment. Many commentators concur that far
more harrowing for Luther was the acute depression and anxiety that periodically
afflicted him throughout his life and which he referred to as *Anfechtungen* (spiritual
trials). The character of such attacks was specific: 'an unnerving and enervating fear
that God had turned his back on him once and for all, had repudiated his repentance
and prayers, and had abandoned him to suffer the pains of hell'. See David
Steinmetz, *Luther in Context* (Bloomington: Indiana University Press, 1986).

is necessary for our salvation but otherwise Luther cannot find a way of acknowledging humanity itself as gift.

Is it possible then to judge between these two tendencies within Luther's sermons on the Johannine Prologue? Luther is undeniably on the side of a Christian orthodoxy that repudiates dualism and hatred of the God-created flesh. He knows that the spiritual strength of the Church is sustained through words and symbols shared within ecclesiastical structures and a responsible ordering of human relationships. But his passionate disgust and suspicion of human claims to consequence and autonomy is counterindicative, since the balance of worth is necessarily all on one side.

Given the long-standing associations that may be traced out between flesh, inferiority, sin and death—that is to say a particular view of humanity—and the symbols of woman and the feminine, it seems worth investigating what Luther is doing more precisely at such places as these symbols enter into the interpretation of this key passage.

3. *The First Riddle: The Absence of Christ's Mother*

Luther was born a Roman Catholic and surrounded by evidence of the honour, love and tremendous respect commanded by Christ's mother Mary. Alongside widespread popular devotion, mediaeval scholasticism developed more specifically theological debates. These debates concerned, most notably, Mary's virgin conception of God's Son, her agreement or cooperation with God in the Incarnation of the Word, her ability to mediate or even gain advantage with her son on behalf of sinners and her own freedom from the consequences of original sin.

Thus the Church had taught Mary's Immaculate Conception[37] from the thirteenth century onwards and the understanding that she was not bound by death as the consequences of original sin[38] was implicit in a general acceptance—in the Roman Catholic Church from about the

37. 'the most Blessed Virgin Mary, in the first instant of her Conception, by a singular grace and privilege granted by Almighty God, in view of the merits of Jesus Christ, the Saviour of the human race, was preserved free from all stain of original sin.' Papal Bull, *Ineffabilis Deus*. It should be noted, however, that the Immaculate Conception was not finally formulated as a dogma of the Roman Catholic Church until 8 December 1854. It was first defended by Duns Scotus (1264–1308).

38. See Michael O'Carroll, *Theotokos: A Theological Encyclopedia of the Blessed Virgin Mary* (Wilmington, DE: Michael Glazier, rev. edn, 1983), p. 58.

same time—of her bodily assumption into heaven. Faith in her perpetual virginity—before, during and after Christ's birth—was also widespread from the thirteenth century. Belief in the necessity of Mary's
consent to the Incarnation was a feature of Bernard of Clairvaux's
Mariology,[39] becoming influential from the twelfth century. The
Catholic Church's rich Marian traditions stress the importance of Mary's
cooperation with the divine plan for Incarnation. In mediaeval religious
art, for example, Mary is imaged as the container or the bearer of Christ
or even as the celebrant offering the saving flesh of Jesus.[40] Inevitably
she acquired status and significance within the redemptive scheme. A
somewhat earlier figure, Germanus of Constantinople (c. 634–733), is
credited with being the doctor of Mary's universal mediation. For
example, in his second homily on the Dormition, Germanus writes:

> No one is saved except through you, O Theotokos; no one is ransomed
> save through you, Mother of God [Theometros]; no one secured a gift of
> mercy save through you who hold God.[41]

The figure of Mary as Mediatrix was soon adopted widely by the
Church in the West.

Luther first broke publicly with both popular devotion and the
Church's teaching on Mary in his *Sermon on Mary's Nativity*, delivered in
1522, arguing against her having any special merit not granted to other
people. And from even before that time he was concerned to relegate
Mary to a less significant place in the Church's life.[42] He argued that it
was far more important to give alms to the poor than honour to the

---

39. Bernard of Clairvaux (1090–1153). See, for example, his fourth homily,
Super missus est. Here Bernard speaks of 'the whole world on bended knees' waiting
for Mary's response to the angel's words because the salvation of the whole human
race depends on this.

40. See, for example, *The Priesthood of the Virgin*, French panel painting commis-
sioned for the Cathedral of Amiens (c. 1437), reproduced in Caroline Walker
Bynum, *Fragmentation and Redemption: Essays on Gender and the Human Body in
Medieval Religion* (New York: Zone Books, 1991), p. 219.

41. Quoted in O'Carroll, *Theotokos*, p. 240.

42. Note Marina Warner, *Alone of All her Sex: The Myth and the Cult of the Virgin
Mary* (London: Pan Books, 1990), p. 96. Warner writes that in later years, Luther
struck the feast of Mary's Assumption into heaven (15 August) from his calendar.
The Assumption was a powerful reminder of the unique status of the Virgin. In
proclaiming that she was taken up into heaven, body and soul, it challenged her
solidarity with the rest of mortal humanity. It re-emphasized the particularity of her
relationship with her Son.

Virgin. And he is, more than once, found lamenting that Marian piety had seemed to substitute worship and praise to Mary for the true worship of Christ himself.[43] He came to reject claims that she could mediate or intercede with her son[44] altogether or that salvation rested in any sense upon her willingness to cooperate with God. Within his commentary on Jn 1.1-18, Luther implicitly castigates the sort of Marian devotion encouraged by Bernard of Clairvaux—one of the very few Church saints, it should be said, for whom Luther had any time at all. In what is undoubtedly a reference to Bernard's image of ecstatic, mystical union with Christ—the kiss[45]—he comments with characteristic bluntness:

> Oh, how many kisses we bestowed on Mary! But I do not like Mary's breasts or milk, for she did not redeem and save me.[46]

What then, does Luther make of Mary in these sermons on the Incarnation of the Word? They were preached in 1537, 15 years after he first broke openly with the Marian devotion that, for hundreds of years, had hailed her with a host of exalted—or extravagant—titles: Star of the Sea, Queen of Heaven, Mistress of the World and Port of Salvation.[47] What attitude towards this female character does he express? Does his treatment of *her* give the reader a clearer understanding of his fundamental attitude towards the *humanity* with which she is frequently associated?

One would perhaps at first anticipate that Luther will give Mary scant mention, particularly since the Prologue itself does not mention her at all, as he himself notes:

43. See Pelikan (ed.), *Sermons on the Gospel of John*, p. 136: 'Christendom neglected and, unfortunately, lost this chief fountain and source, which overflows with rich and full grace; and it substituted Christ's mother Mary for Christ, praying to her for grace'.

44. See, for example, Pelikan (ed.), *Sermons on the Gospel of John*, p. 165. Mary appears here among other saints to whom the misguided believer might appeal for help in coping with the burden of sin. The exact phraseology of the translation strikes the modern reader as slightly bizarre! However, the mention of Mary's breasts is presumably intended to remind Christ of his own humanity, by drawing attention to the sense in which he too has shared the helplessness and dependence of a child: 'Then we run to the saints, and we invoke the assistance of the Virgin Mary, saying: "Intercede for me before your Son; show Him your breasts!... But is this not a hideous and terrible blindness?"'

45. See Warner, *Alone of All her Sex*, pp. 129-30.

46. Pelikan (ed.), *Sermons on the Gospel of John*, p. 146.

47. These titles are taken from another attack on Marian devotion, *The Shipwreck*, composed by Luther's contemporary Erasmus of Rotterdam (d. 1536).

John fails to mention Mary, the Lord's mother, with as much as a word.[48]

But, in fact, Luther's sermons continue to refer to her frequently.[49] Of course, Luther has an implicit understanding of the unity of Scripture—the whole of Scripture lies behind or supports conclusions drawn from a single biblical text. In this sense, Mary's absence from the Prologue is immaterial, given its incarnational themes. The Gospels of Matthew and Luke, in particular, fill out her story and her role.

However, undoubtedly feeling a certain *hostility* towards the pretensions of Mary's devotees, Luther appears to regard the absence of Mary from the Prologue as a cause for approbation and almost celebration! Her absence is worth mentioning. In the fourth evangelist, Luther sees a man—and one with authority moreover—who has not substituted Mary for Christ. Here is a man who respects Luther's own teaching of *Christus Solus*. The absence of Mary suggests his superior qualities, since:

> the greater the men of God and the larger the measure of the spirit in them, the greater the diligence and attention they devote to the Son rather than to the mother.[50]

The fundamental objection expressed *here* is that Mary is nothing. A peerless Christ represents the only grounds of hope for eternal life.[51] John had the right idea. The absence of Mary is the perfect way of expressing her nothingness, her lack of saving graces. To honour her properly, Luther suggests in his *Exposition of The Magnificat*,[52] she should 'be stripped completely of everything and only be regarded in her nothingness, afterwards we should admire the overwhelming grace of God who looks so graciously on such a lowly, worthless human

48. Pelikan (ed.), *Sermons on the Gospel of John*, p. 109.

49. See, for example, Pelikan (ed.), *Sermons on the Gospel of John*, pp. 5-26. Mary is mentioned 13 times by name within the first sermon. A further reference in this sermon (Pelikan [ed.], *Sermons on the Gospel of John*, p. 6) speaks of Gal. 4.4: 'God sent forth His Son, born of a woman'.

50. Pelikan (ed.), *Sermons on the Gospel of John*, p. 109.

51. See Pelikan (ed.), *Sermons on the Gospel of John*, p. 65. Luther here distinguishes between fundamentally biblical saints—John the Baptist at this point—and those canonized by the pope. These first should be revered. 'But when compared with Christ, the true Light (and those mad barefooted friars compared their St Francis to Christ, yes, even foisted him on Christendom in Christ's place), then their light is totally eclipsed in the comparison.'

52. 1521.

being'.[53] The brutality of such a description is undoubtedly directed against ecclesiastical institutions composed largely of men. And these are men whom Luther no doubt perceived to be stupid and quite immoral in leading human souls, women and men, perilously astray. But the effect of this description is still very disturbing. The whole description approximates a little too closely for comfort to the forcible humiliation of women in order to shore up an anxious masculinity—divine or otherwise.

4. *The Second Riddle: The Presence of Mary*

Readers note Luther's claim that it is commendable for John to omit all mention of Mary from his key incarnational text. Nonetheless, Luther himself keeps bringing Mary into his own work. If, in salvific terms, she is nothing, what exactly *does* she represent for him?

The majority of references to Mary in these sermons simply relate her to Christ's fleshly humanity, as in 'Before Jesus Christ was Mary's Son and became flesh, He was with God',[54] or 'He was born as a true man from the Virgin Mary'.[55] But they are nevertheless an indication of Mary's theological significance. First of all, then, Mary guarantees Christ's full and necessary humanity: 'the Son... assumed human nature. He was born of the Virgin Mary'.[56] And this belief in the humanity of Christ is as essential for our salvation as is a belief in the divinity of Christ: 'If He is deprived of His humanity we are lost again... if He were not true man, He could not have suffered and died to achieve our salvation.'[57] What guarantees this salvific humanity is the flesh and blood of Mary:

> He must also be a true and natural son of the Virgin Mary... He was conceived of the Holy Spirit, who came upon her and overshadowed her with the power of the Most High, according to Lk. 1.35. However, Mary, the pure virgin, had to contribute of her seed and of the natural blood that coursed from her heart. From her He derived everything, except sin, that a child naturally and normally receives from its mother.[58]

53. Hilda Graef, *Mary: A History of Doctrine and Devotion*. II. *From the Reformation to the Present Day* (London: Sheed & Ward, 1965), p. 8.
54. Pelikan (ed.), *Sermons on the Gospel of John*, p. 16.
55. Pelikan (ed.), *Sermons on the Gospel of John*, p. 113.
56. Pelikan (ed.), *Sermons on the Gospel of John*, p. 6.
57. Pelikan (ed.), *Sermons on the Gospel of John*, pp. 22-23.
58. Pelikan (ed.), *Sermons on the Gospel of John*, p. 23.

How more precisely does this work? Implicitly, Luther makes a distinction between Christ as Son of God and as son of Mary. Calling Christ the Son of God refers to human generation simply in the metaphorical sense. God as begetter and Son as begotten are metaphors or limited analogies. For example, he argues that this illustration or analogy of the nature of the Father's relationship to the Son soon breaks down because

> it fails to portray fully the impartation of the divine majesty. The Father bestows His entire divine nature on the Son. But the human father cannot impart his entire nature to his son; he can give only a part of it.[59]

But for Luther, the relationship of Mary to her son is less an analogy than a metonymy for his entirely distinct human nature. God is not literally a father. Christ cannot have derived his humanity from God then. Luther states quite baldly that Christ has no human father: 'This was without the cooperation of a man.'[60] Thus Christ's human nature—or what is definitively human—must come solely from his human mother.

---

59. Pelikan (ed.), *Sermons on the Gospel of John*, p. 6.

60. Pelikan (ed.), *Sermons on the Gospel of John*, p. 23 n. 23. Luther appears to have believed firmly in Mary's virginal conception and perpetual virginity, although, with regard to the actual birth of Christ, he seems to have discounted the notion of a physical integrity post partum, such as was a part of a popular Catholic belief at the time and later established as Catholic orthodoxy at the Council of Trent (1545–63). Luther suggests something rather more naturalistic: 'It was a true birth…it happened to her as happens to other women, in full consciousness and with the collaboration of her body as happens at any birth; she was a natural mother and he was a natural son' (*D. Martin Luthers Werke: Kritische Gesamtausgabe*, X, p. 3).

While Luther frequently refers to Mary as a virgin in these sermons, he just as frequently leaves the ascription out. Luther's main concern with Mary's virginity appears to be the absence of a human father, a man. See also: 'God's Son was born of a woman i.e. not from a man, as all other children are born. Among all others, this man alone is born only of a woman. There is no emphasis on the fact that he was *born of a virgin*' (*D. Martin Luthers Werke: Kritische Gesamtausgabe*, X, p. 19).

There is, however, some continuing ambivalence in his attitude towards virginity. Luther clearly objected to the *pretension* of sexual asceticism. That is, he thought it foolish and presumptuous for humankind to try to avoid God's commands in the simple, unassuming matter of marrying and bringing up children. However, he still associated physical virginity with wider cultural notions of purity. See Luther's response to popular discussion of virgin births. To have a child implies loss of virginity, and except within marriage, merits the description of 'whore'. Pelikan (ed.), *Sermons on the Gospel of John*, p. 18.

The son's filial relationship to his mother is precisely an index of his humanity. And what Mary gives her son, in the narrative of divine Incarnation that Luther tells through brief, emblematic references to her, is a nature that is under the judgment of the Law. In these cases, Mary is synonymous with nothing other than human nature through its association with sin.

Luther needs to demolish two possible lines of attack at this point. First he has somehow to affirm, even if he cannot explain, that Christ can be fully human and remain untouched by the Augustinian legacy of inherited guilt that his mother's flesh and blood represent. To the end of his life, Luther continued to affirm Mary's perpetual virginity and also her absolute purity at the moment of conception, even if he appears eventually to have abandoned the Roman Catholic Church's understanding of the Immaculate Conception in its full sense.[61] However, it is clear that the impetus behind this conclusion has little to do with a desire to separate Mary herself from the negative associations of humanity. Luther gropes towards this most 'unreasonable' conclusion of orthodox Augustinian Christology that separates Christ's redemptive humanity from that which most quintessentially defines it as human—its commerce with the feminine-identified 'flesh'. Thus, very much as was the case with Augustine, 'flesh' has become for Luther a concept that represents the disturbing perception of a certain autonomous difference or 'otherness', but whose actual transgressive 'reality' is disguised and controlled by its transformation into a spiritual category of (feminine) valuelessness, vanity or even absence.

And, of course, any reference to Mary carries with it the implication—or risk—that feminine-identified flesh and blood might have some virtue or potency in themselves. Secondly, then, references to Mary as an index of humanity are hedged about with qualifications and denials to this effect:

> if Christ were merely a human being like you and me...[h]e could not have overcome devil, death, and sin; He would have proved far too weak for them and could never have helped us. No, we must have a Savior who is true God and Lord over sin, death, devil, and hell.[62]

---

61. Luther preached on the subject in 1516 in a Latin sermon which differed very little from contemporary accounts (see *D. Martin Luthers Werke: Kritische Gesamtausgabe*, I, pp. 106ff.). Commentators argue that after 1528, however, he no longer believed in this. See Graef, *Mary*, II, p. 11 n. 6.

62. Pelikan (ed.), *Sermons on the Gospel of John*, p. 21.

The identifying sign of divine potency is the absence of sin:

> if we are to be saved from the devil's power…it is imperative that we
> have an eternal possession that is perfect and flawless.[63]

The corresponding sign of humankind, stripped to its bare essentials in a
theological sense, becomes the presence, or in an Augustinian sense the
inheritance, of that flaw.

In conclusion, it appears that Mary is being used metonymically to
stand for the whole of sinful human nature. Mary's theological significance takes on the customary associations of the female gender with
flesh and sin and, by implication, the judgment under which an innocent Christ suffers and dies.[64]

Staying for the moment with the absent mother, made present within
this commentary, Luther's reading of Mary of Nazareth within the
Synoptic Gospel accounts is revealing in what it selects, and what, in
this way, it excludes. Luther respected Scripture as God's word and the
means to the mysterious, the miraculous generation of faith. However,
it has to be said that in these examples,[65] Mary functions like a
penumbra around an eclipse. References to her invariably shed a partial
light around her son in a manner that we should expect, given Luther's
strictures on her place in the theological scheme of Incarnation:

> He is our Brother; we are members of His body, flesh and bone of His
> flesh and bone. According to His humanity, He, Christ, our Savior, was
> the real and natural fruit of Mary's virginal womb (of which Elizabeth,
> filled with the Holy Spirit, said to her in Lk. 1.42; 'Blessed is the fruit of
> your womb!').[66]

---

63. Pelikan (ed.), *Sermons on the Gospel of John*, p. 22.

64. See Lienhard, *Luther*, p. 168: 'To be human is to be accused by the law
which can never be completely fulfilled. Without doubt, Christ fulfilled it perfectly,
but in order to be entirely at one with us, he has like us submitted to the
"punishment and the penalty of the law".'

65. See, for example, Pelikan (ed.), *Sermons on the Gospel of John*, p. 17 for
Simeon's words to Mary (Lk. 2.34-35); p. 23 for the account of the conception of
Jesus (Lk. 1.35); pp. 23, 38 for Mary and Elizabeth's conversation concerning the
birth of John the Baptist (Lk. 1.39-45); p. 73 for Mary's reactions to Jesus'
disappearance in Jerusalem (Lk. 2.41-51); p. 74 for Christ's subsequent obedience to
her (Lk. 2.51); p. 74 for Mary's status as the wife of a carpenter (Mt. 13.55; Mk 6.3);
p. 10 for Christ's words to his mother at Cana (Jn 2.4).

66. Pelikan (ed.), *Sermons on the Gospel of John*, p. 23.

But on the other hand, Mary's response, noted in the text of Lk. 1.38 'Behold I am the Handmaid of the Lord', which might be used to emphasize the sense in which she gives her consent, is not featured in this commentary on John's incarnational text.[67] She does not figure here, then, as either an autonomous being or as a representative of a divinely cooperative *modus operandi* as for example Hildegard of Bingen refers to her. The text of the Gospels is being brought under the control of Luther's own presuppositions in this way, while the resulting interpretation is being given the authority that scriptural quotations naturally attract. In saying this, I do no more, of course, than restate the argument within modern feminist hermeneutics, that powerful 'malestream' theological controls on biblical interpretation, such as Luther imposes on the Marian texts of Luke's Gospel for example, have to be contested.

The specific relevance of this interpretative practice here, however, is that this is not simply an interpretation of Mary within the Gospel of Luke, but that Luther uses this particular and selective interpretation of a Lukan Mary to 'fill out' his understanding of her absence in the Prologue of John's Gospel. This absence, however good for Luther in the sense that it cuts the pretensions of Marian devotion and theology down to size, is still, clearly, disturbing. It is perhaps filled with the possibility of many competing Marian figures or the equally unsettling prospect of her total absence. By means of the selective use of Scripture, then, Luther defines this absence by imposing upon it an authoritatively sanctioned and manageable view of Mary the mother of Christ, which is in line with his own theology of the absolute subordination of humankind.

Luther did have some regard for Mary, Christ's mother. He thought her faith and humility exemplary.[68] And for Mary, the 'poor little orphan', the child of no consequence, Luther feels no scorn, and perhaps even some tenderness.[69] But in this mode, of course, Mary does not threaten the uniqueness of Christ's salvific role. She is placed in the same relation to him as every other human being. Her humble bearing

---

67. There are two references to the Annunciation within this commentary on Jn 1.1-18. However, both of them focus on the message of the angel rather than Mary's response to it. Pelikan (ed.), *Sermons on the Gospel of John*, pp. 109, 113.

68. Note sermon on The Magnificat. Her faith and humility are exemplary but no cause for pride: 'his concept of Mary's humility is such a tribute to God that all merit on her part is excluded'. See O'Carroll, *Theotokos*, p. 227.

69. Pelikan (ed.), *Sermons on the Gospel of John*, p. 162 (commentary on Jn 2).

towards her son is exemplary but it does not thereby make her more virtuous or exalt her above others.

In these sermons on the Prologue, Luther draws a picture of a woman who is not there as an ordinary woman and whose indistinguishable ordinariness is a mark of Christ's own 'inexpressible humility'[70] in taking on flesh, the condition of common humanity.[71] Luther is not especially interested in Mary's exemplary humility here in his sermons on the Prologue. But he could be said to be interested in her lack of consequence in so far as this deflates the claims of Marian devotion or exalted Mariological metaphors and images. In commenting on Jn 1.10—'He was in the world, and the world was made through him, yet the world knew him not'—Luther writes:

> It is as if [John] were to say: 'The very same child that lies in the manger, takes its mother Mary's breasts, and later becomes subject to her, is the Life and the Light of man, yes, is God, the Creator of all things; for the world was made through Him'.[72]

The wonder is that God chooses to live this unassuming life with a plain carpenter's wife[73] and not that this woman, Mary, nurses and then disciplines the Christ child as he grows up in the way of humankind.

Luther's desire to make Mary ordinary may have been a reaction to what he saw as the errors of the Roman Catholic Church and of popular Marian devotion. The Church read her consent as a metaphor for synergy, a form of necessary cooperation in redemption between God and humankind. Popular devotion made Mary herself seem potent. But

---

70. Pelikan (ed.), *Sermons on the Gospel of John*, p. 111.

71. Luther appears to define this common humanity in terms of the whole spectrum of emotional and physical need and expression—although, in the context of these sermons, for example, he never suggests explicitly that Christ shared the common lot of human sexuality or sexual appetite. See, for extended analysis of such a 'common lot' Pelikan (ed.), *Sermons on the Gospel of John*, p. 73: 'He ate, drank, slept, awakened, was tired, sad, and happy. He wept and laughed, hungered, thirsted, froze, and perspired. He chatted, worked, and prayed. In brief, He required the same things for life's sustenance and preservation that any other human being does. He labored and suffered as anyone else does. He experienced both fortune and misfortune.'

72. Pelikan (ed.), *Sermons on the Gospel of John*, p. 74. See also, p. 113, 'His mother nursed Him as any other child is nursed'.

73. Pelikan (ed.), *Sermons on the Gospel of John*, p. 74.

in addition it may also be true that Luther was offended by her failure to conform to the cultural norms for women that he favoured.

Luther's assumption in all he writes, says and preaches is that men and women—ordinary men and women—should marry and have children. This is God's plan for humankind, and one which he followed himself:[74]

> On what pretence can man have interdicted marriage, which is a law of nature? 'Tis as though we were forbidden to eat, to drink, to sleep. That which God has ordained and regulated, is no longer a matter of the human will, which we may adopt or reject with impunity.[75]

Women of the Lutheran Reformation were expected to marry and exercise their religious vocations[76] within the limits of a domestic life.[77] Since women were, for Luther, ideally domestic creatures who kept to their place,[78] he did not see them in general as autonomous individuals within society but [78]rather as part of the furniture:

74. Luther married Catherine of Bora, a former nun, on 13 June 1525. The couple had six children from 1526 to 1534. The Luthers seem to have loved their children very much, grieving deeply for the two daughters who died in childhood. Heiko Oberman's account of the Luther's marriage makes it clear, however, that it was the cause of considerable public scandal at the time, and undertaken, at least initially, with a deliberate theological purpose that must have put some considerable strain on actual relations between Martin and Catherine. As letters and *Table Talk* reveal, however, the marriage appears to have developed into a warm and supportive relationship. See Heiko A. Oberman, *Luther: Man between God and the Devil* (trans. Eileen Walliser-Schwarzbart; London: Fontana Press, 1993), p. 272.

75. Hazlitt (trans.), *Table Talk*, p. 335, number 728.

76. See Caroline Walker Bynum, *Holy Feast and Holy Fast: The Religious Significance of Food to Medieval Women* (Berkeley: University of California Press, 1987). Bynum writes about the blossoming of women's religious communities during the mediaeval period, in which women were offered not simply an escape from domestic danger and drudgery, but also the opportunity to affirm their femininity and celibacy in terms of a religious ideal (Walker Bynum, *Fragmentation and Redemption*, p. 20): 'Set apart from the world by intact boundaries, her flesh untouched by ordinary flesh, the virgin [like Christ's mother, the perpetual virgin] was also a bride, destined for a higher consummation. She scintillated with fertility and power.'

77. It should, perhaps, be noted that the scope of women's domestic work in pre-industrial societies in the West tended to be broader than that of modern women. Catherine Luther bridged the gap between her husband's income and annual expenditure on a large house, children and innumerable guests by managing a farm, large garden, pig-breeding and beer-brewing and by taking in lodgers. See Oberman, *Luther*, p. 280.

78. Luther was reported as saying 'Men have broad and large chests, and small

> Marrying cannot be without women, nor can the world subsist without
> them. To marry is physic against incontinence. A woman is, or at least
> should be, a friendly, courteous, and merry companion in life, whence
> they are named, by the Holy Ghost, house-honours, the honour and
> ornament of the house, and inclined to tenderness, for thereunto are they
> chiefly created, to bear children, and be the pleasure, joy, and solace of
> their husbands.[79]

In the sermons, Luther is certainly trying to align a normative view
of womankind with his description of Mary as an ordinary wife and
mother. It is not just an ordinary woman he sketches out briefly within
these sermons, but the outline of an ideal mother who is both nurturing
and authoritative. To this extent, Luther does something familiar. He
makes Mary an exemplar. She is not just a mother, but a 'good' mother.
At the same time, the metaphorical dimensions of her motherhood are
diminished. She has no more authority outside the domestic sphere than
Luther's own wife. Her breasts and her milk are the ordinary means of
suckling a child so that it may be fed and grow. The Son of God, who is
'suckled and carried in her arms', will be cherished and nurtured by
Mary 'as any other mother does her child'.[80] Mary's breasts and milk are
given none of the metaphorical enrichment of Catholic traditions that
made Mary Mother Church herself, nursing the faithful or penitents
with the milk of healing, knowledge and bliss.[81]

Luther understands becoming flesh as the Word's participation in, or
even consumption of, divinely instituted motherhood and female do-
mesticity. That is, he sees the Word as entitled to the same domestic
comforts as any sixteenth-century man or man-child might wish for.
But Luther's unease or discomfort with this female figure still reveals
itself in two particular ways. First of all, he denies Mary any extraordinary *status* in recognition of her exemplary motherhood. Mary's love
for the Christ child—as presented here in Luther's sermons—is simply
'ordinary'. Luther wants to interpret this maternal loving here in the
light of divine humility that condescends to accept from a woman a

narrow hips, and more understanding than the women, who have but small and
narrow breasts, and broad hips, to the end they should remain at home, sit still, keep
house, and bear and bring up children.' Hazlitt (trans.), *Table Talk*, p. 334, number
725.
   79. Hazlitt (trans.), *Table Talk*, p. 335, number 726.
   80. Pelikan (ed.), *Sermons on the Gospel of John*, p. 112.
   81. See, in particular, Warner, *Alone of All her Sex*, pp. 192-205.

place within the context of human life. Perhaps it is that maternal love is a dangerous area for Luther precisely because in the ordinary context of living, defined in cultural terms, it is actually something quite rare and extraordinary, making it appropriate as a representation even a trope of divine love itself, or even of a vision of transcendence beyond self.

The second sense in which Luther's unease about this ordinary woman is revealed is, of course, the fact that Mary is assumed to be, and is largely referred to as, a virgin. Luther's rebellion against the Roman Catholic Church had included a truly ground-breaking rebellion against the imposition of celibacy on priests and religious. The mature Luther was sceptical about the religious value of extreme forms of asceticism including total sexual abstinence. He believed, somewhat in opposition to his Augustinian inheritance, that the sexual impulse had a God-given purpose, and spoke with refreshing candour of 'the passionate, natural inclination toward woman' that, in marriage, is God's word and work[82] —for men. He certainly regarded many of the Fathers of the Church as far too preoccupied with abstinences[83] and thought virginity was not in itself a particular virtue. And yet, even to support his own view of Mary as just an ordinary woman, he was not prepared to compromise the teaching of her virginity. The solution to the riddle must lie, as I have already suggested, in the nature of Luther's theology as a whole. Mary's virginity is, for Luther, a theological mechanism which supports Christ's redemptive divinity[84] and power over death as the inheritance of guilt. Given Luther's dismissive view of human reason, it is not too hard for him to set aside its evident lack in that respect. The consequence, however, of such theology is to undercut whatever of autonomy or separate significance that this female character might have and to turn

---

82. See *D. Martin Luthers Werke: Kritische Gesamtausgabe*, XVIII, pp. 275, 19-28.

83. See, for example, Tappert (trans. and ed.), *Table Talk*. There are various occasions in *Table Talk* when Luther attacks the Fathers for their failure to say anything useful or appropriate about marriage, castigating Jerome, for example, for being a 'real monk's warden' (Tappert [trans. and ed.], *Table Talk*, p. 177), and dismissing him as 'less profitable than Aesop': 'I wish he had had a wife, for then he would have written many things differently... If only Jerome had encouraged the works of faith and the fruits of the gospel! But he spoke only of fasting, etc.' (Tappert [trans. and ed.], *Table Talk*, p. 177).

84. See Pelikan (ed.), *Sermon on the Gospel of John*, p. 22: 'if Christ is divested of His divinity, there remains no help against God's wrath and no rescue from His judgement. Our sin, misery and distress are so enormous that they require a ransom too great for angels, patriarchs, or prophets to pay.'

her female 'flesh', body and soul, into what is effectively a metaphor for human sin and death.

In the familiar fairy tale of Rumpelstiltskin, the riddle set for the Queen was to guess the name of a man who had once helped her in great danger and now came to claim his reward. If she could guess his name, then she could keep her child. If she could not, the child was forfeit to him. Unfortunately for Rumpelstiltskin, the Queen was re-sourceful and not above cheating. She discovered his name, and the industrious spinner left empty-handed.

To name Rumpelstiltskin was to limit his power, even the power to claim what was his due. Perhaps Luther felt that to leave potential without a name and outwith his own 'text' would have endowed absence with a power for subverting his theological position in relation to the Incarnate Word. The text of the Prologue could not be said decisively to rule out, for example, a view of the Word incarnate as a divine disguise or mask. It could not be said to exclude a vision of a synergetic Mariology in which the mother represents the cooperation of humankind and God for salvation. It is clear, from the way in which he presents her here, that Luther wished to contest both these options. In order to claim that the Word was fully incarnate in human flesh he had to name a physical mother to all our fleshly abilities to hear and act upon the revelation of the redemptive Word in Scripture. In order to deprive the fleshly humanity that she represented of any grounds for complacency or self-reliance he had to name one more ordinary (virgin) mother. Finally, in order to turn away the threat posed by the 'oth-erness' that threatens the masculine singularity of Luther's vision of the divine and of which the woman Mary is a symbol, she had to relinquish her individuality altogether and be named as nothing more than the (feminine) representative of a spiritual fault.

5. Finally, Yet Another Riddle: When Is a Relationship not a Relationship?

Luther's public and passionate protest against the Roman Catholic Church—echoed by many contemporary Christians—began, of course, with his rebuke of the papacy on 31 October 1517 on the matter of 'indulgences'.[85] That he should have felt such anger and passion about

---

85. The practice of granting indulgences at that time related to the remission of

this practice is unsurprising. He felt his own insignificance before God and his own inability to fulfil God's law[86] so acutely. His anger was directed against the theological model that suggested salvation could be bought. Luther wished to dismiss all reckoning from the account of a divine/human relationship. For Luther, not only could salvation not be bought with money, but there was also nothing to be gained from good behaviour, acts of piety and charity or anything pertaining to fleshly humanity at all. And there was no justification for the depth of God's love, demonstrated in becoming flesh.

> With that word 'flesh' the evangelist wanted to indicate this inexpressible humiliation ... we are not to assume that the evangelist used the word 'flesh' lightly. Human reason cannot comprehend the magnitude of God's anger over sin. Therefore it does not fathom Paul's full meaning when he says that God had made Christ a sin and curse for our sakes (2 Cor. 5.21, Gal. 3.13).[87]

temporal punishment for sins already forgiven. This remission was granted by the Church on the basis of what it saw as the accumulated 'treasure' of superabundant merits accrued by Christ and the saints. Luther objected to the unscrupulous misuse of this practice, but more substantially, to the practice itself. He believed that it challenged the sense in which Jesus Christ was the sole source of salvation and assurance, and was also at fault in suggesting that the Church 'owned' this treasure. He argued that faith was pre-eminently a matter of having a relationship with Christ, the consequence of which was that the individual believer was transformed into the image of the Son of God because of a form of loving, suffering participation in the cross, unrelated to effort. His anxiety was that saving grace was thus cheapened and misrepresented as something to be achieved by a little effort, or even a little money. The actual occasion for this outburst was the preaching of J. Tetzel, who publicized the granting of indulgences by Pope Leo X as a reward for contributions towards renovations at St Peter's Cathedral in Rome. Oberman notes that barely two weeks after being posted, Luther recorded that his theses against indulgences had circulated all over Germany. See Oberman, *Luther*, p. 191.

86. Steinmetz's description is powerful: 'Luther felt alone in the universe, battered by the demands of God's law and beyond the reach of the gospel. He doubted his own faith, his own mission, and the goodness of God—doubts which, because they verged on blasphemy, drove him deeper and deeper into the Slough of Despond. Election ceased to be a doctrine of comfort and became a sentence of death. No prayer he uttered could penetrate the wall of indifferent silence with which God had surrounded himself. Condemned by his own conscience, Luther despised himself and murmured against God' (Steinmetz, *Luther in Context*, p. 1).

87. Pelikan (ed.), *Sermons on the Gospel of John*, p. 110.

The obligation to love and serve others could only be fulfilled by God's grace obtained through faith so that living a moral and caring life was an indication of salvation rather than a precondition.

Luther then reads the Prologue as a hymn to God as Creator but primarily as saviour, mediated and revealed above all, in the intervening time, through the Word of God in Scripture. That Word, of course, has already appeared in the world—hidden within the human life of a man, plain and unassuming, enjoying no great reputation[88] for pomp, asceticism or messianic might. This hiddenness within the world, within the body of a woman, Luther relates to divine humility which is itself an effective and unfathomable *saving* miracle. Hiddenness remains the divine *modus operandi*. In blindness and ignorance we 'know him not' (Jn 1.10-11), and, Luther argues, forever rush heedlessly after deceptive appearances. As one contemporary example he holds up the fraudulent holiness or sanctity presented by the monastic life.[89]

But it is, of course, only the humility of God's Word in becoming hidden as a man that has saved us and not the work or participation of humankind. And a theology that reduces all human potentialities to the state of dependence upon divine grace that Luther demands is disturbing. In terms of a position that calls itself feminist, it is disturbing because of the suggestion that it is a divinization and idolatry of the masculine sign of singularity that excludes and obliterates everything but itself.

To this extent, feminist commentators will note how Luther's sermons resist multiplicity. An alternative or cooperative creativity is ruled out by introducing a suitably subordinate mother figure. Moreover the multiplicity suggested by a more sacramental approach to the divine is also contested. Luther certainly taught that Christians should participate regularly and faithfully in the sacrament of Christ's body and blood. But the nourishing sacrament of Christ's flesh and blood is not a means to salvation. It becomes the occasion for contemplating, once more, the absolute singularity of God, confessing

> with heart and mouth, with ears and eyes, with body and soul that you
> have given nothing to God, nor are able to, but that you have and
> receive each and everything from him, particularly eternal life and infinite

---

88. See, for example, Pelikan (ed.), *Sermons on the Gospel of John*, pp. 54, 75, 77.
89. Pelikan, (ed.), *Sermons on the Gospel of John*, p. 71.

righteousness in Christ. When this takes place, you have made him the
true God for yourself, and by means of such a confession you have
upheld his divine glory.[90]

In the context of these sermons on the Prologue, when Luther comes to
Jn 1.14, 'the Word became flesh', he is anxious to outlaw any suggestion
of a potential and even potent multiplicity of aspects within the
Eucharist. This is all dismissed as sorcery and abuse.[91] Neither elements
nor gestures have significance without faith, itself the gift of God's
grace. Just as blood lines and family name have nothing to do with
being a child of God (Jn 1.12-13), there is nothing of automatic potency or effect ascribable to the words or indeed to the form of the
Incarnation—a particular transformation. What is salvific is that 'the Divine Majesty abased Himself and became like us'.[92] The hiddenness of
Christ in the world is elided with the humility of divine self-abasement.

This rejection of multiplicity reflects the view on Luther's part that
humankind is not in any recognizably human relationship with God at
all. As Daphne Hampson concludes, 'Luther's achievement lay in his
reconceptualization of the human relationship to God'.[93] And this is, as
Hampson says, to conceive of the nature of the human person in a way
that is profoundly antithetical to any sort of relational inter-dependence
or mutual support. As against any sort of inter-dependence, Luther's
vision of the divine/human relationship is a matter of excess attenuating
any form of human value independent of the divine. It is a devastating
description of the divine/human relationship in the sense that it defines
the human other in terms of a total absence. And this is clearly reflected
in Luther's configuration of the Incarnation in these sermons, where to
represent the human nature of Christ, Mary's maternal feminine is
similarly transfixed within the Johannine excision.

6. Conclusions

Elisabeth Schüssler Fiorenza draws attention to Mary's journey into the
hill-country to visit her cousin Elizabeth as a hermeneutical metaphor.

90. *Admonition Concerning the Sacrament of the Body and Blood of Our Lord, 1530*.
See Martin E. Lehmann (ed. and trans.), *Luther's Works*. XXXVIII. *Word and Sacrament*, IV (Philadelphia, Fortress Press, 1971), p. 107.

91. Lehmann (ed. and trans.), *Word and Sacrament*, IV, p. 107.

92. Lehmann (ed. and trans.), *Word and Sacrament*, IV, p. 103.

93. Daphne Hampson, 'Luther on the Self: A Feminist Critique', in Ann Loades
(ed.), *Feminist Theology: A Reader* (London: SPCK, 1990), p. 213.

That is to say, as an example of modern feminist practice, she allows the presence of these two women within Scripture to suggest the parameters for interpretation. And what they suggest is two things: an arduous journey through the hill-country, 'but also the joyous embrace of two women pregnant with the possibilities of new life'.[94] What she sees within the hermeneutical process this suggests is first a strenuous effort. She recognizes, as much as Luther, that significance cannot be derived from Scripture without reflection and study. But secondly she sees a divine initiative that is given form, expression and celebration also within the sharing community of women. This represents for her the possibility of different communities sharing in the reading of Scripture. And this is surely one of the most significant insights of modern feminist theology and biblical interpretation. It represents a different perspective to the sort of tempestuous and lonely monologism sometimes evident in theological traditions stemming from Luther's theology, in which the reading and worshipping community is frequently obliterated from sight and replaced by the existential encounter of the individual with his [*sic*] God. In christological terms, feminist biblical critics and theologians strive to question this tendency virtually to obliterate the humanity of Christ by making it merely a quality or possession (innocent suffering, or 'inexpressible humility' for example) of Christ himself. They stress the sense in which Christ's solidarity with both humanity and divinity needs to be understood as belonging to the interconnected life of the whole person—divine or human. They

> have sought to create a paradigm shift in feminist christological discourse from a 'heroic individualistic' or 'heroic liberationist' christology to a christological construction that privileges right relations, connectedness, mutuality, an 'at-one-ment'. This feminist christological discourse uses key concepts such as redemptive connectedness, power-in-relation, dynamic mutuality, erotic creativity, the language of lovers, mutual inter-dependence, passionate creativity, inclusive wholeness, healing energy of existence, and the ontological priority of relationality.[95]

---

94. Elisabeth Schüssler Fiorenza, *Jesus: Miriam's Child, Sophia's Prophet: Critical Issues in Feminist Christology* (London: SCM Press, 1994), p. 34.
95. Schüssler Fiorenza, *Jesus*, p. 50.

5

Demythologizing (the Feminine) within Rudolf Bultmann's Commentary on the Prologue (John 1.1-18)

1. *A View of Bultmann's Theological and Exegetical Approach*

In his essay of 1974, 'Preface to Bultmann',[1] Paul Ricoeur detects in Bultmann's process of 'demythologization' a crucially important hierarchy of levels of both demythologizing and of myth.[2] By taking this into consideration, he claims that readers can avoid drawing the conclusion that Bultmann (1884–1976) is either inconsistent or doing violence to the biblical texts. Ricoeur sees three different modes of approachin Bultmann's work: that of a man of science,[3] that of an existential philosopher[4] and that of a hearer of the word.[5] In each case his priorities are

1.   Paul Ricoeur, 'Preface to Bultmann', in Don Ihde (ed.), *Paul Ricoeur: The Conflict of Interpretations* (Evanston, IL: Northwestern University Press, 1974), pp. 381-401.

2.   See Ricoeur, 'Preface to Bultmann', pp. 390-91.

3.   By this is certainly implied someone holding a modern scientific world-view in which, for example, we can 'no longer believe in events which are inexplicable in principle by reference to the ordinary laws of nature' (see Robert C. Roberts, *Rudolf Bultmann's Theology: A Critical Interpretation* [London: SPCK, 1977], p. 140). It may in addition—within Ricoeur's essay for example—imply the sense in which Bultmann was prepared to engage in more generally 'philosophical' or 'theoretical' reflections on the doctrines and Scriptures of the Christian Church. Thus, for example, Ricoeur speaks of Bultmann's realization that it is necessary to enter into the hermeneutic circle: 'to understand the text, it is necessary to believe in what the text announces to me; but what the text announces to me is given nowhere but in the text. This is why it is necessary to understand the text in order to believe' (Ricoeur, 'Preface to Bultmann', p. 390).

4.   It has frequently been noted that Rudolf Bultmann was greatly influenced by the existentialist philosophy of his contemporary, Martin Heidegger: 'It was precisely because *Being and Time* was in part the issue of an attempt to formalize the

different as is his understanding of the nature of myth. But the centre or foundation of his position remains his own decision of faith, the making himself dependent on an act which determines him:

> Consequently a circulation is set up among all the forms of demythologization—demythologization as work of science, as work of philosophy, and as proceeding from faith. By turns, it is modern man, then the existential philosopher, and finally the believer who calls the shots. The entire exegetical and theological work of Rudolf Bultmann consists in setting up this great circle in which exegetical science, existential interpretation, and preaching in the style of Paul and Luther exchange roles.[6]

Ricoeur's description would certainly seem to me to be a better analysis of Bultmann's project as a whole than attempts to make it conform to a single pattern or theoretical approach.[7] Moreover Ricoeur's critical

structures of factical Christian life that it was greeted with such enthusiasm by Protestant theologians such as Bultmann (with whom it had in part been worked out during Heidegger's stay at Marburg). When Christian theologians looked into the pages of *Being and Time* they found themselves staring at their own image— formalized, ontologized, or, what amounts to the same thing, 'demythologized'. What *Being and Time* had discovered, Bultmann said, is the very structure of religious and Christian existence but without the ontico-mythical worldview that was an idiosyncratic feature of first-century cosmologies' (John D. Caputo, *Demythologizing Heidegger* [Bloomington: Indiana University Press, 1993], p. 173).

5.   By this term is suggested Bultmann's conclusion that Christian proclamation has the character of 'address'. For one discussion of this notion see Rudolf Bultmann, *Glauben and Verstehen* (Tübingen: J.C.B. Mohr [Paul Siebeck], 1960). By this is implied the sense in which Christian proclamation is only truly understood in the form of an imperative, a demand on the hearer for a decisive response, by which they are judged.

6.   Ricoeur, 'Preface to Bultmann', pp. 393-94.

7.   In Roberts, *Rudolf Bultmann's Theology*, it seems to me that the author takes Bultmann to task for just this tendency to move from level to level of approach and in this way seriously to misunderstand the sense in which Bultmann perceives the difficulties of both reading texts and understanding faith in the post-resurrection community. Roberts puts the whole issue down to what he calls the 'a priori' metaphysical determination of Bultmann to divide the world into 'world' and 'existence', thereby *defining*, as it were, the whole realm of 'objective' experience as irrelevant to faith. What appears to be missing from Roberts' analysis is any critical appreciation or reply to modern theoretical understanding of 'objective experience' as *constructed* experience. See, for example, Roberts' discussion of Bultmann's claim that to speak about God makes faith impossible (*Rudolf Bultmann's Theology*, p. 171).

yet sympathetic analysis highlights Bultmann's insight into important hermeneutical issues in Christian faith:

> Christianity proceeds from a proclamation. It begins with a fundamental preaching that maintains that in Jesus Christ, the kingdom has approached us in decisive fashion. But this fundamental preaching, this word, comes to us through writings, though the Scriptures, and these must constantly be restored as the living word if the primitive word that witnessed to the fundamental and founding event is to remain contemporary.[8]

2. *Feminist Presuppositions*

Robert C. Roberts writes with admiration of him that 'the trumpeters of social change have failed to send Bultmann scampering back to his study to inquire after God's gender or the color of Jesus' skin'.[9] To interpret it charitably, the remark is 'thrown away', intended, in 1976, to emphasize the sense in which Bultmann's work over 50 years displayed a certain consistency of purpose and seriousness of intention. In the United States of the mid-1970s, feminist theology was in its infancy, struggling to be heard let alone be taken seriously. Yet the bottom line of Bultmann's response to the Christian texts is the hermeneutical preoccupation of proclaiming Jesus Christ 'the same yesterday, today and for ever'. So that the question feminist theologians and theorists will ask of Bultmann's theology or, in this instance, his reading of the Johannine Prologue is in what sense it conforms to or, conversely, interrogates the methodology and discourse of the patriarchal context.

3. *The Addressing of (Wo)men?*

The myth of the Pre-existent Redeemer come to earth (in the Johannine Prologue) is presented by Bultmann as confronting us *all*. Identifying a concrete history with a mythic story of redemption prevents us—'all the succeeding generations'[10]—from dismissing that history into the irrelevance of the past or, perhaps, the irrelevance of an alien and incomprehensible culture. This is the scriptural context of 'address'. What Bultmann calls 'address' is the occasion for faith. It is distinguished

---

8. Ricoeur, 'Preface to Bultmann', p. 382.
9. Roberts, *Rudolf Bultmann's Theology*, p. 9.
10. Rudolf Bultmann, *The Gospel of John: A Commentary* (trans. R.W.N Hoare and J.K. Riches; Philadelphia: Westminster Press, 1971), p. 70.

from general truths or statements derived, for example, from Scripture and from dogmatic sentences and confessions as types or genres of communication.[11] It refers to, rather than describes, a disposition in respect of any of these. This is what Bultmann calls *Angstbereitschaft* or readiness for dread.[12] Such address is self-authenticating, both unconditional and beyond human control.

Bultmann uses the expression 'address' to indicate the sense in which God's activity can only truly be detected by the individual who is directly addressed or encountered.[13] It is apparently unrelated to any characteristic human contingency of character, status or historical context. If understanding refers to the process of relating new information to what we already know and experience, the patriarchal context would be relevant of course. However, Bultmann argues that it can only become revelation as 'an event that passes all understanding'.[14] He presents the Prologue as a mythical statement of revelation, as something that occurs 'in the human sphere'[15] but which responds to: 'the knowledge that God does not confront me in my world, and yet that he must confront me if my life is to be a true life'.[16]

Bultmann's use of personal pronouns here reinforces the direct relevance of what the text is saying to *every* reader, every 'me'. The reader is apparently being encouraged to recognize that they are directly addressed by these biblical texts. The theme is that no one can consider themselves in a position of neutrality. If they do this, regarding the biblical texts as addressed, say, to one particular historical context, they will not understand what they are reading.[17]

11. See, for example, Bultmann, *Glauben und Verstehen*, p. 170, quoted in Roberts, *Rudolf Bultmann's Theology*, p. 39.

12. Rudolf Bultmann, 'Bultmann Replies to his Critics', in Hans Werner Bartsch (ed.), *Kerygma and Myth: A Theological Debate* (2 vols.; trans. Reginald H. Fuller; London: SPCK, 2nd edn, 1964), I, pp. 205-206.

13. Bultmann, 'Bultmann Replies', pp. 196-97.

14. Bultmann, *The Gospel of John*, p. 62.

15. Bultmann, *The Gospel of John*, pp. 60, 61, 62.

16. Bultmann, *The Gospel of John*, p. 62.

17. On 'demythologizing' see Rudolf Bultmann, *Jesus Christ and Mythology* (New York: Charles Scribner's Sons, 1958), p. 18, for a definition: 'This method of interpretation of the New Testament which tries to recover the deeper meaning behind the mythological conceptions I call de-mythologising—an unsatisfactory word, to be sure. Its aim is not to eliminate the mythological statements but to interpret them. It is a method of hermeneutics.'

Yet Bultmann, as Ricoeur notes, makes this claim in a hermeneutic context. It is his attempts to demythologize canonical Scripture by framing a question about human existence[18] that leads him to make the claim that God's activity cannot be detected in Scripture, but only in the existential encounter. Thus Scripture—or rather, the interpretation of Scripture—remains central to his enterprise, even though, for Bultmann, its *dynamism* comes from the situation of the individual encountered. And this is a situation which, according to Bultmann's theoretical position, does not lend itself to further interpretation:

> The decisive question is therefore whether man, when confronted by the event of the revelation, will remain true to his genuine prior knowledge of the revelation, whereby he sees it as an other-worldly event which passes judgement on him and his world; or whether he will make his own illusory ideas the criterion by which to judge the revelation, i.e. whether he will choose to judge the revelation only by these worldly standards and human values.[19]

If I am going to defend my own feminist position, I have to show at this point that Bultmann's view of existential encounter with the divine, whatever its theoretical status, is actually determined in some way by gender. It appears that the purpose of this particular description of address and encounter is precisely to rule out the relevance of mere human contingencies. The common assumption is, and in terms of orthodox Christian theology has always been, that gender is a mere contingency which may, eventually or in some ultimate sense, be transcended without substantial loss or damage to our essential redeemed humanity. However, to unpack the idea of a 'patriarchal context' a little, my feminist presupposition is that the hermeneut operates within a linguistic web of symbolism, whose structure is characteristically shaped by patterns of gender. Bultmann's interrelated notions of demythologization and existential encounter will not then, I would argue, be able entirely to escape the influence of these symbolic patterns. Bultmann's insistence on the existential encounter as outside any sphere of human controlling outlaws certain conclusions. That such an address is 'beyond human control' makes it impossible to reduce the encounter[20] to anything within the computation of works or deserts. It seems once more radically dissociated from cultural or historical contexts. All human

---

18. Bultmann, *Jesus Christ and Mythology*, p. 191.
19. Bultmann, *The Gospel of John*, p. 62.
20. Bultmann, *Jesus Christ and Mythology*, pp. 203-204.

significance is collapsed to the point of disappearance except in the need for response seen as obedience. But it is characteristic both of the Western logic of presence and of the operation of phallogocentric discourse in general that this metaphor for self as authentic existence is expounded in terms of love as obedience to God, bringing in its wake loss, self-immolation[21] and absolute dependence:

> the man of faith who loves understands that he first receives his existence from the thou; if the particular claim of the thou that stands before me were completely eliminated, then I would no longer be I.[22]

To be sure, the 'thou' in question here is not 'God' but the neighbour of the biblical text, but as this scenario is perfectly coherently interpreted as illustrative of divine encounter, there is little formal difference to be made between them. And this is, in many respects, exactly the symbolic function of woman and the feminine understood by feminist theory: phallogocentricity entails the notion of masculine normativity and feminine derivativeness.

Feminist writers, of course, are particularly sensitive to the sense in which formal external authorities have been invoked to justify the brutal intimidation of women or the most degraded forms of male self-interest and the notion of obedience, as it is elaborated within Bultmann's work, should certainly not be confused with simple conformity to formal or external authority. Nevertheless, as I read it, Bultmann's understanding of obedience—describing a proper human disposition towards the divine—is still very obviously related to a view of this relationship which is structured according to a gendered symbolism which functions in accordance with phallogocentric pretensions. Thus, for example, in *Jesus and the Word* (1926), it is clear that autonomous humanity disturbs Bultmann far more than arbitrary divinity. And the elimination of that disobedient autonomy is achieved, within Bultmann's writings, by absorption within the perspective of the divine—or faith. Faith is the action of relinquishing autonomy when 'addressed'. Only so, it would seem to me, can such commands become 'intrinsically intelligible'.[23]

---

21. Rudolf Bultmann, *Essays, Philosophical and Theological* (London: SCM Press, 1955), p. 176: 'The real act of love is fundamentally difficult…as I give myself away in it, and attain my being only by losing it in this act'.

22. Schubert Ogden (ed.), *Existence and Faith: Shorter Writings of Rudolf Bultmann* (New York: The World Publishing Company, 1961), p. 101.

23. Rudolf Bultmann, *Jesus and the Word* (New York: Charles Scribner's Son's, 1958 [1926]), p. 77.

And here the idea of obedience is first radically conceived. For so long as obedience is only subjection to an authority which man does not understand, it is no true obedience; something in man still remains outside and does not submit, is not bound by the command of God ... In *this* kind of decision, a man stands outside of his action, he is not completely obedient. Radical obedience exists only when a man inwardly assents to what is required of him, when the thing commanded is seen as intrinsically God's command; when the whole man stands behind what he does; or better, when the whole man is *in* what he does, when he is not *doing something obediently,* but *is* essentially obedient.[24]

And surely, there is little formal difference between being—as believer—grasped by the love of God, and becoming—as a woman—for the gratification of a masculine narcissism. This is, once again, the very pattern of phallogocentrism: the delusion that what is represented by the symbols of woman and the feminine can be situated without significant distortion or remainder, within a desire for masculine singularity.

In answer to such a characterization of address and encounter that reflect the symbolic function of gender, feminist theorists argue that the feminine defines the masculine and remains in a clear sense essential to it even if only in its abnegation. Feminist theory resists the movement towards human absence or the disappearance of the human element of the divine/human encounter, suggesting perhaps also a clearer or more defined view of how hermeneutics and the role of the text is to be understood with relation to this divine/human encounter.

4. *Selection as a Form of Gendered Interpretation?*

In his commentary, Bultmann sees the Logos, the Revealer, as presenting to each individual reader within the Christian community[25] the same sort of personal challenge[26] in this narrative as is found within the New Testament in general. In *Jesus and the Word*, a relatively early statement of his approach to the Synoptic Gospels for example, he says:

---

24. Bultmann, *Jesus and the Word*, p. 77. Within the Commentary on the Prologue, this understanding of obedience is elaborated, I believe, in terms of the overcoming of offence, discussed below.

25. Ogden (ed.), *Existence and Faith*, p. 70.

26. Bultmann, *The Gospel of John*, pp. 61-62, 66.

> When we encounter the words of Jesus in history, *we* do not judge *them*
> by a philosophical system with reference to their rational validity; *they*
> interpret our own existence.[27]

As Ricoeur's man of science, Bultmann appears to address himself to the
argument of those who would dismiss the whole of the Christian
revelation on the grounds that it is contained within documents that
have little claim to historical accuracy[28] or even to literary consistency.
In response, he certainly seems to suggest that the mythological form of
certain biblical passages, such as the Johannine Prologue, does not need
to be consistent with all other mythological passages in the Bible to be
important or significant. Which is to say not so much that he understands the same universal truth to underlie all the mythological expressions within the New Testament canon, but that they may all mediate
the same challenge to the human reader in the perplexities of human
existence.

So, how does Bultmann select his material? This selection should
indicate, more precisely, how he views his hermeneutic questions within the overall priority—that is, the framing of the question of human
existence.[29] He implies that the constructions of the Prologue and the
birth narratives of Matthew and Luke are all 'evidently mythological'.[30]
He includes within this description both 'the concept of the pre-existent
Son of God who descended in human guise into the world to redeem
mankind' and the view of Jesus 'begotten of the Holy Spirit and born of
a virgin'.[31] So we have, in the Prologue and in theory at least, simply
one incarnational narrative that may address us all equally as a direct
existential confrontation with the divine. And it is not enough, for
Bultmann, to distinguish this as a text exclusively for Samaritans or

---

27. Bultmann, *Jesus and the Word*, p. 16.

28. It has been claimed by some that it was Bultmann's critical historical work
on the New Testament that led him towards the existentialist philosophy of Heidegger. This drew attention to an overwhelming sense of eschatological expectation
within the texts. This challenged the emphasis of earlier liberal critics and theologians on the exemplary ethical nature of the historical Jesus and his teachings, particularly since it was an expectation that appeared to have been disappointed.

29. Bultmann, 'Bultmann Replies', pp. 191-92. 'I think I may take for granted
that the right question to frame with regard to the Bible—at any rate within the
Church—is the question of human existence.'

30. Bultmann, *Jesus Christ and Mythology*, p. 17.

31. Bultmann, *Jesus Christ and Mythology*, p. 17.

Christian Gnostics or any other group that might have been responsible for, or influential in producing, this Gospel. Moreover, this implies that not every specific characteristic of the myth is essential for the hermeneutic enterprise, since different incarnational myths are presented as virtually interchangeable in terms of their revelatory suitability.

And yet Bultmann, in common, it must be said, with many other theologians, finds more mileage in the concept of the Word of God made flesh than in the son of Mary or David. There is an implicit preference for theologizing based on the Prologue of John's Gospel as an incarnational narrative and model, over against the birth narratives of Matthew and Luke, for example, or Mark's option of secrecy and silence. In Matthew and Luke, the mythological narrative appears to make Incarnation a more cooperative venture between God and humanity, represented by a number of human individuals including women. Of course it has already been said that Bultmann does not make any explicit claim for the superiority or inferiority of the Prologue, as a vehicle of revelation, over the other mythical accounts of the Incarnation within the canon. But it is clear that, for Bultmann, the concept of the Word of God is a key one, perhaps because of the strong symbolic affinity between word, language and proclamation.

> The Word of God is what it is only in event, and the paradox lies in the fact that this Word is identical with the Word which originated in the apostolic preaching which has been fixed in Scripture and which is handed on by men in the Church's proclamation.[32]

It bridges the gap between divine revelation and the proclamation of the Church with an elegance and economy that the more diffuse birth narratives do not possess. (What they do possess is a more overt suggestion of sexuality, kinship and incarnational dependence upon human cooperation.) To conclude then, Bultmann appears to believe that the proclamation of the Church, which is the Word of God, addresses all readers of Scripture. The existential moment of decision for faith cannot be, it would seem, conditioned by a choice of scriptural passage any more than it can be dependent upon any effort of will or 'work'. And yet, Bultmann's theological choices are very far from indiscriminate. There is a process of choice, of symbols and analogies and particular canonical passages under way in his own interpretation. So how does this affect the concept of demythologization as a hermeneutic venture in

---

32. Bultmann, 'Bultmann Replies', p. 209.

Bultmann's work? How is the unconditional address to be related to the specifics of proclamation, given that his work, in itself, expresses a particular hermeneutic dependency or circularity, related, for example, to Lutheran traditions of Pauline interpretation?

5. *Demythologizing (the Marginalized Mother)*

When we come to the specific case of the Prologue, there is some indication that demythologization, as a hermeneutic tool, is also quietly sabotaging Bultmann's interpretation of revelation and eschatological judgment in terms of existential address and individual response. Let us consider the quite distinctive mythological description of divine Incarnation found within the Johannine Prologue. Bultmann argues that it is substantially borrowed from Gnostic philosophy and religion, coloured by Judaic speculations about Wisdom[33] and by the strongly monotheistic conceptions of the Jews.[34] Of course, one way in which this Johannine statement is distinctive is in its failure to make reference to the woman—the mother who figures prominently in the birth narratives of Matthew and Luke and within the tradition of the Christian churches.

If we understand myth not *simply* as the pre-scientific cosmological myth[35] but as something that speaks of self-understanding and the experience of limit[36] and which aims at what it does not say,[37] which is surely implicit in Bultmann's whole project of demythologizing, then we may perhaps suggest that such absences or gaps are, in some sense, bound to be significant. So, let us consider how Bultmann himself demythologizes the mythological statement of 'becoming flesh' (Jn 1.14) in terms of an otherwise absent mother.

In his commentary on the Prologue, of course, there is some incentive for Bultmann to leave the figure of the mother out altogether. Quite clearly she does not appear in the Johannine text of the Prologue

33. Bultmann, *The Gospel of John*, p. 22.

34. Bultmann, *The Gospel of John*, p. 33: 'all polytheistic conceptions and emanationist theories are foreign to the text'.

35. See Bultmann's delimitation of this in 'New Testament and Mythology', in Schubert M. Ogden (ed.), *New Testament and Mythology and Other Basic Writings* (London: SCM Press, 1985).

36. See Bultmann, 'New Testament and Mythology', p. 10.

37. See Ricoeur, 'Preface to Bultmann', p. 391.

in any explicit sense, as Luther noted 400 years or so earlier in his sermons on this text. And whereas a mother figure sometimes plays a part
in the Gnostic mythology[38] which Bultmann believed to underlie this
passage, she is not invariably present. And yet, again like Luther before
him, Bultmann cannot leave her out of his understanding of 'becoming
flesh' altogether. It is as if, finally, Bultmann cannot demythologize this
maternal absence, except in terms of making the absence a sign of her
presence under the heading of 'flesh' following a fundamentally Augustinian process of symbolic representation in gendered terms.

Whereas the text of John's Gospel at this point speaks of the Logos
becoming flesh, Bultmann views the real/historical parents as the
terminus ad quem of the divine Logos. The protective, objectifying scriptural mythology of Incarnation, that modern man, according to Bultmann's first characteristic statement of programmatic demythologization,
believes anyway to be obsolete,[39] suddenly breaks down. 'The Revealer
is nothing but a man',[40] leads Bultmann straight into a consideration of
being a man as a quintessentially generative notion having to do with
real/historical parents. Bultmann understands ὁ λόγος σὰρξ ἐγένετο
(the Word became flesh) (Jn 1.14) to imply the full humanity of the
Revealer and he has already committed himself to a particular index of
humanity:

> For they know his father and mother (6.42; 7.27,28; 1.45) and therefore
> take offence at his claim to be the Revealer (10.33); they cannot tolerate
> the 'man' who tells them the truth (8.40).[41]

It is in this context, of course, that Bultmann cannot do without a
mother. Whatever understanding of the precise relationship between
God and Logos lies within the Johannine text or the Gnostic myth from
which Bultmann says it takes its shape, he commits himself to the model
of human generation as the demythologization of the flesh/absent. And
yet quietly introducing this figure of a mother into his commentary, he
seems not to register any sense of unease about her absence from the
text. The reason for this lack of concern appears to lie in Bultmann's
understanding of flesh—σὰρξ—at Jn 1.14.

Bultmann would have it that this mythical narrative presents us with a

38. See Bultmann, *The Gospel of John*, p. 72, note on Μονογ.
39. Bultmann, 'New Testament and Mythology', p. 3.
40. Bultmann, *The Gospel of John*, p. 62.
41. Bultmann, *The Gospel of John*, p. 63.

vision of divine Incarnation that serves and challenges every individual 'me'. This sense of challenge in Bultmann's interpretation, however, depends on a set of dualities—divisions between divine and human, past and present, real and mythological—being broken down. From a feminist perspective we might note here that while patriarchal culture typically marginalizes the concerns of real, different, individual women making them silent and invisible, symbolically, woman and the feminine serve a vital constitutive purpose within such cultures as the lower term within a dualistic hierarchy of value.

So what Bultmann seems to have done here is to have responded to what he sees as the absence of a term within the mythic narrative of Incarnation in the Prologue, filling the gap by interpreting 'flesh' in terms of what is surely a remythologizing in which a series of symbols with unmistakably gendered complexion play their part. First of all, of course, there are the real/historical parents who embody the reality of material sexuality and generative kinship, but then there are also a series of symbolic equivalents which give the undeniably contingent physicality of this interpretation a particularly transgressive[42] caste or evaluation. Bultmann—in common with many other interpreters it has to be said—refers, for example, to a more general understanding of this concept within the Gospel of John:

> Σάρξ in John refers to the sphere of the human and the worldly... σάρξ stresses its transitoriness, helplessness and vanity.[43]

Bultmann, then, brings together the notion of the 'humanity' of the Revealer in terms of his having parents in an arguably generative sense,[44] with the notion of 'flesh/σάρξ' as the worldly sphere, associated with transitoriness, helplessness and vanity[45] and distinguished clearly from the divine sphere—πνεῦμα.[46] And in terms of the narrative that

42. I want, by this word, to indicate the sense of a certain limitation or indication of difference, rather than any more specifically formulated expression of a moral/ethical sensibility.

43. Bultmann, *The Gospel of John*, p. 62.

44. Bultmann, *The Gospel of John*, p. 62 n. 4: 'To see the ἐγένετο as a miraculous process, that is as a physiological miracle, is to do violence to the main theme of the Gospel, that the Revealer is a man. Moreover 1.45; 6.42; 7.27f., show that the Evangelist knew or wished to know nothing of the legend of the Virgin Birth.'

45. This word translates the German *Nichtigkeit*, vanity in the sense of worthlessness or nullity.

46. Bultmann, *The Gospel of John*, p. 62.

Bultmann constructs in this way, we see that this effectively restricts the mother within the real/historical human sphere of flesh/σάρξ—of transitoriness, helplessness and vanity—while, at least in narrative terms, both father and son are able to move between the worldly and the over against the worldly, appearing as both real/historical and divine/ mythic.[47]

What appears to be happening here is that Bultmann is employing a fundamentally gendered symbolism to represent the opposition of the human sphere to the divine in the process of defining human authenticity. I believe that this symbolism reflects Bultmann's attempts to define authenticity within human existence in terms of divine masculine singularity, excluding the otherness of which woman and the feminine are the symbols.[48] It is particularly difficult to track the moves he makes, of course, because they are framed in terms of his commitment to a demythologized Word made flesh who is so defiantly 'fleshly'. But the drive of his argument is still towards exclusion, and moreover towards the exclusion of whatever it is that woman and the feminine have come to represent so disturbingly within patriarchal reading contexts.

Thus the human sphere is symbolized by σάρξ in the Prologue. Now, according to Bultmann, this is not to be regarded as equivalent to σκότος—darkness—which is the condition of being *at enmity* with God. (To interpret σάρξ in this way would, of course, bring him face to face with the issue I am trying to raise in this study when it comes to reading Jn 1.14a: 'The Word became flesh') So Bultmann argues that σάρξ is simply the condition of being worldly rather than divine. Bultmann has further defined σάρξ in terms of the transitory, helpless and vain.[49] However, if I follow Bultmann's own directions at the point in his commentary on the Prologue, where he refers to the Johannine meaning of σάρξ,[50] I see that he also refers readers to the use of the same word at Jn 3.6 and Jn 6.63. Bultmann's characterization of σάρξ in terms of 'transitoriness, helplessness and vanity'—characteristics that do

47. See Bultmann, *The Gospel of John*, p. 71.

48. See, for example, Toril Moi, *Sexual/Textual Politics: Feminist Literary Theory* (London: Routledge, 1988), p. 167. Moi discusses the marginal position of the symbolic woman within patriarchy, as representing, to a certain extent, the threatening chaos against which they also figure as a protective boundary.

49. Bultmann, *The Gospel of John*, p. 62.

50. Bultmann, *The Gospel of John*, p. 62.

not have particularly strong links with the rest of John's Gospel[51]—is shown in his commentary on Jn 3.6 to belong unambiguously to the project of demythologizing in terms of a polarity between authenticity and nothingness:

> σάρξ refers to the nothingness of man's whole existence; to the fact that man is ultimately a stranger to his fate and to his own acts; that, as he now is, he does not enjoy authentic existence, whether he makes himself aware of the fact or whether he conceals it from himself. Correspondingly 'πνεῦμα' refers to the miracle of a mode of being in which man enjoys authentic existence, in which he understands himself and knows that he is no longer threatened by nothingness.[52]

At Jn 6.63 ('the flesh is of no avail'), Bultmann excises σάρξ from the text altogether, on the grounds that it has been added at this point to support a removal of the scandal or offence of Jn 1.14,[53] in favour of a sacramentalized interpretation of a shocking and revelatory moment (Jn 6.53 'Unless you eat the flesh of the Son of man and drink his blood, you have no life in you'). This indeed is one very clear example of the way in which Bultmann appears extraordinarily sensitive to the radical implications of Incarnation as a way of breaking down the sort of rigid separation between the divine and the human that has encouraged idolatry and limited a sense of human responsibility. On the other hand, it is set up in terms that immediately reimpose rigid separation between authentic human response to the divine and the inauthenticity of human existence without God which is still symbolically feminine, that is to say characterized as transitoriness, emptiness and vanity and crucially *devalued*. Bultmann's new rigid separation between authenticity and inauthenticy is, I believe, partly the product of a prevalent and persistent symbolism within phallogocentric structures, and represents the desire for a new masculine-identified singularity as against the recognition of human existence as lived within a context of feminine-identified multiplicity, which embraces embodiment as well as language and law, and cannot and indeed should not be ultimately resolved.

---

51. ὠφελέω—to profit, gain advantage, prevail. This appears, in the negative sense (in vain, of no avail), at Jn 6.63, describing flesh, and at Jn 12.19, when the Pharisees acknowledge their powerlessness against Jesus' charismatic effect on the world (κόσμος).

52. Bultmann, *The Gospel of John*, p. 141.

53. Bultmann, *The Gospel of John*, p. 237.

In terms of Bultmann's own existentialist interpretation of the Prologue, there is little ground, I think, on which to make a clear distinction between σάρξ as indicative of a worldly sphere of transitoriness,
helplessness and vanity that is somehow neutral or potentially re-
deemable, and σκότος as indicative of an outright opposition. And I
should argue that σάρξ and σκότος are equally indicative of the nothingness that threatens.[54] After all it is not the σάρξ of the Word that
saves humankind, but humankind's response to the revelation it represents. And in terms of feminist analysis and theory, I should also argue
that such a conclusion is predictable, given the persistence and preva-
lence in mythology and symbolic representation of a particular male
anxiety in terms of the female or maternal, the potentially overwhelming other.

6. *An Offensive Gospel*

'Flesh' is given one other indexing quality within Bultmann's commentary on John's Gospel, which appears at first glance to evade and indeed
to challenge the imprint of the rigid and gendered separation that, I
have argued, he reimposes through his project of demythologizing Jn
1.14: 'And the Word became flesh'. This quality is its offensiveness. To
register the offence of the gospel is the 'event of the revelation'.[55] And
the offence is produced by the Revealer's sheer humanity, by his
inability to be recognized as Judge and Revealer except by the eye of
faith. There can be no purely objective recognition because there is no
objective duality. Thus the Revealer becoming 'flesh' is not to be
understood as gracious humility in accepting fleshly limitations but, as it
were, a challenge to the common categories of divine and human which
are used to resist the immediacy of the demand that is being made of
each individual. To see the Revealer as Divine in contradistinction to
what is human lets 'me' off the hook. 'I' insulate myself from the existential demands of the Revealer by excluding the Revealer from the
sphere of the human.

Bultmann's radical commitment to the humanity of Christ should not
be mistaken. And he is ready to abandon the safety net provided by any
sort of body/spirit dualism:

54. Bultmann, *The Gospel of John*, p. 141.
55. Bultmann, *The Gospel of John*, p. 62.

the δόξα is not to be seen *alongside* the σάρξ, nor *through* the σάρξ as
through a window; it is to be seen in the σάρξ and nowhere else. If man
wishes to see the δόξα, then it is on the σάρξ that he must concentrate
his attention, without allowing himself to fall a victim to appearances.
The revelation is present in a peculiar *hiddenness*.[56]

He is ready to take tremendous theological risks in defence of this hiddenness:

the incarnation is not understood as the decisive revelation-event.
Accordingly in the Johannine portrayal of the incarnate Revealer there is
no attempt to present him as a visible figure.[57]

However, the sense of 'offence' produced by this humanity could be
said to be dependent upon the reversal or obliteration of a primary distinction between human and divine which thus, so to speak, re-inscribes
the gendered hierarchy in a negative sense. Or to put it another way,
Bultmann warns against what he calls the 'pietistic misunderstanding'[58]
of the Gnostic construction of the Revealer becoming flesh as an act of
condescension, but there is a sense in which the offence cannot be seen
as *offensive* unless we first accept the boundary or distinction between the
divine and the human, and this, as I have already argued, is already
constructed by Bultmann in culturally gendered terms. It seems that
Bultmann wants to argue for the dynamic operation of a powerful liminality[59] at this point. If the liminality of the Incarnation is indeed
structured in such gendered terms, understanding its offence comes to
be inscribed within a phallogocentric, culturally acquired sensitivity to a
male 'descent' into the female sphere. The hierarchicalism he appears to
want to bypass would be getting in by the back door.

Bultmann seems able to account for the overcoming of its offensiveness in a purely scientific sense, for example, by references to 'eye-
witnesses' who become the σκάνδαλον for future generations,[60] but not

56. Bultmann, *The Gospel of John*, p. 63.
57. Bultmann, *The Gospel of John*, p. 66.
58. Bultmann, *The Gospel of John*, p. 66.
59. Liminality defined as 'a moment of suspension of normal rules and roles, a
crossing of boundaries and violating of norms, that enables us to understand those
norms'. See Caroline Walker Bynum, *Fragmentation and Redemption: Essays on Gender
and the Human Body in Medieval Religion* (New York: Zone Books, 1991), p. 30.
Here, Bynum is referring to liminality, defined after Van Gennep, as an aspect of
Victor Turner's social drama approach to history.
60. Bultmann, *The Gospel of John*, p. 70.

in terms that address the semiotic implications already noted. Thus he admits that our knowledge that this man is the Logos must 'come from elsewhere'.[61] In other words, although the Incarnate is in very truth a man like any other, being a man like any other (wo)man is not *in itself* enough. There must still be the element of surplus, constructed, I would argue, in terms of a fundamentally gendered symbolism. I understand Bultmann to claim that this 'surplus' is located in our existential 'encounter', the authenticity of which is determined by the overcoming of offence. This is the disposition of obedience, of allowing oneself to be loved by being remodelled to play a particular role within a divine economy. And, of course, this is the very disposition required of woman and the feminine within the phallogocentric economy of patriarchy too:

> For χάρις and ἀλήθεια describe God's being; not 'in itself', but as it is open to man (in his receptivity) and in its activity towards man: they refer, that is, to the benefits in which God (or the Revealer) abounds, and which he bestows *on the believer* [emphasis mine].[62]

7. *Seductive or Intimidating Otherness?*

Bultmann is concerned with issues of self-understanding—of identity. For self-understanding comes in choosing who to be,[63] a process which reflects the possibility of a wrong choice, defined in terms of refusing knowledge of our creatureliness.[64] Human creatureliness is contrasted with the 'absolute otherness' of the Logos:

> The Logos has become flesh in Jesus of Nazareth. That is to say: in the person and word of Jesus one does not encounter anything that has its origin in the world or in time; the encounter is with the reality that lies beyond the world and time. Jesus and his word not only brings release from the world and from time, they are also the means whereby the world and time are judged.[65]

We judge, assess, understand what we are, in relationship and contrast to what God is. To evade this particular dualism is equivalent to 'self-glorification'.[66] And yet it is also described in terms that are marked by

---

61. Bultmann, *The Gospel of John*, p. 66.
62. Bultmann, *The Gospel of John*, p. 73.
63. Bultmann, *The Gospel of John*, p. 47.
64. Bultmann, *The Gospel of John*, p. 47.
65. Bultmann, *The Gospel of John*, p. 32.
66. Bultmann, *The Gospel of John*, p. 64.

the presence or absence of power. God's inaccessibility or otherness is described as lying beyond man's control or his desire to turn God into an object of our knowledge. Human weakness and false understanding is an inability to 'master' ourselves and the illusory desire to 'gain control over' oneself and God. This is the content of 'self-understanding' and 'true knowledge' of oneself. In other words, the sense in which God and humankind are different or other—and this is the content of true self-understanding—is seen in terms of the imposition or acceptance of mastery or control of the one by the Other. And those who are judged are the spiritually blind and the poor,[67] tolerated if they know their place, but to be sentenced should they imagine themselves spiritually rich and healthy. Again, although it is used in an inverted sense, here is the language of inequality, the structuring of spiritual worth on the basis of an extremely patriarchal hierarchy of values, placing God in the realm of the rich, the healthy and the powerful and humanity in general in the space usually occupied, culturally, by women, children, slaves, barbarians[68] and in-valids.

So, the Incarnation is presented as a strategy in this particular game of power. It guards against the desire to control God. The invisibility of God in the Incarnation is held by Bultmann to frustrate the desire for power, but faith called forth in this way is also cast in the mould of capitulation, however positive a concept he claims it to be.[69] In this context, then, it is interesting to note that Robert C. Roberts identifies physical nature—with its strong and persistent association with woman and the feminine—within the context of Bultmann's preoccupation with controllability,[70] as having a relatively insignificant role to play in

---

67. Bultmann, *The Gospel of John*, p. 81.

68. See Fiorenza's diagrammatic mappings of patriarchal Greek democracy in Elisabeth Schüssler Fiorenza, *But She Said: Feminist Practices of Biblical Interpretation* (Boston: Beacon Press, 1992), pp. 116-17.

69. Bultmann, *The Gospel of John*, p. 81.

70. Roberts, *Rudolf Bultmann's Theology*, pp. 29-30: 'The concept of controllability is fundamental to Bultmann's concept of the world and ...is capable of explaining most of the other features almost directly.' Thus, Roberts argues that physical nature, general truths, the past and qualities of the soul are all in some sense seen by Bultmann as within human control, and according to his own analysis of Bultmann, constitute the dichotomy of World as against Existence as potentiality to be.

Bultmann's theology as a whole, and that as 'something like a paradigm of the controllable'.[71]

8. *Suspicious Conclusions*

Historically, it would appear that Bultmann's interest in existential philosophy coincided with his conclusions that liberal Protestantism had tended fatally to dilute and colonize elements of New Testament theology with values and features of fundamentally nineteenth-century liberal rationalism, exemplified in the oft-quoted 'Jesus of History' school of theology.[72] As early as 1926 he was writing in his introduction to *Jesus and the Word*:

> Accordingly, this book lacks all the phraseology which speaks of Jesus as great man, genius, or hero; he appears neither as inspired nor as inspiring, his sayings are not called profound, nor his faith mighty, nor his nature child-like. There is also no consideration of the eternal values of his message, of his discovery of the infinite depths of the human soul, or the like.[73]

This tendency he believed to be partly the consequence of failing to face up to the extent to which the New Testament texts constituted a mythology and were not directly available to readers or interpreters in a modern scientific culture. Methods derived from the History of Religions school of interpretation made it impossible for him to regard these texts as even largely historical. Thus Bultmann is revealed in this sense to be very much the man of modern scientific culture who does not seek simply to set his up his theological position against such culture, but equally does not wish to lose its 'edge', its critical distinctiveness, its dynamism.

The philosophy of Martin Heidegger (1889–1976) in particular, then, gave Bultmann a platform from which to claw back the initiative because its concentration on a certain human inwardness could be related to the business of interpreting the biblical texts in a way that was

71. Roberts, *Rudolf Bultmann's Theology*, p. 38.

72. See, for example, John Macquarrie, *Twentieth Century Religious Thought* (London: SCM Press, rev. edn, 1971), from p. 84, on work of W. Herrmann, T. Haering, J. Kaftan and A. Harnack. Of Harnack he writes, p. 88: Adolf Harnack (1850–1931) 'stresses the ethical side of Christianity, reduces doctrine to a bare minimum, and has come to be regarded as the typical exponent of liberal Protestantism'.

73. Bultmann, *Jesus and the Word*, p. 8.

substantially unrelated to whether or not these texts were historically/ scientifically verifiable. Demythologization, the hermeneutic procedure he adopted, provided Bultmann with the cover he needed to develop a scientific method of rigorous biblical textual criticism that might satisfy what John Riches refers to as his 'cultured despisers',[74] while apparently still allowing him to accord an ultimate authority to those texts. Thus, for example, in relation to the eschatology of the New Testament, Bultmann wishes absolutely to concur that any realistic expectation that the world might be coming to an end shortly after the events surrounding Jesus' crucifixion would have been absolutely disappointed. For the modern reader, however, the eschatological force of such expectation was rather to be associated with the existential eschatology of readiness for address or encounter with God.

To return, at the end, to Paul Ricoeur: Ricoeur, in distinguishing between differing levels of demythologization and myth in Bultmann's work, draws attention to what I see as the problem with Bultmann's approach for modern feminists. Bultmann is, in a sense, aware of more than one level of demythologization; there are cosmological myths composed of 'pictures' and 'symbols', for example,[75] that may be interpreted into non-mythological language, but Bultmann also recognizes in theory that we may use mythological language because—at least provisionally—we have no other.[76] In addition, his own fear of objectifying religious language and concepts itself draws attention to the sense in which there is also a real problem with 'non-mythological' language.

Ricoeur argues that the problem with Bultmann is that there is no reflection on language in general, but only on 'objectification'. The sense in which language is itself a form of control is missing:

---

74. John K. Riches, *A Century of New Testament Study* (Cambridge: Lutterworth, 1993), p. 57.

75. Ogden (ed.), *New Testament and Mythology*, p. 100. Bultmann argues that 'symbols' and 'pictures' must be interpretable non-mythologically since the notion of their having a point at all entails this.

76. Ogden (ed.), *New Testament and Mythology*, p. 100: Bultmann argues that mythological representations may be indispensable 'in a provisional sense insofar as truths are intended in them that cannot be expressed in the language of objectifying science. In that case mythological language provisionally expresses that for which adequate language must still be found. Thus the task that is set for thinking...can be formulated in mythological language in the way in which this happens in the Platonic myths.'

It is striking that Bultmann makes hardly any demands on this language of faith, whereas he was so suspicious about the language of myth. From the moment language ceases to 'objectify', when it escapes from worldly 'representations', every interrogation seems superfluous concerning the meaning of this *Dass*—of this event of encounter—which follows on the *Was*—on general statements and on objectifying representations.[77]

My contention is, with Ricoeur, that Bultmann's work is far from done, though again, with Ricoeur, some of its conclusions and presuppositions seem highly suggestive and useful to feminist attempts at biblical interpretation. However, as Ricoeur notes:

A theory of interpretation which at the outset runs straight to the moment of decision moves too fast. It leaps over the moment of meaning, which is the objective stage, in the non worldly sense of 'objective'. There is no exegesis without a 'bearer [teneur] of meaning', which belongs to the text and not to the author of the text.[78]

At this point occupied, as it were, by Bultmann's own exegesis of the Johannine text of the Prologue, my own analysis has suggested a tendency to remythologize in the terms of a symbolism of gender. This gender symbolism has frequently been 'objectified' within patriarchal culture in terms of values and political actions that affect women as a class.

The aim of Bultmann's hermeneutic is, surely, to enable the reader to be 'addressed' or 'encountered'. Phrased in this way, the problem for him is revealed, since, in Ricoeur's words, Bultmann above all else wants to proclaim that

What 'lays claim to me' comes to man and does not proceed from him.[79]

Ricoeur argues that what Bultmann needed to do, and substantially failed to do in using Heidegger, was to address himself like Heidegger to the philosophical task of the question of being as the primary work. And so it seems to me that exercising a hermeneutic of suspicion[80] in reading

77. Ricoeur, 'Preface to Bultmann', p. 395.
78. Ricoeur, 'Preface to Bultmann', p. 397.
79. Ricoeur, 'Preface to Bultmann', p. 399.
80. See Ihde (ed.), *Paul Ricoeur*, p. 442. Ricoeur hones his defence of a Kantian-like notion of the will and of the 'subject' against those current philosophies which challenge the ideas. This process he undertakes with 'an attitude of suspicion and cautious critical scrutiny', examining these ideas by referring closely to the work of such notable critics of Kant as Nietzsche, Freud and Marx. The phrase has been

Bultmann reading the text of John's Gospel, that 'being' which is brought to light here is still substantially occupying the place set up by cultural patriarchy and its phallogocentric constructions, including that of the divine in relation to the human.

taken up by would-be feminist hermeneuts as similarly a means of determining how far it is realistic and profitable to maintain a distinctively feminist method of interpreting the Bible, against those who apparently see no need to do so.

6

A Second Glance at Adrienne von Speyr

1. *Mystic or Masochist?*

Today, Adrienne von Speyr is not very much known or read, certainly in the English-speaking world. She was born in Switzerland in 1902 and died there in 1967. She qualified and practised, for a period of her life, as a doctor. She was married twice, first to Emil Dürr, a professor of history at the University of Basle, and, two years after his death in 1934, to his successor at the University, Werner Kaegi. But she would undoubtedly have seen the most substantive work of her life in terms of spiritual direction, mystic contemplation and the foundation of a secular religious community, the Community of St John, 'a form of life that seeks to follow the inner essence of religious life (vows, celibacy, etc.) but in an entirely hidden way, without external supports, while being fully engaged in the secular world of work'.[1]

In 1940, at the age of 38, she suffered a heart attack from which she seems never to have completely recovered. Her condition was soon aggravated by diabetes and, increasingly, by arthritis that eventually brought her work as a doctor to an end. In the same year as she suffered this first debilitating heart attack she met Hans Urs von Balthasar (1905–88), the Catholic theologian, who was at that time a member of the Society of Jesus and a student chaplain in Basle. Von Balthasar became her friend, preparing her at her earnest request for entry into the Roman Catholic Church in November 1940. Subsequently, he worked with her as confessor and amanuensis and as co-founder of the Community of St John, for which work he left the Society of Jesus in 1950.[2]

1. Edward T. Oakes, *Pattern of Redemption: The Theology of Hans Urs von Balthasar* (New York: Continuum, 1994), p. 3.
2. Von Balthasar writes of von Speyr's involvement in this decision: 'But truly superhuman strength was demanded of her by the part she assumed in the responsibility for persuading me to leave the Jesuit Order when it became evident that it would be impossible to carry out within the framework of the Society of Jesus the

It is largely due to his efforts, that a proportion of her work has been translated and published in English.[3] He was in no doubt about her various charisms, and was, in his own mind at least,[4] deeply indebted to her theological insights, writing in 1984 that:

> I want to try to prevent anyone after my death from undertaking the task of separating my work from that of Adrienne von Speyr. This is not in the least possible, either theologically or in regard to the secular institute now underway.[5]

From 1942 onwards, von Speyr experienced the stigmata—visible and sensible marks of Christ's crucifixion in her own person—a phenomenon first noted in the thirteenth century, most famously in the case of St Francis of Assisi and subsequently reported in every century up to the present one.[6] She confessed to having had a mark under her left breast from the age of 15 and long before her conversion to Roman Catholicism, following a vision of Mary, the Mother[7] of the Lord. But the regular experience of the wounds in the hands, and—invisibly—of the crown of thorns around her head, together with the intense experience of an interior suffering she compared to the passage through hell, did not commence until her fortieth year.[8] Her experience of the

mission with which we had been charged in founding the new community' (Hans Urs von Balthasar, *First Glance at Adrienne von Speyr* [San Francisco: Ignatius Press, 1981], p. 43).

3.   Von Balthasar was clearly disappointed by a general lack of interest in von Speyr's work: 'Although at the time of Adrienne's death thirty-seven of her books were in print, and thirty-four of them available in bookstores, up to now no one has taken serious notice of her writings.' See von Balthasar, *First Glance*, pp. 11-12. In his book about von Speyr, von Balthasar includes a comprehensive bibliography of all her works, both published and in manuscript form. See von Balthasar, *First Glance*, pp. 102-11.

4.   See Oakes, *Pattern of Redemption*, p. 4. Oakes believes that in his preoccupation with von Speyr, 'we have before us the single most telling factor responsible for Balthasar's isolation from the rest of twentieth-century theology'.

5.   Hans Urs von Balthasar, *Unser Auftrag: Bericht und Entwurf* (Einsiedeln: Johannes Verlag, 1984), p. 11.

6.   Ian Wilson lists the best-attested cases in an appendix in *The Bleeding Mind: An Investigation into the Mysterious Phenomenon of Stigmata* (London: Paladin, 1991). The majority of reported stigmatics have been women.

7.   This is how von Speyr refers to her in relation to her own spiritual economy: 'Statements about Herself', in von Balthasar, *First Glance*, p. 156.

8.   She seems also to have undergone some sort of experience of 'bi-location', whereby she had experience of places which she had not actually visited. Von

stigmata was particularly acute during Holy Week each year.[9]

It is, perhaps, unfortunate that there should be so little written about von Speyr[10] since von Balthasar's frankly hagiographic account of her life and thought[11] is at all points strained to present this in an exemplary light. There is much within her writings and the picture of her that he presents, however, that is seriously off-putting. And this is clearly a common reaction. For even von Balthasar felt called upon to defend her:

> In the totality of Adrienne's theological work there are individual parts that can, if taken out of context, occasionally alienate. Readers of her works are urgently requested not to lose sight of the whole of the theology on account of individual statements. The inner coherence of all the parts will become that much more obvious the more one concentrates on this whole.[12]

2. *A Modern Feminist Reading Context*

To characterize von Speyr as a mystic is useful from my perspective since it provides a clue as to why she represents something both arresting and repellent. In so far as mysticism represents a tendency towards experience of God that lies beyond intellect or rationality, it finds itself in sympathy with those feminist approaches that, 'argue that

---

Balthasar reports that she 'travelled' in this way particularly in a mission to re-invigorate the spiritual lives of members of religious orders, but also supporting and praying with prisoners in concentration camps during the war, or praying in forgotten churches. He says that this 'travelling' continued into her final years when she was herself physically weak, becoming a tremendous drain on her own inner resources. See von Balthasar, *First Glance*, pp. 39-40, 45. A comparable report is made of the stigmatic Padre Pio, whose 'bi-locations' have been, in one or two cases, confirmed by those to whom he appeared. See Wilson, *The Bleeding Mind*.

9. Von Balthasar, *First Glance*, pp. 33-37.

10. German readers might pursue, for example, Barbara Albrecht, *Eine Theologie des Katholischen: Einfuhrung in das Werk Adrienne von Speyrs* (2 vols.; Einsiedeln: Johannes Verlag, 1972–73).

11. See, for example, von Balthasar, *First Glance*, p. 47: 'the influence of grace was so pronounced in her, the supernatural dimension in no way effaced her natural individuality: rather it underlined it. But it is one thing to see this individuality and another to describe it in words, for the magic of her personality can be expressed in almost no other way but in paradoxes and by uniting apparent extremes.'

12. Von Balthasar, *Unser Auftrag*, pp. 12-13.

there are distinctive "female" forms of reasoning and that "neutral" standards of rationality are male biased'.[13]

However, in so far as mysticism also entails absorption within or consumption by an absolute divinity, feminist analysis offers some criticism. In particular, it draws attention to the dangers of amplifying the capacity of patriarchal culture—including its religious forms of expression—to define every life and every quality of life according to the specific needs and anxieties of its male priests and patriarchs.

Von Speyr on John 1.4: Life and Death and Light

Just as human words have been accounted vacillating and lying[14] on their own without God's *imprimatur*, in comparison with the creative word of God, so the fruitfulness of life as understood in God is compared with life exemplified in humankind on its own terms. God's eternal life 'is the fullness of life, and consequently perfect peace, power and authority, the absolute affirmation of being and becoming'.[15] In contrast human life without that divine superfluity is striving and growing and dying. Human life on its own is an anxious affair characterized by poverty and need and in all this, von Speyr's deluded human hero— or anti-hero—becomes once more the victim of a divine violence, 'flung to the ground by the power that surpasses all things'.[16]

To challenge, as it were, the mystic understanding of an ecstasy of abasement before God, for example, bear in mind the—albeit highly rhetorical—writing of Mary Daly about the degradation of women's lives and bodies in *Gyn/Ecology*:

> If the general situation of widowhood in India was not a sufficient inducement for the woman of higher caste to throw herself gratefully and ceremoniously into the fire, she was often pushed and poked in with long stakes after having been bathed, ritually attired, and drugged out of her mind. In case these facts should interfere with our clear misunderstanding of the situation, Webster's invites us to re-*cover* women's history with the following definition of *suttee*: 'the act or custom of a Hindu woman *willingly* cremating herself or being cremated on the funeral pyre of her husband as an indication of her *devotion* to him'. It is thought-provoking

---

13. See Maggie Humm (ed.), *The Dictionary of Feminist Theory* (New York: Harvester Wheatsheaf, 2nd edn, 1995), p. 236.

14. Adrienne von Speyr, *The Word: A Meditation on the Prologue to St. John's Gospel* (trans. Alexander Dru; London: Collins, 1953), p. 31.

15. Von Speyr, *The Word*, pp. 36-37.

16. Von Speyr, *The Word*, pp. 38-39.

to consider the reality behind the term devotion, for indeed a wife must have shown signs of extraordinarily slavish *devotion* during her husband's lifetime, since her very life depended upon her husband's state of health. A thirteen-year-old wife might well be concerned over the health of her sixty-year-old husband [emphasis M. Daly].[17]

Of course, von Speyr herself would hardly have wished to make any direct comparisons between the God she believed demanded her loving obedience and the cultural demands laid upon young Indian widows. But the associations with what is overbearing and in some sense unwelcome are, within von Speyr's reflections on the Prologue of John's Gospel, just strong enough to remain disconcerting:

Word and fire are one, and we are drawn to the flame to be utterly consumed. The word and the demand are one, and understanding the word we take everything upon ourselves in order to fulfil its demand...

At first the word which God addresses to us looks harmless, like a human word. But instantly the fire within it begins to stir, insatiably embracing everything, demanding everything, consuming everything.[18]

Within the modern feminist reading context, reservations about von Speyr's religious disposition are inevitable. For example, there are numerous references to the nakedness of the Christian before God, particularly in relation to confession.[19] The stripping-down von Speyr appears to demand—either of herself or the reader—in regard to God, is one-sided: passionately irrational and gloriously self-abandoned. But it is also clearly intoxicated with the divine (male) gaze:

I have the feeling that the entire confession stands within the framework of a demand whose dimensions are no longer within my view at all ... my truth is taken up into the greater truth of God. If God should demand of me that I confess that I am avaricious (which to my knowledge I am not), then I would confess it. And I would do this also for the reason that the concept of avarice has at this moment been infinitely expanded and no longer has anything in common with my narrow concept of it. When God looks at avarice, things become evident in it which I had not as yet perceived. And in this nakedness even I see something of what I had not

---

17. Mary Daly, *Gyn/Ecology: The Metaethics of Radical Feminism* (London: The Women's Press, 1991), p. 116.

18. Von Speyr, *The Word*, p. 18.

19. Von Speyr, *The Word*, p. 55.

seen until now. It is as if I had a birthmark somewhere on my body
where I could not see. God, however, can undress me and tell me,
'There is a spot which you must confess'.[20]

Nakedness represents lost innocence[21] so that being 'clothed'—like
Adam and Eve, rejected from Eden, becomes equivalent to a form of
darkness—resistance to God:

> with people one does not love one wraps oneself up in a sort of artificial
> darkness. One intentionally displays one or other aspect of one's self, one
> clothes oneself in armour. This armour is, of course, useless against the
> light of God, for his light penetrates our artificial darkness all the same.[22]

Clearly for von Speyr, nakedness is a powerful, evocative symbol of
revelation and surrender. But for modern feminism, it also has more
disturbing associations with the invasive voyeurism of a culture that, as a
matter of course, dresses and undresses women at will.

3. *Opening Some of the Doors*

Reading von Speyr's meditations on the Prologue of John's Gospel is
every bit as difficult as they said it would be![23] It is extremely self-
referential and uniformly serious. For all that von Balthasar speaks of
von Speyr's cheerfulness and appreciation of the amusing,[24] there is not
the slightest hint of humour or the remotest indication of self-irony in
this text. The theology is intense, both in tone and construction, and
aside from one or two central analogies, there is not much in the way of
metaphor or illustration to aid reflection. I am therefore suggesting a
series of analyses and intertextualities as a way of weaving this interpretative text into patterns that will, hopefully, be fruitful and significant, both in relation to the biblical text and in relation to von Speyr as
(female) reader.

Von Balthasar gives the readers what is, perhaps, an important key to
the text in question by reminding them that the *hierarchical* symbolism of
gender is of great importance to von Speyr. It is not simply present in

20. Von Speyr, *The Word*, p. 174.
21. Von Balthasar, *First Glance*, p. 175.
22. Von Speyr, *The Word*, p. 54.
23. See von Balthasar, *First Glance*, pp. 11-14, 248-49. See Oakes, *Pattern of Redemption*, p. 4.
24. Von Balthasar, *First Glance*, p. 47.

her work but a conscious element of her whole theology. Metaphors of surrender and of Marian obedience, of abandonment and of nakedness are constituted and exist within this context:

> Adrienne praised virginity in many places in her works; of course she always saw it (in a Marian way) in a functional relationship to obedience. But she equally understood the sexual relationship between man and woman—and, in fact precisely in the highest possible opposition of their functions and attitudes, with no leveling of differences—which she described in the Pauline sense as a *magnum mysterium*: 'I mean this in reference to Christ and the Church' (Eph. 5.32).[25]

In other words, this identification, both of Marian obedience, and of the Church with the 'other' gender in a fundamentally hierarchical relationship, implies that what she has in mind is the underlying relationship of Creator to creature. This relationship has to be, if not necessarily beneficial, certainly beyond creaturely question. The problem for the majority of feminists who might try to engage seriously with this theological text as it stands would be, I imagine, that it appears to have already 'sold out' to the forces of phallogocentric mythology that divinizes the *sign* of masculinity. All attempts to mitigate the harshness of this distinction, for example through the implication that the woman (Mary)'s consent is necessary, are formulated in terms of a derivative non-masculinity. *All that is left* for humankind is the role of passivity, of acceptance, impressionability, of being created, under the *sign* of the feminine. And in this respect, von Speyr's work appears to be determined by a vision of God and of redeemed humanity that is strongly singular and essentially masculine.

This is precisely what feminism, in all its forms, most passionately contests because its trace may be found in all the brutal cruelties and unnecessary burdens that have been laid for centuries on the backs of actual women. Audre Lorde (1934–92), the black American poet and critic, makes it clear how in so many situations, giving assent to anything is dependent upon a freedom to choose—at least in the sense of accepting or rejecting. God's mother chooses to let God use her and to make her suffer. Five-year-old Lorde, like so many other black Americans, like so many women, had no choice. She had to suffer the disgust and hatred her blackness engendered in the white woman she sat next to

---

25. Von Balthasar, *First Glance*, p. 95.

on the train.[26] There are, in Lorde's work, many reference to the experience of being the object of hatred. In her work, avoiding the crushing negativity of such experience, unchosen in any sense, means using her anger to maintain a constant vigilance and a constant denial of the definitions of others. To fail to do this is, she believes, to fail to survive in any meaningful sense at all. In a poem called 'Black Mother Woman',[27] Lorde remembers the 'myths of little worth' and the 'nightmares of weakness' with which her mother was daily assailed and forced to suffer. Lorde's angry refusal to be made to suffer the definitions of others stands in stark contrast to von Speyr's acceptance of the overwhelming definition of God. In a life dedicated to resistance, Lorde writes:

> America's measurement of me has lain like a barrier across the realization of my own powers. It was a barrier which I had to examine and dismantle, piece by painful piece, in order to use my energies fully and creatively.[28]

For Lorde, the definitions of others, when fuelled by anger and hatred, block the energies and prevent people from growing or flourishing. Von Speyr's answer would undoubtedly be that God's definitions cannot be fuelled by anger and hatred. However, she would need to prove that the motivations of God are at all times distinguishable from the motivations of those—largely men—who have had, in the past, the power and the responsibility for interpreting and defining God's word. And this, I believe, she fails to do convincingly in her work.

Von Speyr on the Prologue: John 1.1
The first chapter of her meditation sets out the sense in which God and word are beginning and fulfilment. And yet this is a progression that is constantly being re-enacted, as the word takes different forms or concretizes in different ways—in the Church and sacraments, in Scripture, 'When God takes away what a man holds dearest'.[29] And from the

---

26. Audre Lorde, 'Eye to Eye: Black Women, Hatred and Anger', in Audre Lorde, *Sister Outsider: Essays and Speeches by Audre Lorde* (Freedom, CA: The Crossing Press, 1984), p. 172.

27. Audre Lorde, *Undersong: Chosen Poems Old and New* (London: Virago Press, 1993), pp. 100-101.

28. Lorde, *Sister Outsider*, p. 147.

29. Von Speyr, *The Word*, p. 16.

beginning, there is a sense in which von Speyr sees fulfilment as a pattern or arrangement of joy and suffering.[30]

Within von Speyr's text, there are a number of formal patterns or models of divine activity; beginning and fulfilment, or beginning, centre and fire for example.[31] In her meditations on the Prologue of John's Gospel, von Speyr frequently uses the analogy of marriage and generation to describe divine activity and, at the same time, authorize the proper functioning of human relationships. The analogy concentrates on the formal, theological features of marriage within the Roman Catholic Church in which love has *already* been constructed as divine activity within a symbolically gendered, hierarchical context. This reference to married love and generation, then, is more of a poetics of theological analogy than anything else. That is to say that it functions less as a hermeneutical tool or imaginative metaphor and more as a celebration of marriage as related mimetically to divine activity.[32] This, perhaps, accounts for the sensation one has that von Speyr's view of marriage, sexuality and parenthood is both highly prescriptive and, in a contingent, human sense, curiously unformed within this text.

Similarly, I would argue that for von Speyr the 'introduction' of the absent mother into the Prologue is formally related to a particular kind of Marian obedience and suffering understood in parallel to Christ's obedience and crucifixion. As mother/woman, she lives out of a centre which is formally and *theologically* related to conception and suffering.[33] Thus, for example, the mother of God is described in terms of the

---

30. Von Speyr, *The Word*, p. 17.

31. See von Speyr, *The Word*, pp. 11-20.

32. Given von Balthasar's insistence that his theological approach was at one with von Speyr's, it would seem likely that she would share his understanding of analogical thinking. While this is a vastly complicated concept, it is above all clear that 'all striving towards and all experience of God must assume rather than prove the relationship to God', Erich Przywara, *Polarity* (Oxford: Oxford University Press, 1935), p. 36.

33. Von Balthasar recalls that von Speyr once had a vision of a woman, whose characteristics she related, at his suggestion, to the woman clothed with the sun from Revelation and whom von Balthasar told her represented both the mother (Mary) and the Church. In this vision, von Speyr recalled assisting at a birth—something with which as a doctor, she was familiar. Her interpretation of the woman's cries was that 'in labor she suffers in advance a portion of her Son's suffering'. See von Balthasar, *First Glance*, pp. 92-93.

conception of her child—her very 'being as a woman' is that of victim
from the start:

> At the foot of the cross is the *Mother of the Lord*, who participates in the
> sacrifice. Though in her case the sequence is lived in the reverse order.
> She gives her consent at the foot of the cross; the birth of the child in
> Bethlehem is the consummation of the sacrifice; and when the child was
> conceived in Nazareth she was already the victim given to God. This end
> is already in her beginning. Her whole destiny as a mother is sealed and
> consummated in conceiving; she lives *from* the cross, while Christ, being
> man, lives in the opposite direction, *towards* the cross.[34]

Theologically then, a woman has a particular vocation as woman. There
are two forms of life for individuals within the Church: the priesthood
and marriage. A woman's lack of choice in this matter is balanced, as
von Speyr sees it, by her particular participation in a 'hidden priesthood.
She stands next to the priest like Mary next to John beneath the cross',[35]
characterized by unlimited devotion to the community, poverty and
selflessness, producing a gracious, transformative effect.

The analogical mode of von Speyr's theology is again illustrated in her
treatment of the sacraments as love objectified: 'God desires the love
between him and man to have this form'.[36] And the risks of this approach are perhaps nowhere more apparent. Von Speyr's sometimes
repetitive insistence upon our forlorn condition and the grace and
superfluity of God assails the flagging spirits of readers unaccustomed to
her fundamental disposition. Thus, for example, in her description of
the sacraments as love she—not unreasonably—suggests that love needs
to be enacted and given some concrete form. But the suggestion that
'caritative' love is somehow more overflowing and infinite in its consequences[37] than 'sensual' love surely amounts to little more than the statement of a general presentiment of sensuality and sexuality as something
always potentially greedy for its own fulfilment[38] within a fundamentally
hierarchical vision of the relationship between body and spirit. That the
institution of sacraments reflects this greed, this appetite just as much, is
reflected in her comments that they make us thirst for more. But the
word 'thirst' is itself likely to drown in its own canonical sanctity in

---

34. Von Speyr, *The Word*, p. 55.
35. Von Speyr, *The Word*, p. 98.
36. Von Speyr, *The Word*, p. 83.
37. Von Speyr, *The Word*, p. 85.
38. Von Speyr, *The Word*, p. 83.

reflections on the text of John's Gospel and is, moreover, all set about with predictable conditions:

> It is the sacraments that make and keep love healthy, so that it is always thirsty for more, not for the sake of augmenting itself (which would only lead to an egotistical attitude imprisoned in the I) but for the sake of belonging increasingly to God.[39]

Von Speyr on John 1.2

Von Speyr's Trinitarian concept of God is fundamentally a formal analogy of love between a woman and a man resulting in the birth of a child. This 'Trinitarian' family history is, for von Speyr, a description of the movement referred to in the Johannine Prologue from God/Word in the beginning (Jn 1.1-12) to Word in the world (Jn 1.3-18). The love of the Father and the Son constantly flows in a circle between them. The Spirit bursts open the circle forcing their love for each other to find new directions that nevertheless continually refer back to a union as originating love. This is also clearly related to von Speyr's whole devotional approach, whereby there is no rest or standing still, but an endless succession of new initiatives and outcomes. The Son returns to the Father in joy, and there is a new beginning in the Holy Spirit:

> so too the child appears between man and woman. For it is the child which enables the love between man and woman to become eternal movement, transforms the seemingly complete into a true beginning, and bursts open the circle that threatened to close—and it is also the child that reveals the supernatural character of love as grace by pointing to its divine origin (for the child is a gift of God).[40]

This choice of analogy is revealing in that it marks the first point at which von Speyr, like so many other commentators, brings the woman, absent from the text, back into the interpretative picture. The fruitfulness of love is characterized as the conventional and feminine fruitfulness of pregnancy and birth,[41] but the sense of painful violent parturition

---

39. Von Speyr, *The Word*, p. 83.
40. Von Speyr, *The Word*, p. 26.
41. Note too that she adds a homily on grace to her analogy. It seems, leaping somewhat inconsequentially from the meditative point of her theme, to have returned the reader to the sphere of spiritual instruction. We are suddenly thrust into the consciousness of someone who wants or has wanted a child, and is reminded that its conception is not within the human gift. Perhaps she is speaking to herself.

is also never far away, nor is the parallelism between crucifixion and labour. Moreover, in *The Word* the figure of the mother of Jesus is paradigmatic for the Church in her openness to God and in the fruit-fulness that is the result of such openness:

> Before she conceived, Mary seemed perfectly open to God, and the in-carnation seemed to mark the limit of her possibilities. But in fact these were infinitely expanded: she became virgin and mother simultaneously, and fulfilled the being of woman beyond all expectation. Moreover the birth of the Son did not limit her vocation as mother, but sowed a beginning beyond all hope, her call to universal motherhood.[42]

The mother's unquestioning but essentially passive assent becomes the highest virtue and it is called 'freedom'. In von Speyr's terms, of course, the mother's assent to God *is* liberating—it is a saying yes to the most fulfilling relationship which is, by definition, sustaining and fruitful be-cause, formally speaking, God is the highest good imaginable. Analogical thinking, of course, as Edward Oakes puts it, 'begins inside the act of faith'.[43]

Von Speyr introduces the mother into the Prologue—re-introduces her, we might say, into the incarnational narrative of John as paradig-matic of both the loving reciprocity and the loving outreach of the Trinitarian God and of the Church in relation to God. She has made the Incarnation dependent upon her assent, her 'yes', and she has likened this 'yes' to the assent and to the obedience of Christ himself. For von Speyr, it comes quite naturally, in reading the Prologue of John's Gos-pel, to see the mother there. Clearly, the mother of God, the handmaid of the Lord, whatever her scriptural sources, is integral to von Speyr's understanding of the nature of God's relationship with the world. It is a relationship which cannot do without 'the mother'. It goes without saying, however, that 'the mother' is strictly defined under the *sign* of the feminine.

Von Speyr on John 1.6-8

John the Baptist represents for von Speyr the neighbour through whom 'I' come to know God.[44] The man sent from God becomes the image of

---

42. Von Speyr, *The Word*, pp. 26-27.
43. Oakes, *Pattern of Redemption*, p. 35. This occurs in Oakes's discussion of the influence of Erich Przywara's discussion of analogy on the work of von Balthasar.
44. Von Speyr, *The Word*, p. 73.

the Word and the model for the Christian life.[45] That is, his life formally reflects the nature of divine 'mission'; the Incarnation. Above all this mission is characterized by 'fluidity'—almost unpredictability—'the ever-new message is always opaque and formless, and neither Church nor individual understand it fully'.[46] It is a restless readiness for ever new challenges. And, as it is only through the consent of Mary that the Incarnation became an actual, human mission, so—says von Speyr—it is only through contact with the Mother of God that John's becomes a human mission. Thus she draws, once again, the human involvement of the divine Word into a formally feminine vision of mission as openness, readiness, acceptance of God's Word.

Von Speyr on John 1.9

The light that enlightens every man is understood by von Speyr to represent the sacraments of the Roman Catholic Church. For von Speyr they represent the objectivity of love for another which does not (divine)/should not (human) remain 'concealed in the private sphere of the I':[47] 'they preserve love from the danger of exhausting itself in a private and subjective world'.[48]

With communion, von Speyr once more returns to the realm of 'purely one-sided prodigality'.[49] With confession, while she expressly denies that its purpose is to become preoccupied with sins, the abasement, the exposure continue apace. Confession in the Church leads back to the Father through the cross—suffering and exposure combined:

> The way back to the centre of the Church is a return to the centre of the Father. Into the burning light of the Father. Whether the sinner comes from the outer darkness or was already in the light, he will certainly be consumed and burnt by the inmost light.[50]

As a third interpretative key, or possible 'arrangement' of the textual symphony, I would suggest that von Speyr's stigmata might themselves be viewed as a form of intertextuality. It has to be said from the start that it is hard to do this without, so to speak, incurring the—posthumous—displeasure of von Balthasar, who anticipated attempts to

45. Von Speyr, *The Word*, p. 74.
46. Von Speyr, *The Word*, p. 78.
47. Von Speyr, *The Word*, p. 82.
48. Von Speyr, *The Word*, p. 83.
49. Von Speyr, *The Word*, p. 91.
50. Von Speyr, *The Word*, p. 90.

illuminate von Speyr's writing in terms of 'depth psychology'[51] and heartily deplored any such attempts. I would not, however, claim that this intertextuality could makes her work 'understandable' in any fixed or final sense. It does, however, offer insights to the critical reader.

The phenomena collectively described as stigmata are regarded from the perspective of psychoanalysis as symptoms of 'conversion hysteria'. Hysteria is widely understood as a general form of psychological disturbance. It is expressed within individuals in many different forms and has different ways or mechanisms of operating, for example, by repression and, or, by conversion:

> Conversion consists in a transposition of a psychical conflict into, and its attempted resolution through, somatic symptoms which may be either of a motor nature or of a sensory one ... Freud's sense of conversion is tied to an economic approach: the libido detached from the repressed idea is transformed into an innervational energy. But what specifies conversion symptoms is their symbolic meaning: they express repressed ideas through the medium of the body.[52]

In other words, the particular somatic symptoms depend upon the richness or intensity, for the individual concerned, of its associations—its semiotic, archaic connections with infantile motivations. As Nitza Yarom writes in her study of the first documented stigmatic, St Francis, such symptoms are not incompatible with a high level of competence, vision and energy, and indeed human compassion, all of which von Speyr seems to have possessed in good measure.[53] But it does have to be said, even on the evidence of the little published about her and generally available in English,[54] there are indications that her disposition and

51. Von Balthasar, *First Glance*, p. 11.

52. J. Laplanche and J.-B. Pontalis, *The Language of Psycho-Analysis* (London: The Hogarth Press and The Institute of Psychoanalysis, 1985), p. 90.

53. See Nitza Yarom, *Body, Blood and Sexuality: A Psychoanalytic Study of St. Francis' Stigmata and their Historical Context* (New York: Peter Lang, 1992).

54. For the purposes of this brief study, I have referred only to von Balthasar's recollections of his conversations with von Speyr, together with her own statements about herself, collected, translated and published in the same volume, *First Glance*. A brief and necessarily somewhat impressionistic comparison between these accounts and the extended analysis of St Francis published by Nitza Yarom in *Body, Blood and Sexuality* reveals several parallel elements to those that, Yarom argues, led to the development of this characteristic form of conversion hysteria in the case of St Francis. Among these are undoubtedly a sense of deep-seated conflict with a parent, her mother (see von Balthasar, *First Glance*, pp. 24-25, 27, 32, 122, 132), serious

experiences are at least potentially explicable in terms of a serious form of psychological disturbance.[55]

Von Speyr's experience of the wounds of Christ's crucifixion[56] is relevant to a discussion of her interpretation of the Prologue of John's Gospel because it illustrates something both central and apparently contradictory within von Speyr's work, which relates closely to the theme of the Word made flesh. Von Speyr accepted, apparently quite unequivocally, the hierarchical relationship between flesh and spirit, which appeared to belong to each other in terms that, once again, are described by formal analogy with the sacramentality of Roman Catholic marriage as itself the form of divine, Trinitarian love. In Roman Catholic marriage the sacrament is not imposed from without by any sort of priestly intervention but belongs to the love between a man and a woman:

> The whole sphere of body and spirit is open to Catholic man, and neither of them is forgotten. There is on the one hand the balanced harmony between the two whereby the centre of gravity in a life, in a marriage, may at one time, and during a particular phase of life, be more

sickness in youth (von Balthasar, *First Glance*, p. 123), some evidence of difficulty with sexual relationships (von Balthasar, *First Glance*, pp. 29, 160), and the distancing of family through public religious conversion (von Balthasar, *First Glance*, p. 32) that brought some significant relief to inner tensions.

55. Both von Balthasar's recollections in *First Glance* and the autobiographical sketch 'Statements about Herself' included in that volume make many allusions to factors within her life, and particularly during her childhood and youth, that might have contributed to the development of hysterical symptoms in someone so clearly intelligent and sensitive as Adrienne von Speyr. Von Speyr's extremely poor health as a child, and her closeness to death as a young girl, her mother's strictness, lack of affection towards her, favouritism of her older sister and vehement objections to her daughter's choice of career, her love for her father who died during her teenage years, her delicately alluded to difficulties with sexuality within marriage, the death of her first husband and her conversion to Roman Catholicism in spite of the disapproval of her family, her childhood visions of the saints, constant fantasies of helping the poor and needy, and her self-inflicted penances on their behalf, her sense of being very special from her earliest days, and her increasing physical immobility in middle age are all factors that might be paralleled in the annals of Freudian analysis, or in the characteristic descriptions of other stigmatics.

56. Von Balthasar, *First Glance*, pp. 34-35. Von Balthasar describes how von Speyr was 'prepared' for this experience a year before it actually occurred: 'by an angel who stood by her bedside at night and said most earnestly: Now it will soon begin. During the following nights she was asked for a consent that would extend itself blindly to everything that God might ordain for her.'

in the spirit or more in the flesh. Both are in order within the framework of the subordination of the flesh to the spirit. And then too, since
the word was spiritual in its incarnation and since we must reach the
Father through the incarnate word, there is also the possibility that in the
place of this balanced harmony—marriage—the centre of gravity may be
entirely transposed into the spirit. Then the flesh may be absorbed into
the spirit and almost forgotten, or it may be utterly separated from the
spirit, and borne as a burden on earth, a penance, a thorn that we must
bear with us,—and the rebellion of the impulses and the struggle with
them lasts a life-time. The whole breadth of these possibilities is embraced in the fact that the Lord was in the flesh, and that he was so in
pure love.[57]

The issues of Incarnation and the hierarchical balance between flesh and
spirit in both Christ and every believing Christian are thus controlled by
a formal analogy with divine love in the Trinity, whereby flesh is
subject to spirit, but nevertheless, so to speak, holds its place as the
expression of that divine love. What, however, von Speyr seems to have
embodied in her stigmata, rather than conceptualized in her words, was
precisely the theological intuition that the Incarnation has to represent a
radical challenge to this hierarchy. Whatever the particular history of
von Speyr's hysterical symptoms—I am assuming, of course, that hysteria is a plausible explanation—they convey, for her, a double burden. I
believe that it is possible to say, for example, that for von Speyr the *sign*
of the crucifixion—her stigmata—is transgressive in the sense that it
causes a fraction in the cultural and, crucially, the religious structures
within which she, as a woman, understands herself as 'subject'. Within
these structures, woman and the feminine and their symbolic equivalents—body, humanity-not-divinity, incarnate divinity, bride, mother,
death, debility and the status of victim—have become over-determined
as forms of passivity and suffering. This stigmatic *transgression* is transgressive, because its primary effective reference is to the male and authoritative Christ as Word. Thus this transgression is also, and for von
Speyr quite literally 'crucially', empowering, because it enables her to
'speak' the Word—not simply spoken in her dictation[58] to von Balthasar
or published in books, but written visibly, displayed, branded on her
body; the mark of ownership and power.

57. Von Speyr, *The Word*, pp. 136-37.
58. Von Balthasar recalls that as von Speyr's health deteriorated she gave up
writing in favour of dictating to him as her secretary. See von Balthasar, *First Glance*,
p. 37.

This is dissemination of the Word with the undeniably divinely masculine authority of Christ, because she bears his scars and wears his name on her suffering (female) body.[59] And of course, without this suffering, she could not otherwise speak, given her own acceptance of the fundamental hierarchical division of divine gender economy, and her fundamental formal definition of woman within that economy. In other words, she has invested *heavily* in this gender economy, in terms of her own spiritual disposition towards God. And the stigmata allow her a way of getting around this bondage to silent passive subjection and obedience, while still affirming its validity in terms of a largely hidden suffering.

To reiterate then, in theological terms, and concentrating here upon her reflections on the Prologue, she becomes the Word of that Prologue made, through her crucifixion/stigmata, flesh, that is, *female flesh*; passive and suffering, the symbolic representation of humankind—particularly as taken up by Christ himself on the cross, but also by his mother in labour and mourning. But, of course, as transgression, this is a double-edged sword for her. In order to be word—to be able to proclaim authoritatively within structures that demand absolute obedience—she must be also passive, painful suffering flesh and partake of the common lot of both woman and the flesh, as obedient and compliant within patriarchal structures whether familial or ecclesiastical.[60]

It is perhaps for this very reason that confession in particular takes on for her the—itself crucifying—role of drawing together the physically unavoidable and emotionally crushing imperative to proclaim a faith,

---

59. See Rev. 22.4-5. It seems that the book of Revelation had considerable significance for von Speyr.

60. One of the perhaps more disagreeable and counterindicative aspects of von Speyr's life and experience for this reader is to be found in connection with her apparently insatiable demand for penance. According to von Balthasar, von Speyr would give him instructions concerning her own penitential exercises, and then 'under obedience' forget all about this programme. Then he would impose these exercises on her, 'with authority'. He was clearly uncomfortable with such practices, and it is hardly surprising when they read like a form of sado-masochism: 'As part of the "program", moreover, it was often necessary for me to turn myself into "sheer authority" in my behavior towards Adrienne. Every "dialogue-situation" was excluded—by a corresponding agreement of Adrienne's soul—so that it became experientially clear that the obedience of the Church can and at times must have all the reality and the relentlessness of the Cross itself.' See von Balthasar, *First Glance*, pp. 69-70.

and the straitjacket of submission to authority which had yet in a fundamental sense enabled her to validate the divine seal within her own silent, suffering, female body. It cannot be surprising either, that, consciously at any rate, she found the stigmata highly disconcerting—von Balthasar says she prayed over the years that the marks might become less visible[61] but not less painful. In other words, it is not surprising that she sought to hide the wounds, and yet to reveal, indeed *display* the inner suffering and the hiddenness to her confessor.[62] Again, it does not seem to me at all surprising that she lived out her days after 1940 in a state of increasing debility. She was herself, as it were, perhaps bound to become the incarnation of divine suffering and female passivity. She had, according to the conflictual *theological* pressures working upon her, to reconcile and do justice both to God's divinely ordained gender economy, according to which woman and the feminine represent the passive, obedient and surrendering, the Marian,[63] disposition of humankind towards God, and also to the actual virility and potency of his Word, hidden in a secular world. I believe, then, that one could say she became a quite brilliant exponent of a certain sort of mystical and Johannine theology, an embodied proclamation of the Gospel as a hidden crucifixion, in the world, but not of it. And in the light of this intertextuality, it also becomes more acutely obvious why von Balthasar speaks of the frightening intensity of her experiences and, so to speak, her need of courage.

Von Speyr on John 1.3

Within the third chapter, von Speyr's tendency to move from meditation to direction is more marked. God's word is creative, his *modus operandi* is dialogic. However, this 'dialogic' is based upon a proper attentiveness, and von Speyr takes to task any reader who fails to account for this, in tones reminiscent of the schoolroom:

61. Von Balthasar, *First Glance*, p. 35.

62. There is some indication that von Balthasar found von Speyr's insistence upon certain forms of penance following confession somewhat disconcerting. It sometimes appears that his cooperation was rather unwilling. See, for example, *First Glance*, p. 45.

63. See by way of definition von Balthasar, *First Glance*, p. 51: 'She is infinitely at the disposal of the Infinite. She is absolutely ready for everything… Coming…from man, it is also the highest achievement made possible by grace: unconditional, definitive self-surrender.'

> God does not desire man's self-made word, he does not want man to 'express himself'. Man should not suppose that God depends upon him and wishes to be informed about him. What God wishes to hear is simply the answer to his word. Naturally the whole person may, and even should, be contained in the answer, but the whole person only interests God in so far as it is the answer to his word.

The severity of tone continues through the chapter. Added to this is the perhaps rather sentimental vision of the innocent child, whose babblings are apparently untouched by desire and selfishness[64] (or Freudian analysis!) and the dying Christian, faced with the sobering prospect of death, who has forgotten himself again and returned to the first stammerings of infancy. Otherwise, she dismisses all our words as vacillating utterances, except as sanctified by Christ. And yet, and at the same time, the word —understood as in some sense the blueprint—of each individual remains within the compass of God's word, and she anticipates purgatorial sufferings if 'his' words do not accord with that word:

> There, in fire, he will lay aside his irresolution and his vacillation and conform to God's thought; he will have to learn to love through the painful expansion of love until he becomes one with his word deposited in God.[65]

Von Speyr on John 1.13

Von Speyr's definition of Jn 1.13 is in many ways revealing. Within the human economy there is a clear dualism as between the impulsive, instinctual drive for satisfaction, associated with pleasure and generation, and the spiritual man who is looking for devotion.[66] In a distinction that is Augustinian in tone, procreation properly ordered in marriage produces a child different or other than a child of pleasure, but there is still no relationship between such a procreation and the child of God, born of God. Von Speyr describes the birth of the child born of God in terms of its hiddenness and secrecy before the 'majority' of men,[67] and then

---

64. It should be noted that she never gave birth herself—at least as far as her published works or works about her allow us to say, she never gave birth to a live child. Her second husband was a widower and already had a child or children. But, again, it is not clear how far von Speyr took responsibility for them upon herself. If contact was relatively restricted it might, in some way, account for her tendency to slightly sentimental generalizations about children in general.

65. Von Speyr, *The Word*, p. 35.

66. Von Speyr, *The Word*, p. 126.

67. Von Speyr, *The Word*, p. 127.

follows an extended description of this 'man'. After that birth 'he knows that he is saved, but no longer knows who he is. He is a man whom God has overwhelmed'.[68] The experience is distressing[69] but momentous. The Man Born of God bursts open the framework of tradition against the Church's initial resistance:

> At first the Church regards a catastrophe of this order as a misfortune, until she has learnt through the blessings it brings, that God has revealed himself. Until she gradually comes to see that her forms only retain their vitality and life if her tradition and framework are from time to time burst open.[70]

This violent unseen birth results in an overwhelming trauma, a jarring of the whole person. People born in this way become out of step with the Church and the community, altered in their expectations and vision, sometimes psychically and even physically weakened:

> But the man of whom we are speaking looks upon his work as straw, only fit for the fire. His faith takes the form of impossibility, his love the form of unattainability. But the fire of the impossible is his very life, and it makes him creative. This does not mean to say that everything will work out well, and that all the consequences of his experience are willed by God. The gulf between feeling and doing is perhaps all too great. Men who have been buried alive, or barely escaped from a burning house, bear the wound permanently in their soul. For the rest of their lives they bear the stigma of the catastrophe. For ever after they are left trembling, and that may often be a hindrance for much that is good.[71]

The power God gives to become his children is seen as radically unsettling and demanding for the individual and also disturbing for the whole community which may find such people very hard to cope with. And yet they offer the rest a sight of God: 'God reveals himself through the opening created, and generations of men live on that revelation'.[72]

Yet even the effects of the volcanic upheaval von Speyr envisages are restricted within traditional theological and spiritual limits. The theoretical possibility of bursting through traditional spiritualities and theological presupposition is belied in von Speyr's writing on the Prologue by the imperialistic moves she seems to make to conquer even this

68. Von Speyr, *The Word*, p. 129.
69. Von Speyr, *The Word*, p. 131.
70. Von Speyr, *The Word*, p. 134.
71. Von Speyr, *The Word*, p. 131.
72. Von Speyr, *The Word*, p. 133.

territory of new possibilities. Those who are empowered to become God's children (Jn 1.13) are, characteristically, thrown into contemplation of their own unworthiness, the distance separating them from God, the thought of all that has not been done.[73] But while they may be spiritually shell-shocked, wounded in their souls, and 'an unbearable member of the community', the explosion originates in God, and for this reason, the Church by the apparently painless procedure of 'gradually coming to see'[74] sails on re-formed, reinvigorated and blessed by the bloodletting. The variety of human differences has been reduced to the one inconceivable crushing difference between God and humankind, as defined within Christian patriarchy, a relationship within which there is no room for negotiation or change.

Von Speyr on John 1.14
The Incarnation is understood, in its normality and comparability to our own existence, to consist initially in having an earthly mother. The divine analogy of Christian procreation and birth is once again invoked.

> The word became flesh means, finally, that Christian parents in their sacramental marriage not only beget the body and flesh of their child. The child of Christian parents is also born and begotten of the spirit, of the sacramental word of their marriage. So that even before it is baptised, it is a different child from the child of pagan parents.[75]

It is, I believe, confusing and misleading to regard this as a description of a human child, since its implicit understanding of sacramentality assumes the prior enactment of the divine Incarnation. It is rather the analogical description of divine Incarnation, of sacramental word made flesh. And that is a fairly concise description both of her own stigmatized predicament and perhaps of her own family romance.[76]

73. Von Speyr, *The Word*, p. 130.
74. Von Speyr, *The Word*, p. 134.
75. Von Speyr, *The Word*, p. 138.
76. Sigmund Freud's essay called 'Der Familienroman der Neurotiker' first appeared in a series of brief papers during the years 1907–1909, having to do less with neurotics than with the general context of child/parent relationships. It was initially something of a plea for candour and honesty, particularly in sexual matters. It outlined his theory that in liberating themselves from the authority of parents, children first experience a variety of dissatisfactions—sexual rivalry, a desire for revenge and retaliation for example—with their parents and then commonly express this dissatisfaction in fantasies which consciously or unconsciously replace parents

In many ways, what Audre Lorde wrote about the erotic and about
poetry is sharply opposite and yet also apposite in any discussion of von
Speyr's 'psycho-theology':

> When we live outside ourselves, and by that I mean on external direc-
> tives only rather than from our internal knowledge and needs, when we
> live away from those erotic guides from within ourselves, then our lives
> are limited by external and alien forms, and we conform to the needs of a
> structure that is not based on human need, let alone an individual's. But
> when we begin to live from within outward, in touch with the power of
> the erotic, within ourselves, and allowing that power to inform and illu-
> minate our actions upon the world around us, then we begin to be
> responsible to ourselves in the deepest sense. For as we begin to recog-
> nize our deepest feelings, we begin to give up, of necessity, being satisfied
> with suffering and self-negation, and with the numbness which so often
> seems like their only alternative in our society. Our acts against oppres-
> sion become integral with self, motivated and empowered from within.[77]

Von Speyr's writing is characterized by an excess and explosiveness that
would seem to have its roots in the erotic impulse as Lorde sees it, to
experience the empowerment of great joy and connection:

> God is love because he is the fulfilment. He is all this to us in the
> sacraments which pour forth grace and exhaust themselves in love. But
> when everything is resolved into love, it enters the mystery of explosive
> unity. Prior to love everything is disjointed and cannot become one ...
> those who are born of God are touched by the surpassing mystery of the
> unity of love—infinitely above distinctions and beyond notions.[78]

Within von Speyr's framework of faith, however, the Roman Catholic
Church is the bride of Christ, whose sacramental libido, so to speak, is
expressed through the eroticism of obedience and suffering. Arguably,
what von Speyr seems to have internalized in a very specific way is this
erotic dynamic. What distresses Lorde is the sense in which, within our
Western culture, we refuse to look the need we have, for sharing deep
feelings, in the face. Instead, we conspire to look away. For Lorde, the
erotic belongs to the context of sharing and empowerment. And as she
notes:

with more exalted figures—Lords of the Manor or Emperors, for example.

77. Audre Lorde, 'Uses of the Erotic', in Audre Lorde, *Sister Outsider: Essays and
Speeches by Audre Lorde* (Freedom, CA: The Crossing Press, 1984), p. 58.

78. Von Speyr, *The Word*, p. 127.

> To share the power of each other's feelings is different from using an-
> other's feelings as we would use a kleenex. When we look the other way
> from our experience, erotic or otherwise, we use rather than share the
> feelings of those others who participate in the experience with us. And
> use without consent of the used is abuse.[79]

The relevance of this criticism to the work of von Speyr is that, in some
ways, she might be seen to have treated Scripture, Church and sacraments, especially the sacrament of confession, as objects of her own
erotic satisfaction without 'sharing in the satisfying', without discussion
without argument without question, simply 'under obedience'. Arguably, the tremendous and crippling knowledge of her own undeniable
secret was the 'looking away' from what she was doing, in refusing to
look—in making it impossible to look—beyond the means of her own
satisfaction.

The crux of the problem for me, then, is a sort of potential misuse or
misdirection of eroticism, a blindness at best, an obscenity at worst.
Once again, Lorde is to the point. She explains her understanding of the
erotic—it is the power that comes from sharing deeply any pursuit with
another,[80] it is the underlining of a capacity for joy and it is empowering. But she also points to the way in which it has been commonly
restricted within certain limits and deeply feared, because once we recognize our need and capacity for joy and deeply shared communion,
this becomes a lens through which we examine all aspects of our lives:

> And this is a grave responsibility, projected within each of us, not to
> settle for the convenient, the shoddy, the conventionally expected, nor
> the merely safe.[81]

Von Speyr on John 1.5: Light Shining in the Darkness
God, she concludes, is the light shining in the darkness. This is not simply enmity towards God or even what is not God but rather it is, itself,
the divine mystery of love, 'a shell, a veil, a hiding place for the essential
mystery, as a protection for its love'.[82] Von Speyr seems here to be
speaking with reference to human loving. For the human lover to seek
to know too much appears to indicate a lack of trust and respect—an
impious unwillingness to be deprived of anything, including knowledge.

---

79. Lorde, *Sister Outsider*, p. 58.
80. Lorde, *Sister Outsider*, p. 56.
81. Von Speyr, *The Word*, p. 57.
82. Von Speyr, *The Word*, p. 53.

The source of the analogy is, for von Speyr, to be found in God: the darkness is necessary because 'the light needs it in order to flow on eternally, in order to have still more space to penetrate, conquer and measure'.[83] Thus, darkness becomes the necessary mystery of those we seek to love.

In her meditation on the darkness of Jn 1.5, von Speyr taps into another powerful symbolic equivalent in terms of the sacrifice that has considerable relevance for her own stigmatized body. This is understood in terms of the life (Incarnation/consent), crucifixion (surrender/consummation) and descent into hell (emptiness and death/victim given to God) of Christ. This is strongly associated, in a reversed form, to the sacrifice seen as the conception, birth and faithful vigil of Christ's mother.[84] Finally darkness is understood by von Speyr in terms of the mutual abandonment of Father and Son, 'the period in which the most secret mystery of their love is fulfilled. Their estrangement is a form of their supreme intimacy'.[85] In this the Holy Spirit becomes witness to that dark night and guarantor, as it were, of its validity.

There is a curious parallel current in the work of Lorde and von Speyr at this point. In her call for a disciplined attention to our feelings,[86] Lorde is talking about the bringing to birth of poetry:

> this is poetry as illumination, for it is through poetry that we give name to those ideas which are—until the poem—nameless and formless, about to be birthed, but already felt.[87]

These ideas, expressed in poetic terms, generate the light 'by which we scrutinize our lives' and which have 'a direct bearing upon the product which we live, and upon the changes which we hope to bring about through those lives'.[88] In her meditation on the Prologue of John, with its rich attention to the metaphor of light and darkness, von Speyr sees 'disciplined attention' to the voice and light of God as the guarantee of 'fruitfulness' in the life of the Christian believer and within the Church.[89] Lorde equally scrutinizes the distillation of experience, that is

---

83. Von Speyr, *The Word*, pp. 52-53.

84. Von Speyr, *The Word*, p. 55.

85. Von Speyr, *The Word*, p. 61.

86. Audre Lorde, 'Poetry is not a Luxury', in Audre Lorde, *Sister Outsider: Essays and Speeches by Audre Lorde* (Freedom, CA: The Crossing Press, 1984), p. 37.

87. Lorde, *Sister Outsider*, p. 36.

88. Lorde, *Sister Outsider*, p. 36.

89. Von Speyr, *The Word*, p. 48.

the feeling of rightness, as the grounds for a further poetic product. Lorde clearly has some appreciation of the searing quality of intimate scrutiny but still couches her thoughts about poetry as actively birthing 'thought as dream ... concept, as feeling ... idea, as knowledge',[90] von Speyr sees the divine light as primarily overwhelming:

> we soon have enough light, it is more than we can bear. We always cry out for more life...but we are shy of more light because it overwhelms us.[91]

And to be able to cope with the life God reveals, she presents her readers with an increasingly unresisting passivity to that overwhelming light:

> When God reveals one aspect of his life to us, he creates more room in us, an opening for something greater. But even if we were entirely open, if there were nothing left in us to be expanded, we should still be completely shut in and imprisoned compared with him ... Nevertheless there will be nothing humiliating in learning more and more about him, because his very being is the 'ever more', and our apprehension of God will be a growing capacity to allow ourselves to be filled by the abundance of his light.[92]

For Lorde, the creation of poetry is a necessity of survival because it forms the quality of light by which we see how to act politically. For von Speyr, the light of the Word is revealed to us only by passive contemplation, described in highly sensuous terms. It is radiated like the beauty of someone we love,[93] it is something in which to bask[94] or bathe,[95] and it is something graciously offered and poured out by God,[96] regardless of whether it is gathered up or not.

4. Conclusions

In describing Adrienne von Speyr's work as 'psycho-theology'—an admittedly very curious expression—I wanted to be able to make reference to her extraordinary stigmatic symptoms. Understood as the signs

90. Lorde, *Sister Outsider*, p. 36.
91. Von Speyr, *The Word*, p. 46.
92. Von Speyr, *The Word*, p. 49.
93. Von Speyr, *The Word*, p. 46.
94. Von Speyr, *The Word*, p. 45.
95. Von Speyr, *The Word*, p. 47.
96. Von Speyr, *The Word*, p. 47

of conversion hysteria, they point to the development of subjectivity during childhood and adolescence. While it seems to me that the available information is suggestive, I am not qualified to make a judgment in this respect. However, as a form of intertextuality and as a reading of the Prologue of St John that takes into account—at least theoretically—the unconscious as well as the conscious motivations of commentators, it seemed to me well worth investigating as a form of theological interpretation. It enables me to suggest that von Speyr manipulated the analogical theology so suited to her own disposition—the conviction that her suffering mirrored, in an objective sense, the feminine dimension of divine love—to her own advantage, demonstrating, in her own flesh as word, the most radically authoritative challenge to any absolute or final hierarchy as between body and spirit or thus to any hierarchy of gender.

That her sincerity was absolute, in every conscious sense, goes without saying. That she felt compassion towards the suffering of others and believed that her own sufferings might—objectively—mitigate theirs, is indisputable. Ultimately, however, there is a sense in which her interpretation was questionable. The price in suffering she paid herself and the price she demanded, not least, of von Balthasar was, arguably, demonically overinflated in a world already choking on suffering. And her interpretation might still be seen as a form of what Audre Lorde calls 'looking away', a disguised form of erotic satisfying or a perversion which is an abuse of feeling. While one might say that such experience comes under the heading of what Caroline Walker Bynum has described, in the context of mediaeval spirituality, as a particular attempt to both gain power and give meaning,[97] von Speyr's intriguing reading practices are not really such as a modern feminist reader could seriously wish to imitate.

---

97. See Caroline Walker Bynum, *Holy Feast and Holy Fast: The Religious Significance of Food to Medieval Women* (Berkeley: University of California Press, 1987), pp. 208-18.

PART II

7

Which Came First: Word or the Words?
Towards a Feminist Transformation

Only the one who is sent can reveal the one who has sent him.[1]

1. *Some Introductory Remarks to Part II*

In the course of this study so far, I have read a number of different in-terpretations of a single biblical text and found them all, to some degree or other, determined by the tendency to collapse all traces of woman or the feminine within the Prologue into either descriptions of emptiness and absence, or evil and moral failure. I think that the women readers among the five figures analysed probably go farther towards valorizing feminine-identified images or modes of action than the men. In the case of Hildegard von Bingen, for example, there are striking references in her extended commentary on Jn 1.1-14 to the female figure of divine, creative Wisdom. Moreover, Hildegard's incarnational theology as read within Part One of *Liber divinorum operum* embraces the whole of creation, in its earthly and bodily materiality as well as in its ultimate subjection to divine judgment, as a divine revelation. And Adrienne von Speyr makes the principle of cooperative obedience, of consent, com-parable to the obedience of Mary in accepting God's Son within her body, a characteristic of the Trinitarian economy itself. And, perhaps, these women go even further by literally embodying the Word in the physical and bodily symptoms of migraine attacks and stigmatic suffering which accompanied their personal experiences of the divine.

However, even Hildegard's theology is still strongly coloured by an Augustinian anxiety about 'fleshly' desires that were particularly asso-ciated by him with genital sexuality. Moreover her female figures are

---

1. Ernst Käsemann, *The Testament of Jesus: A Study of the Gospel of John in the Light of Chapter 17* (London: SCM Press, 1968), p. 23.

maternal and virginal, not autonomous or sexually active. Divine revelation and physical incapacity and pain seem linked within the religious experience of both women, compromising the expression of an undoubtedly heightened bodily and physical sensibility. And finally, of course, neither Hildegard nor Adrienne von Speyr appear willing or able to abandon the hierarchical and gendered vision of the divine in relation to humanity, closely related to the hierarchy of masculine over feminine values, roles and modes or existence in general. This vision is projected, by both women, upon humankind in relationship to God, giving divine accreditation to the hierarchy of ecclesiastical structures and making it normative for male and female living in general.

I would say that the three men whose work on the Prologue I have dealt with in detail demonstrate a similar anxiety about divine embodiment and the challenge to the singular, spiritual identity of the divine that this constitutes at one level or another. It would be quite unfair to these commentators not to recognize that they wrestle to find this embodiment a central role within their work on the Prologue. In all three cases, however, it seems to me that they finally resolve the difficulty raised by the fleshly Incarnation of the Word by, in some way or another, reimposing a hierarchical division between Word and flesh as a means of supporting a singular standard of divine perfection or human perfectibility. Thus Augustine ultimately finds no place for the irrationality of human desires and particularly that of embodied sexual desire. He takes the view that subjection to such irrational desires is the central and identifying factor of human life apart from God. Ultimately, in other words, he thinks that it is dangerous to any sort of human perfection. Luther attempts to obliterate the significance of human being, except in so far as it is defined as the consequence of faith in the divine. And finally, Bultmann, in obliterating the separated divinity of Jesus' existence in favour of a revelation of the divine through his sheer humanity, still seems to me to relate the significance of the Word's fleshly Incarnation largely to its role in a 'divine' rescue mission. In other words I do not believe that Bultmann's reading of this passage evaluates human existence, in itself, any higher than a number of other interpretations that are far more equivocal than he is about the humanity of the Word. Without or outside the existential and unmediated encounter with the divine, human existence—its traditional relationship to woman and the feminine faint but still traceable—continues to be regarded as transitory, empty and vain. And even if we may say that

Bultmann allows us to describe the supercharged existence of the human creature who has responded to the divine address as being entirely within the sphere of existence that is human, the divine/human distinction is still being used by him to describe a hierarchy of values that designates the negative pole as *human* flesh without divine Word, and the positive pole as *divine* Word made flesh.

2. Part II—The Possibilities of New Readings?

The aim within this second part is to find new readings of the Prologue of John's Gospel that recognize the traces of an 'otherness' symbolized by woman and the feminine without copying into the interpretative text the devaluation of this feminine-identified 'otherness' that is evident in all the readings examined so far.[2] In these three attempts to read the Prologue self-consciously as a feminist critic, I continue exploring the model of interpretation as a collaborative effort between text and reader. I want to 'try on' this textual garment in order to see whether it might be read to fit and suit women readers as well as men.

In view of my conclusion that many existing readings of the Prologue tend to give support to 'phallogocentrism'—seeing the feminine as merely part of the definition of masculine and trying to derive all meaning from a single, masculine transcendental truth or essence which necessarily excludes or devalues the feminine—one natural route for me to take would be deconstructive criticism of the text. Deconstructive analysis proceeds by resisting or turning on its head any predetermined scale of values or priorities, such as masculine over feminine, or divine over human. Thus, for example, a biblical text might be interpreted by focusing on the so-called 'minor' characters rather than the character of Jesus or the Word. The main thread of the argument in two of the following three interpretations is deconstructive. In this first interpretative variation, my focus is on the figure of John the Baptist, rather than the Word, as the Revealer. In the second variation, the focus is the despised 'flesh' of Jn 1.13 as opposed to that of the glorified 'flesh' of Jn 1.14.

But finally, given my underlying commitment to interpretative multiplicity, I have attempted to give one reading of the Prologue that is

2.   It should, of course, be noted that an analysis of five readings can hardly be accounted exhaustive. It is possible that there are already other readings—even historical readings—that serve this purpose.

not so much deconstructive as constructive, or even, to some extent, structuralist. I read the Prologue as a description of the human self or subject, in Julia Kristeva's term, *en procès*. This makes sense in so far as becoming a human subject or self would appear, by common agreement, to be the theme of the Johannine text. This third reading does have a deconstructive element. Kristeva's fundamentally psycho-analytic discourse of the developing subject accounts for the drive towards singularity that I have detected in a series of historical readings in terms of a realm of symbol, language/articulation and law/control, identified with the masculine, which is constantly under threat from the feminine-identified realm of the semiotic. The semiotic realm is con-cerned with bodily rhythms and drives, with desire and satisfaction, having their origins in the pre-linguistic relations of an infant with its mother. A violent and necessary division is made between the two, driving the maternal, so to speak, underground. However, Kristeva con-tinues to maintain the autonomously creative and even 'salvific' poten-tiality of this abject maternal in constantly breaching and breaking down the boundaries of the order of symbol and law. In this way, while she accounts within her theoretical framework for the persistently negative evaluation of the maternal feminine, she does not thereby adopt it.

3. *A Feminist Critique of the Prologue*

In this first reading I want to do two things. First of all I shall describe the patriarchal myth which I believe existing interpretations of this passage have supported. In other words, I want to describe what might be called the 'rhetorical mythology' which I believe underpins much patriarchal interpretation of this passage. I define 'rhetorical mythology' as a mythological narrative which is reproduced in individual interpre-tations of authoritative texts, for example, passages from Scripture, and then used rhetorically to persuade readers to support its instantiation within the institutions of the wider culture, including those that regulate any further reading of Scripture. The particular mythological narrative I relate to the interpretation of the Prologue of John's Gospel is undoubtedly based on a close reading of the text. But I want to argue that it is not the *only* narrative to be found by reading the text. Sec-ondly, then, I want to begin the process of identifying a new mytho-logical narrative, in order to challenge both existing interpretations of this passage and the myth it has cherished.

I believe that the issue of much concourse between this text (Jn 1.1-
18) and its interpreters is a broadly mythic summary of God's self-
sufficiency in creation and disinterestedness in undertaking human salvation. This is the story told, to an extent, by all the commentators
whose work on the Prologue I have looked at so far. While the
mythological narrative certainly concerns divinity in relationship with
humankind, I am also arguing, of course, that it is closely related to a
common understanding of the relationship between male and female.

Typically, then, the relationship between divine and human is asymmetrical: God's mission is central to concepts of human history and self
but the creation and self-understanding of humanity-in-the-world
cannot define what is meant by God's mission. In a formal sense, humanity lacks all autonomous value or relevance. This asymmetrical
pattern clearly mirrors what modern feminist theory describes as
'phallogocentricity', in which the feminine is simply defined in terms of
a masculine view of it. Once again, it has no autonomous value or
relevance. The feminine becomes symbolic of an absence or lack (of the
masculine or masculine sign—in Lacanian terms, the phallus).[3] But the
more formal sense of lack or absence or of emptiness associated with
woman and the feminine is elaborated within the patriarchal context in
terms of a matrix of connecting associations with bodily desire,
materiality, death, decay, and sexuality, which is given a negative construction. These descriptions appear to function, more or less effectively,
as the means to articulate and control a disturbing presence whose
necessity is perceived but still resisted—expressed rather neatly in a col-
loquialism on the subject of women: 'Can't live with them! Can't live
without them!'

In this context, Ernst Käsemann's reading of the Gospel of John
(1968) is interesting and relevant. Käsemann concluded that the unorthodox and Docetic implications of the whole of the Fourth Gospel
were clear and unmistakable:

> I am not interested in completely denying features of the lowliness of the
> earthly Jesus in the Fourth Gospel. But do they characterize John's
> Christology in such a manner that through them the 'true man' of later
> incarnational theology becomes believable? Or do not those features of

3.   For a discussion of this pattern of phallogocentricity, see, for example,
Elisabeth Grosz, 'Contemporary Theories of Power and Subjectivity', in Sneja
Gunew (ed.), *Feminist Knowledge: Critique and Construct* (London: Routledge, 1990).

his lowliness rather represent the absolute minimum of the costume designed for the one who dwelt for a little while among men, appearing to
be one of them, yet without himself being subjected to earthly conditions? His death, to be sure, takes place on the cross, as tradition
demands. But this cross is no longer the pillory, the tree of shame, on
which hangs the one who had become the companion of thieves. His
death is rather the manifestation of divine self-giving love and his vic-
torious return from the alien realm below to the Father who had sent
him.[4]

Käsemann argues, then, that the Gospel of John is not, in a straightforward sense, a text about incarnation in the flesh at all but the narrative of divine glory revealed in the world. This reading of the Prologue reproduces in a very vivid way the myth that I am claiming lies
behind much traditional interpretation of the Prologue. This mythic
construction enables the divine to condescend to humanity without
needing to become involved in, or compromised by, the condition of
humankind, disturbingly symbolized by woman or the feminine. God
lays claim to divine (masculine) self-sufficiency, omnipotence and self-
containment[5] while a prevailing fear of death and dissipation continues
to be located within the symbolic matrix of male-defined concepts of
female gender and sexuality, including, of course, human flesh and
humanity as a whole (male and female) in its relationship to the divine.[6]

What Käsemann seemed to read in the Gospel of John was the
representation of an absolute exclusion of the human 'other' exalted as
the principle of divinity. All that is revealed is the Revealer, the non-
embodied self-sufficient masculine subjectivity of the divine. As Raymond Brown puts it, against Bultmann, Käsemann 'sees not so much
that the Revealer is only a man, but that God is present in the human

---

4.   See Käsemann, *The Testament of Jesus*, pp. 9-10.

5.   This is, of course, to place the argument within the context of current
debates about self and subjectivity in which it is held that 'selfhood', in terms of
both individual and community identity, is defined in terms of a significant reaction
to, and frequently a rejection of, 'otherness'. See in particular Pamela Sue Anderson,
'Wrestling with Strangers: Julia Kristeva and Paul Ricoeur on the Other', in Alison
E. Jasper and Alastair G. Hunter (eds.), *Talking It Over: Perspectives on Women and
Religion 1993–5* (Glasgow: Trinity St Mungo Press, 1996), pp. 129-49.

6.   In this context, such a symbolic matrix would incorporate male as well as
female identity since, in hierarchical relationship to the divine, all humanity would,
symbolically, become identified with the feminine.

sphere'.[7] All the rest is the mere placental garbage of the defining and banished feminine. This is the stuff of feminist nightmares!

However, of course, Käsemann does not claim that this radically Docetic interpretation of the Prologue and the Gospel of John could be acceptable as a teaching of the Christian Church. He makes these claims about the text in the course of an argument against his scholarly colleagues, whom he accuses of interpreting the text rhetorically to support a particular theological position. He seeks to convince his colleagues in 1968 that historical criticism had been domesticated in the service of theological conservatism. In fine and rhetorical style he declares that

> The 'happy ending' is not merely wishful thinking, but the condition tacitly agreed upon for the historical-critical enterprise, and even satires of this technique of transformation would offend against good manners. The Gospel of John is the favourite playground for such practice.[8]

Käsemann's reading is persuasive in many ways. After all, it is quite possible that the author(s) of the Gospel viewed Christology in a far from 'orthodox' manner. In the final analysis, however, Käsemann's reading seems to be open to the criticism that it is rhetorical, that is, driven by his desire to reconcile the Docetic and unorthodox text with its canonical authority in order to produce an ending which is 'happy' in so far as it supports his own position. For example, he raises most acutely the question of how the unmediated encounter between believer and glorified Word, in which he believes the Gospel's 'kerygma' to consist, can be reconciled with the necessary mediation of the Gospel itself as somehow authoritative. This point is itself germane to the feminist argument. Within a gendered vision of the divine/human relationship, the mediation of the Gospel as a text written and expounded by embodied human creatures can become the focus for an argument about the necessity of human agency. Käsemann however concludes that John's Gospel is only the medium of a demand that we 'continually surrender ourselves anew to the Word of Jesus' and evaluate every church 'in the light of the one question, do we know Jesus?'[9] It is, he

---

7.   Raymond E. Brown, *The Gospel According to John I–XII: A New Translation with Introduction and Commentary* (AB, 29; New York: Doubleday, 1966), p. 35.

8.   Käsemann, *The Testament of Jesus*, p. 8.

9.   Käsemann, *The Testament of Jesus*, p. 77.

claims, the demand and our faithful response to it that matters. Moreover, the very fact that John's 'church' produced this naïvely Docetic Gospel is itself indicative that, for Käsemann at least, the kerygmatic core in some sense transcends the text—he suggests that 'unorthodoxy' can function in a dialectic sense, balancing what he argues are 'no less dangerous extremes'. So, although he appears to have regarded the rhetorical mythology of a Docetic Johannine text as 'unorthodox', his own rhetorical reading seems to be leading back in the direction of a divine Word to which humankind has little to contribute except in the sense of a spiritualized reception. That is to say, his work is moving towards the vision of a self-sufficient divinity which he himself has already argued can be read in an authoritative biblical text. And his concluding words place this Docetic rejection of the feminine symbolic, that is the humanity of the Word, at the service of that (rhetorically constructed) phallogocentric totalitarianism by stating that the purpose of John's christological proclamation, and perhaps also the earthly Jesus, is to call us 'into our creatureliness',[10] a word which identifies us entirely in terms of our relationship to what we are not, that is, the Creator.

Käsemann is not proposing any alterations to orthodox Christology on the basis of his reading of the Johannine text, and yet curiously he appears to have doubly inscribed it with a patriarchal myth of divine self-sufficiency. (Is he representing or resisting orthodox Christian teaching here?)

4. *Rhetorical Readings for Woman and the Feminine*

In order to transform interpretation of the text, I believe that feminist readers need to steer clear of this rhetorical myth of divine (male) self-sufficiency or presence—if they can. It seems potentially fruitful, then, to read the Prologue (Jn 1.1-18) from a point of 'focalization'[11] other than that of God, Word or narrator, whose undeniable presences within the text lend themselves to what might be called phallogocentric tendencies within orthodox traditions of interpretation.

---

10. Käsemann, *The Testament of Jesus*, p. 78.

11. The term 'focalization' is used in the sense proposed by Mieke Bal in *Narratology: Introduction to the Theory of Narrative* (Toronto: University of Toronto Press, 1985), pp. 100-15. Bal uses the term 'focalization' to distinguish 'visions' of a passage from any overtly narratorial voice or vision.

Orthodox traditions of interpretation begin at the beginning of the Prologue with ἐν ἀρχῇ ('in the beginning...') and frequently link these words to that other famous opening passage in Gen. 1.1. Raymond Brown writes:

> In the Hebrew Bible the first book (Genesis) is named by its opening words, 'in the beginning'; therefore, the parallel between the Prologue and Genesis would be easily seen. The parallel continues into the next verses, where the themes of creation and light and darkness are recalled from Genesis.[12]

However, though the theme of creation is clearly referred to at this point, it is not developed within the mainstream of modern critical scholarship in terms of a reflection on the nature of the Word's humanity *in the world*. Commentary on the Prologue tends to devote attention to the relationship between God and the human Word rather than to the role of Word in creating humanity and humanity in the world (Jn 1.3).[13] It is much more to do with laying out the parameters of the discussion, beginning with the absolute fundamental of God. In other words, much critical scholarship at this point is preoccupied with emphasizing the *presence* of God and Word. Raymond Brown, for example, agrees with Rudolf Schnackenburg that 'beginning', as it occurs in the Prologue of John's Gospel, has little to do with temporality and indicates, rather, limitless divine dominion:

> This is not, as in Genesis, the beginning of creation, for creation comes in v. 3. Rather the 'beginning' refers to the period before creation and is a designation, more qualitative than temporal, of the sphere of God.[14]

> The phrase 'in the beginning' contains no reflection on the concept and problem of time... The phrase does not mark the coming into existence of the created world. It expresses the being of the Logos as it was before the world. That which already existed 'in the beginning' has precedence over all creation.[15]

---

12. Brown, *The Gospel According to John*, p. 4.

13. It should be noted that Barnabas Lindars, *The Gospel of John* (NCB Commentary; Grand Rapids: Eerdmans, 1972), p. 82, sees Jn 1.1 as a possible reference to Prov. 8.22 and that Rudolf Schnackenburg, *The Gospel According to St. John* (trans. K. Smyth; 3 vols.; New York: Herder & Herder, 1968), I, pp. 228, 233, assumes a reference to Wisdom traditions. Brown, *The Gospel According to John*, however, makes no reference to this passage at this point.

14. Brown, *The Gospel According to John*, p. 4.

15. Schnackenburg, *The Gospel According to St. John*, I, p. 232.

Barnabas Lindars sees the Prologue as providing the cosmic setting[16] for the entry of the Word into the world and points to the past continuous tense of ἦν (Jn 1.1: 'In the beginning *was* the Word...'), distinguishing this, as descriptive of the 'virtually timeless', from the historic ἐγένετο of Jn 1.3 and 6 (Jn 1.3 translated as: 'all things were made through him...'; Jn 1.6 translated as: 'There was a man sent...'). Once again the emphasis is laid on such timelessness as descriptive or predicative of divinity.

Mark Stibbe is a reader who uses many of the insights of modern literary criticism and theory in his work on John's Gospel. He too draws attention to the reference to Gen. 1.1 at Jn 1.1. He is rather more interested in the intertextual implications of relating the narratives of Genesis and John than either Brown or Schnackenburg, for example. But even Stibbe seems preoccupied with the Prologue as marking out the context, the presence of God in an authoritative sense, when he draws attention, for example, to the role of the narrator's voice within the text:

> From now on the relationship will be one of an omniscient narrator communicating with a privileged reader.[17]

Readers should believe what they are being told. Certainly, none of the readers referred to so far seems at all inclined to doubt that readers— real, intended or implied[18]—are being addressed in a very straight-forward manner indeed about the absolute presence and authority of God the Word.

It seems to me, however, that 'In the beginning' is reminiscent of the tradition of folk tales in which the teller, by a description that in itself appears to be making claims in terms of time and space, simply loosens the tale from any particular temporal or spatial moorings: 'Long ago and far away, there lived...' or 'A man once...'. The effect is to make the story more universal in its application or perhaps more relevant to a whole host of different listeners. And, of course, it also alerts the listener or reader to the possibility that the following tale never actually happened, or never happened quite like this! Of course, the persistence and popularity of folk tales are not based on claims to authority in the same way as canonical Scripture. Folk tales, at first glance, do not appear

---

16. Lindars, *The Gospel of John*, p. 76.
17. Mark W.G. Stibbe, *John* (Sheffield: Sheffield Academic Press, 1993), p. 22.
18. See Chapter 1, pp. 29-30, for a definition of these various concepts.

to impose the same task on the reader. And, of course, the word ἀρχη ('beginning') used within the Johannine text[19] as a whole could easily seem to bear the impress of something rather more portentous than a conventional literary device for getting started. On the other hand, 'In the beginning…' as it occurs at the opening of the creation myths within the book of Genesis seems to operate in precisely this sort of folkloric manner.

If the 'implied readers', the hypothetical 'target' readers within the mind of the author(s) of this Gospel, are equipped with all the correct cultural, theological and literary apparatus necessary for understanding what that mind intended to convey within the text, actual readers are very frequently not so provided. This does not mean that they will not be able to find some significance that is rooted in the text, although it might well be unpredictable if the intention of the author is regarded as the only reliable guide to its meaning. I should like to explore the idea of reading the Prologue, from the beginning, in this more oblique and folkloric sense, particularly for the benefit of actual readers and women who may be suspicious of absolute presences and especially disinclined to treat this text as authoritative for them.

'In the beginning' (Jn 1.1) itself, I would suggest, may perhaps be read in a different way from the interpretation that says it is a reminder that God is foundational, the grounds as much as the means of creation. In its reference to the Hebrew Bible, it is also a reminder that the arduous work of creation—humanity in the world—narratively speaking led God directly into a risk-laden relational exercise with two different human beings (female and male). It also involved delegation (Gen. 1.28) and trust (Gen. 2.15-17), since God could not himself, apparently, live in or tend to the world. Such an interpretation may or may not lie within the realm of 'authorial intention'. Nevertheless the Prologue may yet perhaps be read as the narrative of a similar risk-laden enterprise; not the proclamation of God's self-sufficiency and ineffability but of dependence on human desire and imagination. This then is an attempt at transforming a myth of patriarchal self-sufficiency brought to birth and nurtured through interpretation of the Prologue.

If the narrator's authority is in question, the reader needs some other clues to the significance of this passage. Within the Gospel of Luke is the story of the Rich Fool. The man is a fool, not because he is rich but

---

19. Cf. Jn 2.11; 6.64; 8.2, 44; 15.27; 16.4.

because he is complacent. He has it all worked out and sown up. His death, according to the text (Lk. 12.21), is God's judgment on the wrong use of his riches. But it is also the punchline of the joke: he forgot that he wasn't going to live forever!

Some have chosen to read the first five verses of John's Gospel as the incomparable poetry of a devout believer.[20] And so it may be. But what if all those inclusive terms that seek to contain or reduce to the darkness of non-existence what lies outside God/Word are read as the setting up of human complacency or dangerous illusions about cosmic or symbolic certainties that, like the Rich Fool's plans, are about to be blown away, necessarily abandoned and submerged in the confusion of human imagination and desire?

To propose this reading is, of course, to have recourse to irony as a focus for interpretation. It is a commonplace of modern literary biblical scholarship that the author of John's Gospel is an accomplished ironist. The reasons why he [*sic*] should be so described are not really very hard to discover given certain ground-rules about how to identify irony. George Macrae[21] defines irony in John's Gospel as a form of literary device to be largely, though not entirely, distinguished from humorous (satire), Socratic (dialectic), Sophoclean (tragic irony), or modern 'metaphysical' irony (a modern ironic vision? Nietzschean Hilarity?).[22] Macrae, among other commentators,[23] limits Johannine irony to something that is relatively straightforward:

> Johannine irony is first of all dramatic irony in that it presumes upon the superior knowledge of the reader to recognise the true perspective within which the Gospel's assertions are ironical.[24]

However, what Macrae sees Johannine irony to have in common with modern metaphysical irony is the view that 'the world itself and the

---

20. See, for example, Lindars, *The Gospel of John*, p. 77. Raymond Brown indulges in similar 'purple prose' in Brown, *The Gospel According to John*, p. 18.

21. George W. Macrae, 'Theology and Irony in the Fourth Gospel', in Mark W.G. Stibbe (ed.), *The Gospel of John as Literature: An Anthology of Twentieth Century Perspectives* (Leiden: E.J. Brill, 1993), pp. 103-14.

22. See David Jasper, *Rhetoric, Power and Community* (London: Macmillan, 1993), pp. 1-13.

23. See, for example, Paul D. Duke, *Irony in the Fourth Gospel* (Atlanta, GA: John Knox Press, 1985).

24. Macrae, 'Theology and Irony', p. 107.

symbols it uses are ambiguous'.[25] Macrae draws the readers' attention to the trial scene and to the figure of Pilate:

> he may represent…the state faced with the option of yielding to the world or confronting the issue of the source of its own authority, or he may represent the Gentile faced with the option of a decision when confronted with Jesus. In any case, Pilate plays the role of an ironical figure.[26]

The sort of irony that I am interested in exploring in my reading of the Prologue, however, is closer to modern metaphysical irony and cannot really be contained within descriptions of what Paul Duke calls 'communicated irony',[27] as it were to gloss Wayne Booth's understanding of 'stable irony' within literature as a whole:

> If there were victims (and there usually were) they were never the implied author (whatever victimized masks he assumed in passing) and they did not include the true implied reader; the reader and author were intended to stand, after their work was done, firmly and securely together.[28]

This would have to refer to the kind of irony within John's Gospel that was transparent to any reader accepting the claims of Christian belief.

Nevertheless, it appears to me that interpretation in a more metaphysically ironical mode can be justified and may be revealing for readers who are disturbed by the insistent authoritative presences to which traditional interpretations of this passage tend to give expression. Appropriately enough, if I treat the claim of these verses (Jn 1.1-18) as if it were made ironically, what first breaks up the balanced poetic text (Jn 1.6)[29] is the appearance of a man, John. John is just an ordinary man (ἄνθρωπος—'man' as a generic masculine, not man as opposed to woman), like any other Adam, Elijah or Samson. His nature whether fleshly or divine is not at issue (nor yet is his gender). He does not come in for the scandal-sheet treatment of Jn 1.14: 'The Word became flesh…' But I am told that he is sent from God (ἀπεσταλμένος παρὰ

---

25. Macrae, 'Theology and Irony', p. 109.

26. Macrae, 'Theology and Irony', p. 110.

27. Duke, *Irony*, p. 19.

28. Wayne C. Booth, *A Rhetoric of Irony* (Chicago: University of Chicago Press, 1974), p. 233.

29. See in Brown, *The Gospel According to John*, pp. 3-4. John the Baptist's contribution to the Prologue is understood as an interruption, to the extent that these verses are parenthesized.

θεοῦ, Jn 1.6). And I am reminded that, whatever I tell myself about cosmic certainties, from the human perspective all there is to work on is the human stage. God may or may not be Creator and sustainer of human life but I do not observe this cosmic activity unmediated. Without the human apostle, messenger, witness (reliable or otherwise) midwife or matchmaker, I cannot get into the place or frame of mind to believe (Jn 1.7) or see (Jn 1.8). No one can get *themselves* born even the first time, yet alone the second.

So the punchline to the joke, the point of the irony, would be that however grand—or totalitarian—our vision of God, we are first and foremost related to God through each other as teachers, guides and lovers. And inherent within that realization is the notion that human relatedness is itself God-defining.

But you might still need some further convincing that focusing on John the Baptist in this passage is an interpretative procedure that has much to commend itself! It is not entirely unprecedented. In his work on John's Gospel, Sjef van Tilborg argues that John the Baptist's relationship to Jesus in the text has, until recently, been given less attention than is actually warranted because of

> the (almost) exclusive focus on the historical reconstruction of the baptiser-movement(s). The studies which explicitly treat John the Baptist…are all historically oriented. The texts of the Johannine Gospel are, therefore, exclusively or mainly seen in so far as they can have possible informative value for such an historical reconstruction.[30]

Narratively speaking, van Tilborg argues, John's words have a priority over the words of Jesus as the Evangelist tells the story, he [*sic*] gives John's relationship to Jesus (especially Jn 1.15-36 and Jn 3.22-36) an affective, even formulative dimension:

> [John] is in a certain sense 'the teacher' who brings his 'disciple' to the marriage; he is present at the feast as the most important guest. The happiness he experiences is a kind of evaluation; there is complete inner agreement. That John (the Baptist), then, uses the same words as Jesus has used before shows that, between these two friends, we have μία ψυχὴ δύο σώμασιν ἐνοικοῦσα, one soul inhabiting two bodies: the Aristotelian ideal of friendship.[31]

---

30. Sjef van Tilborg, *Imaginative Love in John* (Leiden: E.J. Brill, 1993), pp. 59-60.

31. Van Tilborg, *Imaginative Love in John*, p. 77.

My reading of the role of John the Baptist is related to van Tilborg's in its implicit promotion of the significance, for the figure of Jesus, of relational contexts within this Gospel. But I would push the significance of John the Baptist further. It appears that John the Baptist's relationship to his hearers is defined by the narrator as that of witness (Jn 1.7, 15) and also facilitator (Jn 1.7). Yet John's own description of the role he plays in relation to his listeners is, at this point in the Gospel, riddling and largely a matter of denial. 'This was he of whom I said, "He who comes after me ranks before me, for he was before me"' (Jn 1.15). He says that he is not the Christ (Jn 1.20) and answers 'I am not', when the priests and Levites ask if he is Elijah (Jn 1.21). His association with prophecy is ambiguous. At Jn 1.20-21 he denies that he is the prophet[32] and yet his answer to the insistent interrogation of the priests and Levites sent from Jerusalem makes reference to prophetic Scripture (Isa. 40.3), 'I am the voice of one crying in the wilderness "Make straight the way of the Lord" as the prophet Isaiah said' (Jn 1.23). At Jn 1.29-34, he finally and explicitly accepts the description of witness to the Son of God and role of facilitator. But a note of ambiguity remains: 'I myself did not know him; but for this I came baptising with water, that he might be revealed to Israel' (Jn 1.31).

I would argue then, that the man John materializes (Jn 1.6) to challenge the closed system of Jn 1.1-5 with the reminder he presents of the significance of human work, both in the struggle to understand and to interpret divine commissioning (whether his own or Jesus') for his listeners. In other words, this narrative of John the Baptist bears witness—John speaks first as if to authorize Jesus—to the crucial or even prior significance of human participation (Jn 1.29-34) for divine revelation.

Of course, the theme of subversion, of challenge to the ways of the world's knowledge, reception, belief and culture (Jn 1.9-13) is subsequently and most explicitly attached to the figure of Jesus in this Gospel. But within the Prologue, and arguably elsewhere in the Gospel, Jesus' humanity is far more ambivalent than that of John (Jn 1.14a, b). And certainly, here at the beginning of the Gospel, the narrator makes

---

32. See Schnackenburg, *The Gospel According to St. John*, I, pp. 289-90, on the identity of 'the prophet'. He agrees that the precise designation of this term is difficult to pin down, since 'there were in fact various ideas current among the people about the coming of a prophet in the days of salvation'. He suggests, however, a stronger connection with the prophet of Deut. 18.18.

some differentiation between bearing witness to the creative (Jn 1.10), regenerative (Jn 1.12, 13), culturally radical (Jn 1.13) light/Word and the agency of the Word/Son of the Father understood as something particularly invested in Jesus (Jn 1.14-15). Yet the narrative of the Prologue weaves these two stories of witness and agency together in systematic interdependence. Thus, Jn 1.18, 19 seems to bear interpretation along similar lines as at Jn 1.5, 6, and Jn 1.14, 15. Whatever the narrator speaks of certainty and assurance, the witness of John the Baptist is its conclusion and indeed, at Jn 1.15 and Jn 1.19, it is also the resolution and definition of an otherwise invisible or inaudible divinity (Jn 1.10, 11 and Jn 1.18). Even if, following van Tilborg, I take Jn 1.18 as part of John the Baptist's own words and I construct the divine as self-enclosed autism: 'No one has ever seen God/No one has ever seen God the only Son/God, who is in the bosom of the Father' (Jn 1.18), it seems that the revelation of God by the Son: 'he has made him known' (Jn 1.18) is not enough. At Jn 1.19 we read 'And this is the testimony of John'. Again, in terms of the narrative, John's gradual revelation of his own role and that of Jesus (Jn 1.20, 21, 23, 26, 27, 29-34) functions, perhaps, as an ironic parallel, characterized by elusiveness, ambiguity and slow development. It challenges the far less nuanced understanding of Jesus as divine light/Word presented by the narrator in Jn 1.9-14 and at Jn 1.15-18.

5. *A Rhetorical Myth of Feminist Interpretation:*
God as Desiring and Inarticulate

What does this all represent? I suggest that it may illustrate the words of George Macrae:

> Johannine irony shares the view that the world itself and the symbols it
> uses are ambiguous.[33]

The irony that appears outwith the point of view of the narrator is for me, then, the derisive, riddling chicken and egg motif. Which came first, is more fundamental, divine Word or human witness to it, divine glory or human vision of it? And it would have to be situated outwith and beyond the point of view of the authoritative narrator because the joke or riddle is precisely, I am saying, the ironic overturning of any attempt to manhandle the opening 'In the beginning was the Word'

33. Macrae, 'Theology and Irony', p. 109.

into a mere manifestation of stifling religious and intellectual singularity. By introducing the Baptist and his witness, the authority of the narrator is questioned and undermined, the narrator is revealed as the construction of imagination and desire both in structural authoritativeness and imaginative scope. But equally, it becomes possible to read the narrator's words as a commentary on the words and actions of John the Baptist (Jn 1.7-8). After all, what possible reason should we have for listening to words which do not, in any sense, reflect the fecundity of our imaginations or the richness of our desires? They work together. John is unworthy even to untie the thong of Jesus' sandal (Jn 1.15, 27) and he ranks after Jesus but, without his witness, how should the readers and listeners know, in a world that otherwise knows him not, how to read the actions and words of a man who ends up being executed?

I am reading the text of the Prologue in order to reveal a God who is necessarily dependent upon the materiality (Jn 1.14) of both word (witness) and flesh (glorified presence), in order to enter into relationship with humankind. It is, after all, only those who receive and believe in the light whom the divine light is able to empower (Jn 1.12). This is an implication of an orthodox Christian position but it demands a much stronger reading of dependence in which the patriarchal mythology of cosmic presence and divine (masculine) self-sufficiency is not, so to speak, permitted to 'mark the cards'—determine the limits of 'dependence'—before the game begins.

Once again, Sjef van Tilborg's work is suggestive:

> embedded in the imaginary reality of the story as told, the main character of the narrative creates an imaginary world in which he and God appear in a father–son relationship which is accessible only from the imagination of the main character, from the fantasy, the imagery and desires of Jesus.[34]

What van Tilborg suggests, albeit tentatively, is that embedded within this Gospel is the narrative of Jesus' self-exploration. This illustrates, rather well, the implications of my own ironical reading of the Prologue. Van Tilborg's reading of Jesus as divinely accepted humanity is perceptive and persuasive. His Jesus is left entirely on his own to draw his own conclusions about who he is and what he is doing. His cards are unmarked. And, of course, within the narrative of both Prologue and Gospel, his divine authority is derived finally, not from pre-knowledge or signs or from his own words, all of which might be understood to

---

34. Van Tilborg, *Imaginative Love in John*, p. 22.

belong to the narrative of Jesus' own self-exploration and self-reflection, but from the agreement, affirmation or witness of his friends,[35] including John the Baptist.

At this point I want to return to the Prologue and suggest that readers could derive a mythology from it to challenge divine (masculine) presence and self-sufficiency. The new myth would relate to a divine desire for birth and for deliverance from inarticulateness that, in effect, can only be achieved through relatedness and mutual dependence. In other words, the Prologue could perhaps be better read as the epilogue, the conclusion of a narrative in which divine authority is ultimately only able to be articulated through the witnessing words of human women and men.

6. Women Readers?

And what has this reading to do with feminist theory or the concerns of women readers? (Chicken and egg is a nicely feminine metaphor—both in its relationship to maternal birthing and nurturing, and in its relationship to domestic slavery!) The challenge from a feminist perspective is to open out the varieties of acceptable human relatedness that may bear fruit (or bring to birth) in terms of a human understanding of God. This is an alternative to beginning with a notion of God, defined according to the values of patriarchal culture, that can be used still further to limit the types of relatedness that can be seen as potentially God-defining or revealing. Thus it might become the task of the feminist biblical critic, at this point, to create from his or her imagination and desire an interpretation of the Prologue that sees John the Baptist as the proto-incarnate, lending fully human authority to the embryonic divine.

Of course, it might be said that though he is introduced (Jn 1.6) in the Greek of the first century as generic (ἄνθρωπος) and not gendered man (ἀνήρ), he still bears the imprint of a wider patriarchal definition of generic humanity as normatively masculine. My attempts to restore the absent mother in terms of John the Baptist's necessary human priority might appear questionable, given that he is male. But, as Elisabeth Schüssler Fiorenza argues, perhaps we should not be deterred from deactivating 'masculine/feminine gender contextualization in favor of an abstract degenderized reading'[36] provided that we remain aware that

---

35. Jn 1.29, 35, 45; 2.5; 6.68; 11.27; 20.28.
36. Elisabeth Schüssler Fiorenza, *But She Said: Feminist Practices of Biblical Inter-*

non-feminist readers may well try to *re*activate this contextualization. Here, in other words, we should as readers recognize John the Baptist as potentially representative of humanity in both its male and female forms and expressions. And in narrative terms, this interpretation of John the Baptist as a birthing and incubating human, male mother might appear to circumvent some of the more divisive hierarchializing tendencies of orthodox Christian theology. In contrast to the presentation of Jesus' mother in the Gospel of Luke, where divine dependence on humankind is signified in Mary's acceptance of the message sent to her (Lk. 1.38) and of the child in her womb, this necessary dependence in the Prologue is expressed in terms of the giving of a message. The necessary human relatedness refers to a divine need for words and language, and not simply an empty space waiting to be filled up.

7. *Conclusions*

If, speaking rhetorically, this Prologue can be seen as the ironical delimitation of God as desiring and inarticulate divinity, rather than as a mythological tale of pre-existence, cosmic closure or (masculine) divine self-sufficiency, then it is perhaps no longer so important that the first instance of revealing relatedness is in the witness of a man, since there are other witnesses too, some of them women.[37] The narrative priority of John (ἄνθρωπος) is still disturbing, however. This interpretation—as potentially deconstructive of hierarchical dualism between male and female—depends on the underlying identification of the dualisms of divine/human and masculine/feminine in which the divine/masculine and the human/feminine are seen to be mutually dependent. But its implications for relations between male and female have to be formulated quite carefully.

It would be quite simple for such an interpretation to be understood as implying an extremely inequitable mutuality, when the concepts of equity and mutuality are defined, say, in terms of the values of patriarchy. Thus, the biblical texts already contain many instances of the symbolic identification of the divine/human relationship in terms of marriage. Such a relationship undoubtedly reflects elements of interdependence but very often they are interpreted in terms that embody,

---

pretation (Boston: Beacon Press, 1992), p. 200.
    37. Most notably, of course, Martha of Bethany, Jn 11.27.

for example, typically male anxieties about female infidelity or the dangerous 'otherness' of women.[38]

It is for this reason that a reading of the narrator's commentary in the Prologue that entertains the possibility of an ironic focalization, or point of view, is important to my argument. What the narrator bears witness to is the ontological status of the divine but it is, at the same time, a narrative of faith. In terms of the stable, communicated irony of the text, it is faith that things are not as they seem. It is then a reflection of human desire for certainty. And the reason that I believe this description may be charged with irony is indicated in the pattern of this text (Jn 1.1-18) as a whole, by the insistent interruption of a human witness into passages in which it would seem, were the Prologue simply concerned with stating the ontological truth about a self-sufficient divinity without irony, no further witness would be actually required. The implications of this irony then, for the issue of identification between divine/masculine and human/feminine, is that it is able to relativize or destabilize certainties described within the passage as pertaining to the divine. Mutual dependence itself lies revealed within the realm of desire and not ontological certainty. There is everything still to play for.

> So, on this interpretation, is our theological existence...delivered up to the impulses and whims of the moment, no longer knowing anything except what can just as well be found outside the canon...?[39]

Does it make sense to talk about being misled into the tyranny of arbitrary interpretations?[40] My anxiety is evident. And yet there are again some nuances of interpretation that seem appropriate to note. The implicit violence of canonicity—whether in terms of scriptural texts or of their interpretation—is no better an extreme. The combination of canonical texts and canonical interpretation has nourished some powerful configurations of the world, humankind and God that arguably continue to serve predominantly patriarchal values and culture. These, I believe, have to be questioned. Given the understanding of interpretation that I have adopted, the product of the interaction between text and interpreter/reader need not conform to any one particular form

---

38. See for example, Mieke Bal, *Lethal Love: Feminist Literary Readings of Biblical Love Stories* (Bloomington: Indiana University Press, 1987), especially her analysis of the Samson narratives, Judg. 13–16.

39. Käsemann, *The Testament of Jesus*, p. 77.

40. Käsemann, *The Testament of Jesus*, p. 77.

of rhetorical mythology, though it cannot exist outwith any. What au-
thorizes or guarantees such interpretations is, fundamentally, the relations of power exercised by the interpreter/reader. Like the inarticulate
divinity of my rhetorically constructed interpretation of the Prologue,
the text is, of itself, entirely mute and powerless. Which is to leave the
final responsibility of not turning the text into a whore (male or female)
with those who, so to speak, pick it up.

8

Flesh Insights on the Prologue of John's Gospel

ὅσοι δὲ ἔλαβον αὐτόν, ἔδωκεν αὐτοῖς ἐξουσίαν τέκνα θεοῦ γενέσθαι, τοῖς πιστεύουσιν εἰς τὸ ὄνομα αὐτοῦ, οἳ οὐκ ἐξ αἱμάτων οὐδὲ ἐκ θελήματος σαρκὸς οὐδὲ ἐκ θελήματος ἀνδρὸς ἀλλ᾽ ἐκ θεοῦ ἐγεννήθησαν. Καὶ ὁ λόγος σὰρξ ἐγένετο (Jn 1.12-14).

1. *A Second 'New' Reading of the Prologue*

In this chapter, I want to give a second reading of this biblical passage that also recognizes the traces of an 'otherness' within the patriarchal context. This 'otherness' is, as I have already said, very often symbolized by woman and the feminine carrying a devalued sense. Again, within this chapter, my method could be broadly termed 'deconstructive' in the sense that I concentrate on the more obviously devalued sense of the term 'flesh' at Jn 1.13 as the key to its significance within the incarnational statement of Jn 1.14: 'And the Word became flesh'.

2. *Word Become Flesh*

Within the Prologue, Word (λόγος) is acknowledged as creative and powerful in an ultimate sense (Jn 1.3: 'all things were made through him, and without him was not anything made'). But then at Jn 1.14, Word becomes flesh (σάρξ). I believe that the attitude of Christian readers to the concept of σάρξ has always been extremely ambivalent. Whether σάρξ implies a quality of material sensuality, an attitude of fundamental opposition to God or even a reference to the earthly sphere that is only a source of sin if the Christian trusts in it alone, I believe that these definitions rarely, if ever, escape entirely from negative connotations. There is then, at first glance, some cause to balk at the verse Jn 1.14. And, of course, it is interesting that this passage has retained its place at the core of a canonical text. So what exactly is going on?

Divine Incarnation as a theological concept has always disturbed Christian thinkers and readers in spite of fifth-century efforts to resolve difficulties by bringing in the doctrinal formulation of Christ's two natures.[1] And it seems to me that this sense of unease or anxiety, both for Christian thinkers in general and for readers of John's Prologue, has a good deal to do with the phallogocentric context in which interpreters are trying to define meaning or truth by excluding, marginalizing or devaluing—as feminine—whatever they cannot articulate or control.

Some feminist analysis identifies the determination[2] of the divine Word as being essentially masculine. On this basis, it makes sense to argue that the anxiety generated by a doctrine of divine Incarnation is related to the perceived dangers of contaminating and confusing the singular masculine identity of the divine with feminine-identified flesh and thus setting up some sort of unavoidable multiplicity. Multiplicity would challenge the very identity of God as essentially different from humankind and, crucially, different in the sense of an ascription of value—being good for example.

The reason for the symbolic identification of 'flesh' as feminine has clearly to do with the bodily and material site of human sexual desire, fragility and subjection to death. Feminist writers and commentators argue that the roots of the association lie in perceptions of woman as connected with male sexual desire but also with birth and nurturing,[3]

1.   The definition of the Person of Christ agreed in Chalcedon at the Fourth Ecumenical Council of 451 CE was of two natures—divine and human—which were inseparable but not confused. It was a decision drawn up, in part, against the teaching of Eutychus (373–454) that the humanity of Christ was not consubstantial with the rest of humankind, which orthodox Christians took to imply the impossibility of human redemption through Christ.

2.   For a treatment of the masculinity of orthodox Christian teaching about God, see, for example, Luce Irigaray, 'Divine Women', in her *Sexes and Genealogies* (trans. Gillian C. Gill; London: Routledge, 1993), pp. 57-72 (61-62): 'man has sought out a unique male God. God has been created out of man's gender. He scarcely sets limits within Himself and between Himself: He is father, son, spirit. Man has not allowed himself to be defined by another gender: the female. His unique God is assumed to correspond to the human race (*genre humain*), which we know is not neuter or neutral from the point of view of the difference of the sexes.' In this essay, Irigaray's point is that women cannot find their own 'divine' potential by contemplating such a uniquely masculine divinity.

3.   See, for example, Rosemary Radford Ruether, *Sexism and God-Talk* (London: SCM Press, 1983), especially Chapter 3, 'Woman, Body and Nature', pp. 72-92 .

with sickness and death. Women, traditionally, are those who deal with the very young, the sick and the very old. These associations are then extended to the sometimes terrifying power of an uncontrolled nature, which deals out life and death, as opposed to male-identified institutions of culture and law by which that power is, to some extent, tamed.[4]

These sorts of associations are illustrated, for example, in interpretations of the myth of Adam and Eve. In one example, from his commentary on Genesis, Philo argued that before the creation of Eve, the bodily component of Adam was kept under the control of his spiritual self but that her creation represented his separation into soul and a lower self, susceptible to sexual desire, which

> is the beginning of iniquities and transgressions, and it is owing to this that men have exchanged their previously immortal and happy existence for one which is mortal and full of misfortune.[5]

And, within the Church, the story of Adam and Eve has sometimes been debased into an aetiology of evil with Eve as scapegoat:

> You are the Devil's gateway. You are the unsealer of that forbidden tree. You are the first deserter of the divine law. You are she who persuaded him whom the Devil was not valiant enough to attack. You destroyed so easily God's image, man. On account of your desert, that is death, even the Son of God had to die.[6]

What I am suggesting is that the incarnational text of the Prologue is itself representative of a multiplicity that many interpreters find exceptionally difficult to cope with. In interpretative practices, I believe that they have usually sought to disguise or confine the difficulty by claiming, when it suits the argument, that a feminine-identified 'flesh' rather than an extremely negative category or even the absolute lack of any value to the point of exclusion is really a category of relatively benign neutrality. However, I would go on to suggest that a reading of the Incarnate Word in terms of a radical and gendered difference retains sufficient coherence to challenge readings that would resolve the difficulty into yet one more form of divine masculine singularity.

---

4.   See, for example, Sherry Ortner's influential essay 'Is Female to Male as Nature Is to Culture?', reprinted in M. Rosaldo and L. Lamphere (eds.), *Woman Culture and Society* (Stanford, CA: Stanford University Press, 1974 [1972]).

5.   Philo, *Quaest. in Gen.* 46.53.

6.   Tertullian, *De cultu feminarum* 1.1.

So I have argued that σάρξ is invariably read as somehow or other negative and that it is associated with the symbols of woman and the feminine which, within the phallogocentric vision, constitute the definition of what is to be valued positively—that is to say that whatever is male or masculine-identified is defined by its not being, or its being superior to, whatever is female or feminine-identified. However, some readers might still need convincing that this view of σάρξ (flesh) genuinely represents the use of the term in the Prologue. Some commentators, for example, have argued that the concept of σάρξ is essentially neutral—capable of being *both* corrupted *and* redeemed. They might say that to think otherwise is to fall into a dualism that has never been a part of orthodox Christian anthropology.

The word σάρξ is probably associated most strongly within the New Testament world, with the Pauline and 'deutero-Pauline' literature. This—rightly or wrongly—has not had a 'great deal of street credibility with feminists'.[7] Not unnaturally, feminists tend to be disturbed by a commonly perceived 'Pauline' attitude towards women. This is seen as an attempt to reduce women to the troubling objects of male sexual appetite—marry or burn[8]—or to align their role within the early Church to their role within the broader patriarchal societies of the first-century world—covering their heads[9] and keeping silence.[10]

In a recent study of Pauline[11] literature, however, the Jewish writer Daniel Boyarin argues that the word σάρξ does not have to be read in a

7.   Angela West, 'Sex and Salvation: A Christian Feminist Bible Study on 1 Corinthians 6.12–7.39', in Ann Loades (ed.), *Feminist Theology: A Reader* (London: SPCK, 1990), p. 72.

8.   1 Cor. 7.9: 'But if they cannot exercise self-control, they should marry. For it is better to marry than to be aflame with passion.'

9.   1 Cor. 11.5: 'but any woman who prays or prophesies with her head unveiled dishonours her head' (i.e. her husband).

10.   1 Tim. 4.12: 'I permit no woman to teach or to have authority over men; she is to keep silent.' It should be noted that few modern biblical critics would account this text as part of the original or authentic Pauline material in the New Testament. (Susanne Heine even goes so far as to claim that the Pastoral Epistles—of which 1 Timothy is one—are, because of the attitudes towards women that they evince, self-evidently beyond the pale of Christian praxis. See Susanne Heine, *Women and Early Christianity: Are the Feminist Scholars Right?* [trans. John Bowden; London: SCM Press, 1987], p. 153.)

11.   This is a convenient form of reference to a collection of epistles preserved in

way which supports this popularist conception of Pauline misogyny. He believes that σάρξ belongs within a complex body/spirit framework which combines a number of oppositions.[12] But Boyarin also believes that this apparently dualistic framework does not necessarily imply that Paul regards σάρξ or its symbolic representation in terms of woman and the feminine as inherently evil.

According to Boyarin's reading of this Pauline material, then, σάρξ functions—*within* a context of a common, persistent and widespread Western dualism[13]—in a broadly figurative or allegorical sense. The Pauline material constructs an opposition—in which σάρξ is one term —that is rhetorical, illustrative and illuminating. Yet this opposition is not something to be energetically reified. That is to say, in using κατὰ σάρκα ('according to the flesh'), Paul 'refers to an ordinary level of human existence that is, to be sure, lower than that of the spirit but not by any means stigmatized as being evil, venal, or without reference to God'.[14]

Perhaps it is possible then, to argue that readers may understand σάρξ within the Prologue of John's Gospel in the same way. That is to say, perhaps, that the narrative makes a theological argument—a statement of a hierarchy of values: σάρξ is a *neutral* lower term. Divine λόγος and human σάρξ represent a hierarchy of values belonging to a fundamentally metaphorical context in which metaphors refer to spiritual realities, not material qualities. Thus λόγος becoming σάρξ would indicate a gracious summation, a glorious scooping up of the human into the divine without implying anything about the value of actual bodies.

In a passage that is reminiscent of Paul's discussions of the claims of Torah,[15] gifts of grace and truth (Jn 1.16, 17) are associated, in the Prologue, with Jesus Christ in a form that seems to hint at an opposition of

the New Testament and typically regarded as substantially the work of one author. It does not imply any particular theory about who 'Paul' was.

12. See Daniel Boyarin, *A Radical Jew: Paul and the Politics of Identity* (Berkeley: University of California Press, 1994), p. 78. First of all, for example, he describes a biblically attested opposition—one that can be read within the Christian Old Testament as well as the New—between, for example, 'in the flesh' and 'in the heart'. Then he outlines another opposition between 'the letter' and 'the spirit'. Finally there is the very Hellenistic opposition—much more unambiguously related to Platonic dualism—of 'outer' and 'inner'.

13. See Boyarin, *A Radical Jew*, p. 85.

14. Boyarin, *A Radical Jew*, p. 72.

15. See Paul's comments on the Law in 2 Cor. 3, especially vv. 7-18.

a similar nature between the gifts of the Word that are associated with true—inner—vision and revelation, and those received through Moses and, as it were, the outer letter of the Law. In the Prologue, as in the passage in 2 Corinthians, this gift of the Law is contrasted with the grace and truth that come through Jesus Christ but not so strongly that it may not still be understood as gift, perhaps of a lesser or intermediary nature (Jn 1.17).

Other oppositions within the Prologue featuring the concept of σάρξ, however, seem less amenable to analysis in these terms. At Jn 1.13, children born of God are contrasted with children born of the will of the flesh. And in this Johannine context (Jn 1.13), σάρξ certainly *appears* to imply something beyond the merely rhetorical. Those who have been empowered to become 'children' of God are clearly contrasted with the blindness and indifference of the rejecting world of humankind (Jn 1.10-13). They are distinguished emphatically from children born of the will of the flesh in a sense that is similar to the sort of opposition suggested at Jn 3.5-6, which has consequences of the utmost significance for their ultimate destiny. There is an implication that birth in the flesh is not simply a lesser term, commended like the Law as a gift,[16] but rather a term implying emptiness and having no positive significance at all. Without the spirit, no one will enter the kingdom: ἐὰν μή τις γεννηθῇ ἐξ ὕδατος καὶ πνεύματος, οὐ δύναται εἰσελθεῖν εἰς τὴν βασιλείαν τοῦ θεοῦ. τὸ γεγεννημένον ἐκ τῆς σαρκὸς σάρξ ἐστιν, καὶ τὸ γεγεννημένον ἐκ τοῦ πνεύματος πνεῦμά ἐστιν. ('unless one is born of water and the Spirit, he cannot enter the kingdom of God. That which is born of the flesh is flesh, and that which is born of the Spirit is spirit').

In this chapter I shall argue—against the broad direction of Boyarin's definition—that the predominant and underlying association of the word σάρξ in the Prologue is with the symbols of woman and the feminine, representing precisely the devalued terms within any scale of values determined by a phallogocentric context. In other words, it is not that the Pauline usage Boyarin suggests is dualistic in a simple misogynistic sense but that gender and gender identification or association are being employed to mark value up (or down) across the board. In the

16. Raymond Brown reads Jn 1.17 in this way, linking reference to Moses here with what he describes as 'honorific' references to Moses at Jn 1.14; 3.14; 5.46. See Brown, *The Gospel According to John I–XII: A New Translation with Introduction and Commentary* (AB, 29; New York: Doubleday, 1966), p. 16.

case of Boyarin's analysis, moreover, by absorbing all the elements of signification within the flesh/spirit dualism into the figurative/allegorical mode of better and worse rather than good and evil, the gender-identifying process may be clearly observed since it has, in Boyarin's way of looking at flesh, effectively deprived the feminine-identified bodily and material aspect of flesh of expression altogether. This process seems actually more exclusive than a simple spiritual/material dualism. That is to say that denying the relationship between 'flesh' and whatever, in the common dualistic terms of modern Western culture, has been laid out as absolutely negative could be seen as an attempt to eradicate the trace of the 'otherness' symbolized by the feminine altogether, in order to replace it with the male-defined 'female' sign of devaluation or valuelessness.

In summary, then, a definition of σάρξ such as Boyarin offers within the Pauline material of the New Testament appears attractive because it offers some resistance to interpretative traditions that do play up the dualistic relationship of flesh and spirit to the disadvantage of actual women. Dualistic traditions of interpreting σάρξ as female-identified and in opposition to a male-identified πνεῦμα have clearly supported the marginalization and even demonization of women as representatives of an earth-bound, evil materialism. On the other hand, the attempt to neutralize the dualism by regarding the opposite term identified as feminine as merely 'rhetorical' or 'allegorical'—a matter of outlining a hierarchy in a merely metaphorical sense—also runs into problems from a feminist point of view. It cannot escape the gender-identification which is still being employed to describe the comparative value of the two terms. Moreover, it ultimately fails to recognize the sense in which 'otherness' might represent an actual presence, albeit one that cannot be fully articulated or controlled.

Commentators on John's Gospel have been forced to define the word explicitly within the Prologue where its use at Jn 1.13 appears to be different from its use at Jn 1.14. The definitions of the word and the reasons given for this apparent discrepancy are instructive for a feminist critic and reader.

At Jn 1.13, 'flesh' appears to carry a negative inference, being—as it seems—related to generation, but clearly dissociated from the power to become, to be engendered as, children of God who are: 'οὐδὲ ἐκ θελήματος σαρκὸς...ἐγεννήθησαν' ('born...neither of the will of the flesh'). And yet, at Jn 1.14, 'flesh' is the very word used when the divine

Word becomes human: Καὶ ὁ λόγος σὰρξ ἐγένετο... ('And the word became flesh...').

In a number of modern biblical commentaries, readers attempt to play down any contrast that might be perceived between 'flesh' at Jn 1.13 and 'flesh' at Jn 1.14. The reason for this appears to be related to a desire to protect the Word at Jn 1.14 from the suggestion that becoming flesh actually draws the divine Word into the disturbing realm of the feminine-identified 'flesh' regarded as evil and which, at Jn 1.13, it might be seen to do. At Jn 1.13, Raymond Brown, for example, translates σάρξ in conjunction with desire ἐκ θελήματος σαρκὸς, ('of the will of the flesh') in such a way that he claims, like Boyarin in his work on the Pauline material, that 'flesh' retains a complexion of neutrality in parallel with the Hebrew expression 'flesh and blood' that is said to be equivalent to 'man' rather than 'a man'.[17] Brown goes on to define σάρξ at Jn 1.14[18] as a term representing, once again, the 'whole man' clearly distinguished from 'a man'.

So, attempts are made to disguise the more profoundly disturbing implications of flesh by a general trend towards interpreting 'flesh' in the context of both Jn 1.13 and Jn 1.14 as belonging to a metaphorical duality which indicates simply a hierarchy of values. Thus, for example, Margaret Davies links Jn 1.12-13 to a reading of the conversation between Jesus and Nicodemus (Jn 3.1-21). She argues that the narrator intends us to see that Nicodemus is making a mistake by apparently taking Jesus' remarks about the need to be re-born literally: 'How can a man be born when he is old? Can he enter a second time into his mother's womb and be born?' (Jn 3.4). But she goes on to suggest that

17. Since Brown was writing this in 1966, before self-consciousness about gender became more widespread in works of biblical criticism, it is not quite clear what this implies, but it seems to suggest some distinction between becoming human in a general or typical sense (assuming such an idea is coherent), and becoming a single particular—and presumably gendered—individual.

Feminist theory, in conjunction with various modern critiques of subjectivity, poses the question of what exactly 'being human' in this neutral sense implies. Most feminist writers and philosophers argue that, in the past, such expressions of generic humanity, being defined androcentrically, referred to the characteristic aspirations, problems and anxieties of men rather than women. See, for example, Simone de Beauvoir, *The Second Sex* (Harmondsworth: Penguin Books, 1972), p. 16: 'Thus humanity is male and man defines woman not in herself but as relative to him; she is not regarded as an autonomous being'.

18. Brown, *The Gospel According to John*, p. 12.

Nicodemus's mistake is not really to interpret literally when he should interpret metaphorically but to miss the significance of that metaphor which places greater value on the spiritual than on the physical or fleshly as suggested, she says, at Jn 1.12-13.[19]

However, Davies's interpretation of flesh at Jn 1.14 is related, in her words, to the particular human existence of the Word in his 'vulnerability and mortality'.[20] From this description, it would appear that the utter futility of physical birth indicated at Jn 1.13 ought to be challenged since it is a necessary part of the process of Incarnation. Her reading should perhaps be interpreted in the same light as that of Rudolf Schnackenburg. Schnackenburg reads the distinction between 'flesh' at Jn 1.13 and Jn 1.14 as a distinction between birth as a sexual and—as he implies by his references to the book of *Enoch*[21]—a *defiling* process and the miraculous birth through God, a birth that is, perhaps, to be linked to Christian baptism in apologetic or even polemical mode. When it comes to Jn 1.14, however, Schnackenburg contents himself with stating that σάρξ here has no relationship with 'the notion of flesh as sinful, inclined to sin or fettered by sin'.[22] Without explaining precisely why the implication of defiling sexuality and sin has been dropped, Schnackenburg describes the sense of 'flesh' in Jn 1.14 as the 'typical human mode of being'[23] characterized as a participation in transience and perishability,[24] the 'typically human mode of being, as it were, in contrast to all that is divine and spiritual'. And here a quite definite distinction is made between 'flesh' understood as weak and 'flesh' understood as 'sinful' which Schnackenburg argues is an inference belonging to the theology of the Qumran sect and which comes to dominate Pauline thinking.[25] Both C.K. Barrett and Barnabas Lindars favour this sense in which 'flesh' refers to a contrast between humankind and God. And again, both appear anxious not to imply that there is any 'negative' implication. Of Jn 1.13, Lindars writes:

19. Margaret Davies, *Rhetoric and Reference in the Fourth Gospel* (JSNTSup, 69; Sheffield: JSOT Press, 1992), p. 363.

20. Davies, *Rhetoric and Reference*, p. 45.

21. See Rudolf Schnackenburg, *The Gospel According to St. John* (trans. K. Smyth; 3 vols.; New York: Herder & Herder, 1968), I, p. 264.

22. Schnackenburg, *The Gospel According to St. John*, I, p. 267.

23. Schnackenburg, *The Gospel According to St. John*, I, p. 267.

24. Schnackenburg, *The Gospel According to St. John*, I, p. 267.

25. Schnackenburg, *The Gospel According to St. John*, I, p. 267 n. 171.

the will of the flesh means the impulse of man's natural endowment, and so refers to sexual desire. There is no suggestion, however, that flesh is inherently evil; in biblical usage it is applied to the createdness, and therefore weakness, of human or animal nature in contrast with God (cf. Isa. 31.3).[26]

In a similar vein, C.K. Barrett concludes that at Jn 1.13:

σάρξ in John is not evil in itself (see the next verse...), but stands for humanity over against God.[27]

In summary then, these modern biblical commentators appear to want the word σάρξ to function as a reference to humankind or to human existence in its absolute distinction from divinity and the life within the generation or gift of God. But they also wish to deny that it refers to any fundamental difference or distinction that would imply a really radical modification of the divine in order to make sense. In other words, I am asking whether this refusal to go beyond neutrality in defining 'flesh' is simply a blind? If humankind and human existence are insistently regarded as distinct and different from the divine life of the Creator Spirit to which we should aspire, how can humankind or human existence really amount to anything positive? The answer must surely be that to make such reservations any more explicit would, at the same time, raise some exceptionally difficult and disturbing questions about the nature of the Incarnation—the Word become flesh.

---

26. Barnabas Lindars, *The Gospel of John* (NCB Commentary; Grand Rapids: Eerdmans, 1972), p. 92.

27. See C.K. Barrett, *The Gospel According to St John: An Introduction with Commentary and Notes on the Greek Text* (London: SPCK, 2nd edn, 1978 [1955]), p. 164. So also Schnackenburg, *The Gospel According to St. John*, I, p. 263. Schnackenburg sees Jn 1.13 as an emphatic, threefold description of 'the World', to be contrasted with the 'utterly supernatural work of God in *creating children*' (my emphasis). Ernst Haenchen, for example, sees Jn 1.12-13 as an insertion, which he attributes to the last editor, or 'redactor', of the text. These verses are simply an attempt to emphasize the point that one does not become a Christian by a natural process of procreation but by virtue of an act of God. Theological speculation is therefore seen to be unnecessary, the difficulty is caused simply by clumsiness. See Ernst Haenchen, *John: A Commentary on the Gospel of John* (2 vols.; eds. Robert W. Funk and Ulrich Busse; trans. Robert W. Funk; Philadelphia: Fortress Press, 1984), from p. 118. Such an argument, apart from raising questions about the convenience of editorial additions for getting one out of a tight interpretative corner, does not address the substantive issue of how the meaning of flesh is to be taken, given its resonance in such differing contexts.

3. 'Σάρξ' *and its Evil Associates*

If σάρξ characterizes something particularly defining about humanity or the distinction between humanity and divinity, in what more precisely does this distinction consist? Barrett assumes that the Word could not become something 'evil'. But within the brief summary I have already given of some recent biblical analysis there are traces of an anxiety that the word σάρξ carries within it the possibility of a pejorative significance. This pejorative sense is not attached, in the minds of commentators, to the apparently synonymous term ἄνθρωπος which appears repeatedly within the passage (Jn 1.1-18) as a whole. Commentators would undoubtedly have been spared embarrassment had this second generic term for mankind [*sic*] been used at Jn 1.14.

But my argument would be that the distinction between ἄνθρωπος and σάρξ is significant precisely *because* σάρξ introduces associations based upon the fundamental perception of an anomalous (dangerous/repulsive?) but also quite unavoidable (necessary/formative?) area of experience, represented and symbolized by women and the feminine.[28] Arguably, it is difficult to articulate this experience because it must be done by means of the defining reverse and because it is the 'outside' or 'beyond' of the universe defined in phallogocentric terms. This universe of meaning achieves shape and form in relation to what is excluded but not thereby altogether eliminated. Arguably, this exclusion is never complete or secure and that is why there is always an anxiety attached to the use of σάρξ—the feminine-identified register of that unavoidable but excluded element—in conjunction with the Word.

4. *The Prologue*

Perhaps, however, there is a simpler method of reading the Prologue, and the particular summary of Jn 1.14 with its troubling juxtaposition of Word and flesh, in order to discover liberating interpretations for womankind? Perhaps the text is more directly and explicitly offering a

---

28. Interestingly, in his study of the Pauline literature, Daniel Boyarin draws attention to two of the metaphorical senses of 'flesh' allowed by the Bible and Jewish usage: the penis (to be circumcised), and kinship. While such usages do not have any automatically pejorative inference, it is notable that both the penis and the concept of kinship are necessarily related to the bodily roles of women and the symbolic difference of the feminine. See Boyarin, *A Radical Jew*, p. 67.

critique of cultural forms oppressive to women. Taken as a whole, the text of the Prologue could be understood, as Daniel Boyarin understands the corpus of Pauline literature, to imply a theological vision with radical implications for *transcending* differences of gender.[29]

There may be grounds, for example, for reading within the Prologue a radical challenge to cultural barriers such as those that have been set up on the basis of gender. Certainly, within the Gospel of John as a whole, a number of women play roles of central significance as apostles and witnesses.[30] Moreover, the new standard imposed in the Johannine community to which, it is assumed, this Gospel has been addressed[31] is one merely of belief and reception. A remarkably open 'generic' reading of the passage is possible in which:

> There was a human being (Jn 1.6 ἐγένετο ἄνθρωπος ['There was a hu/man']), sent to witness to one who was already the life/light of hu/mankind (Jn 1.4 φῶς τῶν ἀνθρώπων ['light of hu/mankind']), so

29. See Boyarin, *A Radical Jew*, p. 195. Boyarin argues that at 1 Cor. 11.1-16, for example, Paul distinguishes between androgyny on the level of the spirit and the hierarchical construction of gender difference in contemporary cultural terms: 'Another way of saying this is that Paul holds that ontologically—according to the spirit—there is a permanent change in the status of gender at baptism, but insofar as people are still living in their unredeemed bodies, gender transcendence is *not yet* fully realized on the social level. Perhaps, we might say, that final realization awaits the Parousia.' He argues further that this vision had social consequences—women were undoubtedly pursuing active ministry within the contemporary Church—but that the fundamental underlying dualism of his intellectual framework, as it were, 'took the pressure off' pursuing the issue in more practical terms.

30. See, for example, the mission of the Samaritan woman (Jn 4.39), and of Mary Magdalene, known according to tradition as the *Apostola Apostolorum* (Jn 20.17-18). This tradition is thought to date back at least as far as the work of Hippolytus (c. 170–236). See Susan Haskins, *Mary Magdalen* (London: Harper-Collins, 1993), p. 65. See also Martha's confession (Jn 11.27).

31. For recent theories on the nature of the Johannine community, see the comprehensive account given by John Ashton in *Understanding the Fourth Gospel* (Oxford: Oxford University Press, 1991). A summary of the general direction of his treatment is contained within the following quotation: 'The Fourth Gospel was neither a missionary tract destined for Jews or Gentiles nor a work of theology intended as 'a possession for ever'. In its present form, and in any recognizable earlier version or edition, it was written for the encouragement and edification of a group of 'Jewish' Christians who needed to assert their identity over against the local synagogue, which was almost certainly where the Christian group had taken its rise' (p. 111).

that all/hu/mans (Jn 1.7 πάντες),[32] might believe, every hu/man (Jn 1.9 πάντα ἄνθρωπον ['all hu/mankind']) being enlightened. We are assured that, of this 'all hu/mankind',[33] those who have received and believed have the power to become children (Jn 1.12 τέκνα ['children']) not sons (υἱοί) of God.

Indeed, it is perhaps possible to push even further in this direction and to see, in the Prologue, a *resistance* to the cultural barriers erected against women within patriarchy. And what gives such a possibility even greater plausibility is the extended 'unpacking' of the notion of becoming children of God found at Jn 1.13.[34] The children of God are not children defined in terms of blood or lineage, in terms of gender or in terms of a man's[35] desire to satisfy or perpetuate himself. On this reading, the idea of a child/human and thus also, by implication, of a parent/God presented in Jn 1.13 may also be said to define a relationship that rejects, specifically, some of the key culturally determined impositions on actual female existence. In other words, this relationship is not to be conditioned by the sort of ideas of biological determinism (Jn 1.13 ἐξ αἱμάτων ['of blood']), that have been employed to make women prisoners of their sexual biology or by bourgeois patriarchal constructions based upon the acquisition of property and the need to possess it in perpetuity (Jn 1.13 ἐκ θελήματος ἀνδρὸς ['of the will of a man (*sic*)']) or by the sorts of cultural definition that turn women into a means of satisfying male sexual desire (Jn 1.13 ἐκ θελήματος σαρκὸς ['of the will of the flesh']). On this understanding of Jn 1.13, God's parenthood and the childhood of the receiver and believer function together as a critique of the commonest forms of women's oppression within patriarchy.

Within this passage, then, I have read a strong impetus to dismantle the sort of cultural barriers that might be seen as excluding women from the new community. By setting up a single standard or condition for inclusion (Jn 1.12) all other forms of selection are implicitly denied

32. Nom. pl. masc.—leaves it open as to whether ἄνθρωπος or ἀνηρ is implied. However, the former perhaps is more likely, given a comparison with Jn 1.9 πάντα ἄνθρωπον.

33. Jn 1.12 ὅσοι usually goes with πάντες/πάντα. See Haenchen, *John*, I, p. 118.

34. It should be noted that there are a number of biblical critics who regard the verses Jn 1.12-13 as, possibly, editorial additions. See, for example, comments of Schnackenburg, *The Gospel According to St. John*, I, p. 265.

35. Jn 1.13 ἐκ θελήματος **ἀνδρὸς**—of the will of *man*, that is, *not woman*.

legitimacy—at least in theory. In its description of God's new children (Jn 1.13), this impression is reinforced. These are children related to a parent in a new way and one that is not dependent upon the patriarchal cultural expectations that have, typically, fallen so heavily on the lives of women.

However, quite apart from the question of how 'liberated' the earliest Johannine community actually allowed its female members to be, there is another criticism that can be levelled against this reading. If this interpretation of Jn 1.12-13 is chosen as a model for human transcendence and related to socially radical strains within the Christian reading tradition—by which term I include the texts of John's Gospel itself—it cannot altogether escape the criticism that it supports the fundamental normativity of a redeemed humanity as masculine. In Jn 1.13 human engendering—paradigmatically to do with women's biology, work and worth—is presented as irrelevant to the business of becoming God's children. Being a woman, as generally defined within patriarchal culture, is no bar to becoming a child of God but it carries with it absolutely no positive significance either.

It may be more important to recognize the sense in which the Prologue continues to reflect an overriding symbolism of gender related to a concept of difference and implicated in the perception of hierarchies and the exercise of power within a patriarchal society. It is this overriding symbolism, I believe, that offers some explanation of women's many and *varying* experiences within the Christian communities to whose scriptural canon the Gospel of John belongs.

What I am saying is that the above interpretation of Jn 1.12-13 in terms of social radicalism still appears to operate within the same patriarchal and hierarchical frame of symbolic reference in which what is symbolically represented as associated with women and the feminine is given a lower value—or no value at all—in relation to that which is associated with men and the masculine. However, when an interpretation of 'flesh' at Jn 1.12-13, understood in these hierarchical terms, is taken in conjunction with 'flesh' as understood at Jn 1.14, something potentially more challenging occurs.

A number of biblical commentators suggest that the word σάρξ at Jn 1.14 represents a greater degree of palpability or reality,[36] or a more convincing description of what it means to be 'a man among men, a

---

36. See, for example, Schnackenburg, *The Gospel According to St. John*, I, from p. 268.

person among persons'[37] than could be conveyed, for example, by the use of the word ἄνθρωπος. I have argued, of course, that what gives it this greater density and weight is its associations with the symbolic 'feminine' and what that represents of sexuality, bodiliness, the maternal and the material and also with death, all viewed with anxiety or ambivalence. And yet, all this is recognized as structurally inescapable and unavoidable because it represents the defining reverse side of the phallogocentric symbolic universe—that which such definitions *necessarily* exclude or devalue.[38]

Within traditions of reading, the Prologue seems to partake of a certain dualism in which there is a spiritual and a non-spiritual context. In becoming 'flesh' (Jn 1.14), the Word is—to imply no more—revealed in the world of spiritual darkness, characterized, in the Prologue, by human sexual generation and kinship. The Word offers to those who receive and believe an enrichment that is defined, in opposition to this, as spiritual birth and the reception of spiritual gifts. And yet to do this the Word becomes 'flesh'. I believe that this entry into a sphere already negatively constructed represents a recognition of multiplicity within the experience of being human. I think too that it represents a recognition that dualistic boundaries or the common characterization of dualistic spheres in terms of a symbolic hierarchy of gender within patriarchal contexts cannot contain or do justice to this multiplicity. In other words, the Prologue (Jn 1.12-14) functions, whether 'narratively' (what the Word does/becomes) or in theological terms (what the Word constitutes), as a problematizing of any differential hierarchy as, for example, between the bodily and the spiritual.

That this anarchic, boundary-crossing feature of human experience, that perhaps prevents the hardening of patriarchy's symbolic arteries, can realistically be read into Jn 1.14 as a summary of the Prologue may perhaps be determined, more precisely, by examining the word σάρξ through its links with bread and meat in John 6.

---

37. Haenchen, *John*, I, p. 119.

38. To illustrate this notion in cultural terms, we may say, for example, that while, in patriarchal societies, the work and roles ascribed to women tend to carry less status, these are nevertheless represented as an integral part of the social fabric in terms, particularly, of marriage and fertility.

5. *Eating the Flesh That Is of no Avail (John 6)*

The word σάρξ has one other major significance within the Gospel of John which is in its relation to the body of Jesus that must be eaten (Jn 6.53). This is usually interpreted as a reference to Eucharistic feeding.[39] Feeding is, of course, culturally related to the role of women but also, as the discourse within John 6 appears to emphasize, to the nourishment of the body and, within the metaphorical terms of possible readings of this chapter, nourishment of the soul or spirit.

In Jn 1.14, the Word becomes flesh—a term which is vigorously defended against the taint of some unspecified 'evil' which I have argued is ultimately related to the feminine as a male-defined symbol of multiplicity or heterogeneity that challenges the singular masculine determination of God detectable within many reading traditions. In John 6, as in the Prologue, commentators resist interpretations that suggest the term 'flesh' has momentarily escaped from the determining significance of the spiritual which excludes or relegates the bodily as the lower term within a dualistic hierarchy.

In Jn 6.53, the flesh that is to be eaten to sustain life is contained by commentators within Eucharistic descriptions which limit the bodily 'flesh' to a term within a context (the liturgical practice of the early Church) that has already promoted 'spiritualized' feeding and giving nourishment. Raymond Brown argues that only in this way could the apparently unavoidable implication of feeding on, or eating/drinking

---

39. Schnackenburg discusses the sense in which this passage (Jn 6.26-58) has, at various periods of its interpretative history, been understood to refer to Eucharistic feeding along a continuum from magical materialism—a view of the twentieth-century rationalist, linking the words to the mystery cults of the first Christian century—to the sixteenth-century views of the Reformers who, while not abandoning the sense of the real presence of the Lord in the Eucharist, laid great emphasis on the faithful disposition of the communicant, or to the sense in which such feeding is to be understood as related to the ecclesial 'body of Christ' and to the life of faith. Schnackenburg traces the Eucharistic interpretation of Jn 6.53-58 back to the Fathers, including the Alexandrinians; Ammonius and Cyril. Clement appears to have favoured a reading along the lines of Philo's interpretation of the manna in the wilderness as a symbol of the Logos. For Clement, according to Schnackenburg, the symbols of feeding, bread, flesh, blood and milk all relate to the spiritual feeding of believers. See Schnackenburg, *The Gospel According to St. John*, I, pp. 65-67.

flesh and blood, be accounted 'favorable'.[40] As at Jn 1.13, however, Jn 6.63 returns the reader to the more conventional and negative interpretation: 'the flesh is useless'.[41]

These further references to σάρξ occur in the course of a discussion between Jesus and sceptical 'Jews' following the discourse on the bread of life (Jn 6.35 ἐγώ εἰμι ὁ ἄρτος τῆς ζωῆς [I am the bread of life...']). The discourse follows on from the sign of feeding the crowd by the Sea of Galilee with bread and fish. Within the Johannine text itself there is much that points in the direction of a metaphorical interpretation of the act of feeding: 'Do not labour for the food which perishes, but for the food which endures to eternal life' (Jn 6.27); 'Your fathers ate the manna in the wilderness, and they died. This is the bread which comes down from heaven, that a man may eat of it and not die' (Jn 6.49-50). Equally unambiguously, Raymond Brown comments on Jn 6.35:

> The ego eimi with a predicate does not reveal Jesus' essence but reflects his dealings with men; in this instance, his presence nourishes men.[42]

Moreover, Brown argues that the whole 'bread of life' discourse in John 6 is based upon the theme of the consumable, sustaining *word* from Isaiah 55:

> Why do you spend your money
> for that which is not bread,
> and your labour for that which
> does not satisfy?
> Hearken diligently to me, and eat
> what is good,
> and delight yourselves in
> fatness,
> Incline your ear, and come to me;
> hear that your soul may live;
> and I will make with you an
> everlasting covenant (Isa. 55.2-3).[43]

C.K. Barrett summarizes 6.22-27 thus:

> Men are foolishly concerned not with the truth, but with food for their bodies. They must learn that there is a bread which conveys not earthly

---

40. Brown, *The Gospel According to John*, pp. 284-85.
41. Brown, *The Gospel According to John*, p. 295.
42. Brown, *The Gospel According to John*, p. 269.
43. Brown, *The Gospel According to John*, p. 521.

but eternal life, and earn it; yet they will not earn it, for it is the gift of the Son of man.[44]

It is then, perhaps, not so surprising to find that some commentators have had considerable difficulty[45] in deciding whether Jn 6.51-59[46] can be genuinely Johannine, given that it appears so anomalous from the position of readers, including apparently the reader who is the text of the Gospel, who maintain an overall commitment to the 'completely symbolic attitude of the bread discourse in Jn 6.31-51, which contrasts with the 'sacramental realism' of the Eucharistic verses'.[47]

Some commentators have tried to eliminate the troublesome tensions altogether. Ernst Haenchen, for example, offers an extraordinarily clear-cut explanation for the curious contradictions inherent in the use of σάρξ in these passages that employs a sophisticated theory of multiple sources and complex patterns of composition. He argues that the Gospel is substantially the work of a gifted and original theologian, whom he calls the Evangelist (upper case 'E'). In this narrative of composition, the Evangelist's text, based on earlier material that has been his inspiration, is subsequently worked over by an editor of inferior talents and understanding whom Haenchen describes as the redactor (lower case 'r'). Using this as a basic framework, he concludes that the redactor was at odds with the Evangelist. In John 6, he argues that the redactor, whom he castigates as a clumsy 'supplementer'[48] for introducing the same ambivalence in Jn 1.12-14, belonged to a community that was struggling to normalize its sacramental practice and theology. Naturally

---

44. Barrett, *The Gospel According to St. John*, p. 282.

45. Rudolf Bultmann regards Jn 6.51-58 as an addition of the Ecclesiastical Redactor to introduce a non-Johannine sacramental theme. In Brown, *The Gospel According to John*, p. 286, Brown agrees that the passage is an editorial insertion, but argues that it builds on truly Johannine themes. Brown also notes that E. Ruckstuhl, *Die literarische Einheit des Johannesevangeliums* (Freiburg: Paulus, 1951), believes the passage to be genuinely Johannine, but on a similarly stylistic basis Eduard Schweizer, *Ego Eimi* (Göttingen: Vandenhoeck & Ruprecht, 1939), is not convinced.

46. It is not possible to be definitive about the exact determination of the length of this troublesome interlude, since different scholars have different opinions about the exact length of the editorial insertion. Raymond Brown, for example, draws limits at Jn 6.51 and Jn 6.58. Ernst Haenchen makes Jn 6.51b and Jn 6.59 his cut-off point. Schnackenburg goes for Jn 6.51c-58.

47. Schnackenburg, *The Gospel According to St. John*, I, p. 57.

48. See Haenchen, *John*, I, p. 118 and n. 62.

enough, the redactor wanted to give apostolic or evangelical authority to his own views. Given that the Johannine text appears either ignorant or—and this is Haenchen's own view—dismissive of the Eucharistic traditions associated with the Last Supper, Haenchen argues that the interpolation of Jn 6.51b-59 represents another attempt by this redactor to get his own word in. He sees it as intrusive and ill-judged since it is clear to him that:

> [n]othing depends on the flesh and blood of Jesus; his flesh and blood, isolated from his word and the Spirit that is imparted with those words, lack significance.[49]

It is clear that Haenchen is labouring to produce an interpretation of the Gospel that does justice to its undoubted dualities[50]—such as clearly inspire the interpretative extremes of both Docetic and existentialist theologies of the Word. But for him, Jn 6.51b-59 is simply far too materialistic, implying the taking of Jesus' humanity itself into oneself through bread and wine.[51] In other words, for Haenchen, the 'palpability' of the Incarnation is not to be found within a 'naïve' sacramentalism, but the 'sole important thing' is to recognize the *present encounter* with the message of Jesus.[52] And this is the interpretation he attributes to the Evangelist who, he implies, must represent any genuinely *Johannine* (by which he implies 'authoritative') theology.

Haenchen's analysis of John 6 and its use of the word σάρξ offers one persuasive solution to the difficulties of the contrasting evaluations of 'flesh'. But it achieves its end by acting in accordance with a fundamental preference for the spiritual over the fleshly (Jn 6.51b-59) which is removed from the authoritative, 'Johannine' text and transformed into the likeness of marginality and absence. This looks rather like a classic illustration of interpretative phallogocentricity, understood as the centrality, not simply of the masculine sign (phallus), but also of his voice (Logos) in framing the subject. Haenchen's preference is not framed in baldly dualistic terms but relates particularly to the hierarchicalizing tendency within the symbolism of gender to which I have already referred. In other words, once again what happens in this account is that, while recognizing the bodily and material as unavoidable,

---

49. Haenchen, *John*, I, p. 298.
50. See, for example, Jn 3.6, 31; 4.10-15; 6.48-50; 8.23.
51. See Haenchen, *John*, I, p. 298.
52. See Haenchen, *John*, I, p. 299.

it is still rejected as the site or locus of divine communication which can result only from reading his text, that is, man's text.

In this way, perhaps, Haenchen aims to provide another layer of protection for the text as 'authoritative'—let us say, rather, conventional in a patriarchal sense—against the scandalous implication that the description of 'flesh' at Jn 6.53 might represent a challenge to the controlling hierarchical symbolism, an outbreak of anarchic boundary crossing. Such an implication of the hierarchical reversal of the 'flesh' as a feature of the symbolic feminine would be, arguably, at least as disturbing to readers as the literal suggestion of cannibalism[53] in this context.

There was a virulent campaign in the early Church against the Gnostic dualities of Marcion and Montanus.[54] And orthodox Christianity has always, at least officially, taken the line that the human body—male and female—is the creation of God rather than some lesser demiurge or demon. Such would appear indications that, for the Church, there was never any *absolute* duality as between spiritual and bodily. Yet readers of the Gospel of John have detected a strong preference for the spiritual and spiritualizing interpretations. From the time of Clement of Alexandria, there have been those who wanted to categorize the distinction between John and the Synoptic Gospels as a distinction between 'the outward facts' (τα σωματικα—literally 'bodily things') and a 'spiritual Gospel' (ἐύαγγελιον πνευματικον).[55] And such a distinction is very readily seen in terms of an implicit hierarchy in which the bodily is inferior to the spiritual. Thus, one fairly recent commentator remarks in relation to Clement's distinction:

> One could then interpret the Gospel of John as a supplement to the Synoptics, but if one took the relative values into account, the Gospel of

53. See, for example: 'It should be realized that there is no suggestion intended of the horrifying idea involved in a literal interpretation. The choice of phrase is again *entirely controlled* by the tradition of Jesus' words at the Last Supper' (Lindars, *The Gospel of John*, p. 268 [emphasis mine]). Note too that for Jn 6.63, Lindars offers the following definition of the 'flesh' that is of no avail, within the common understanding of 'the anthropology which [John] has received from Judaism': 'flesh here is the earthy part of man, man as he is by nature, his intellect remaining unilluminated by the revelation of God'. See Lindars, *The Gospel of John*, p. 273.

54. It was, for example, Heracleon, a disciple of the Gnostic Valentinus, who first wrote an allegorical commentary on the Gospel of John. A mid-second-century Gnostic movement was led by Montanus, who saw himself as the Paraclete bringing the world to an end.

55. See Eusebius, *Historia Ecclesiastica* 6.14.7.

John had the advantage since 'spiritual' is certainly worth more than 'the bodily'.[56]

But retaining the Eucharistic emphasis on the flesh that must be eaten[57] (Jn 6.53) is a clear option, even within the context of modern biblical criticism. As Ernst Haenchen himself notes, there are biblical critics who are uncertain about dismissing this passage as one more editorial blunder.[58] What I am suggesting is that retaining the uncomfortable and apparently contradictory associations of 'flesh' in John 6, as in the Prologue, ensures the reader maintains a certain sensitivity to what might be called 'embodied spirituality' rather than forcing him or her always and only to view the body and its needs as a metaphor for something more spiritual and thus more profound. Such sensitivity includes the recognition of the multiplicity of human existence which cannot be neatly divided, for example, between the bodily and the spiritual, any more than it can, at all easily, reconcile the claims of both. And in terms of the text, the dissonance is marked, yet more emphatically, by the almost thematic instability of this word, this Word made 'flesh'.

Recent work on the mediaeval period has revealed a far greater emphasis on the body and its significance than at almost any point before or since in the Western world. Mediaeval anthropology, for example, clearly regarded persons—though described with, sometimes, quite radical duality—as both body and soul. It associated body with woman but also with God in imaginative—if, to modern thinking, sometimes bizarre—visions of maternal love and physical signs.[59] As the historian Caroline Walker Bynum notes:

> Medieval men and women did not take the equation of woman with body merely as the basis for misogyny. They also extrapolated from it to an association of woman with the body or the humanity of Christ. Indeed,

---

56. See Haenchen, *John*, I, Introduction, p. 23.

57. The word used is τρωγω, which means to gnaw or chew, especially uncooked foods.

58. Haenchen, *John*, I, p. 297.

59. See Caroline Walker Bynum, 'The Female Body and Religious Practice in the Later Middle Ages', in Michel Feher (ed.), *Fragments for a History of the Human Body* (New York: Zone Books, 1989), p. 171. She notes, for example, 'stigmata, incorruptibility of the cadaver in death, mystical lactations and pregnancies, catatonic trances, ecstatic nosebleeds, miraculous inedia, eating and drinking pus, visions of bleeding hosts'.

they often went so far as to treat Christ's flesh as female, at least in certain of its salvific functions, especially its bleeding and nurturing.[60]

Thus, body was not invariably either of negative or neutral value but sometimes given *positive* significance in relation to the divine, as is, of course, clear in the case of Hildegard of Bingen. In Hildegard's case, as also in the case of a number of other women who were concerned with devotion to the Eucharistic host as Corpus Christi,[61] the emphasis on the materiality of Christ's body was undoubtedly a response to heresy and particularly that of the Cathars. A number of women mystics from the Low Countries who revered the body of Christ in this particular form of devotion aimed to contest the Cathar view that the physical world was the creation of an evil God.[62] And, of course, it is not only mediaeval commentators who deal with the perceived difficulty of 'flesh' in Jn 6.53, as too 'realistic' or bodily a concept, by interpreting it in terms of the need to combat Docetism and unacceptable forms of spiritualization at this point.[63]

Moreover, within the mediaeval period, the very materiality of body sometimes achieved a positive significance in very much the way that modern critics, such as Haenchen, appear to find distasteful. Both the body of the devotee and the body of Christ were seen as channels of direct communication with God. In cases of inedia,[64] for example, the

60. Walter Bynum, 'The Female Body', p. 175.

61. The feast of Corpus Christi was instituted in 1264 by Urban IV, largely in response to the influence of a devout visionary nun of Liége, Juliana (d. 1258).

62. Caroline Walker Bynum, *Holy Feast and Holy Fast: The Religious Significance of Food to Medieval Women* (Berkeley: University of California Press, 1988), p. 253.

63. See, for example, Schnackenburg, *The Gospel According to St. John*, I, p. 67, who quotes the work of Eduard Schweizer approvingly: '[he] says that in John's view the point of the sacraments is to bear witness to the reality of Jesus' incarnation, and that of the Lord's supper in particular is to secure the reality of the incarnation up to and including the crucifixion against any docetic attempts at spritualization.'

64. The claim—or the phenomenon—of being sustained physically over long periods of time, merely by the elements of the Eucharist. See Walker Bynum, *Holy Feast and Holy Fast*, for reflections on the phenomenon during the mediaeval period. For some modern reflections on and investigations of this, see Ian Wilson, *The Bleeding Mind: An Investigation into the Mysterious Phenomenon of Stigmata* (London: Paladin, 1991); Joe Nickell, *Looking for a Miracle: Weeping Icons, Relics, Stigmata, Visions and Healing Cures* (Amherst, NY: Prometheus Books, 1993).

bread and wine of the Eucharist alone apparently sustained physical life and well-being for periods of years at a time.

With this abandonment or violation of boundaries between the bodily and the spiritual, it also became possible, in the iconography of the Church, to depict the body of Christ as a female body, representing his nurturative or life-giving role. Thus, for example, there are miniatures and panel paintings of the fourteenth century that show the Church effectively being born from the side of Christ crucified.[65] Even more striking are the Eucharistic images of Christ, offering the wound in his side and the blood pouring out, in visual parallels to Mary, offering her breast to suckle sinners.[66] It does have to be said, however, that this did not ultimately question the underlying gender hierarchy in which Christ's masculinity remained unquestioned.

Nevertheless the theme is not uncommon. A fourteenth-century monk from Farne pursues the same theme:

> Little ones...run and throw themselves in their mothers' arms...Christ our Lord does the same with men. He stretches out his hands to embrace us, bows down his head to kiss us, and opens his side to give us suck; and though it is blood he offers us to suck we believe that it is health-giving and sweeter than honey and the honey-comb (Ps. 18.11).[67]

It appears then, that Christian readers and interpreters of the biblical text from the twelfth to the fifteenth century in Europe were able to live with a much greater degree of fluidity between spiritual and physical and, indeed, male and female than can be observed today in Western cultures. Of course, the bodies on which it focused tended to be women's bodies[68] which might then still be subsumed under the patriarchal

65. See Feher (ed.), *Fragments*, p. 176, fig. 2: Eve made from the rib of Adam and the Church from the hip of Christ (Paris, Bibliothèque Nationale).

66. See for example, Feher (ed.), *Fragments*, p. 177, fig. 3: Jacob Cornelisz, 'The Man of Sorrows', c. 1510 (Antwerp, Mayer van den Bergh Museum); p. 178, fig. 4: Unknown, 'The Intercession of Christ and the Virgin', c. 1402 (New York, Metropolitan Museum of Art, Cloisters Collection); p. 179, fig. 5: 'Mass of Saint Gregory', Spanish altarpiece, end of the fifteenth century (Spain, Parish Church of Villoido). Also see Caroline Walker Bynum, *Fragmentation and Redemption: Essays on Gender and the Human Body in Medieval Religion* (New York: Zone Books, 1991), p. 110; fig. 3.10: Quirizio of Murano (fl. 1460–1478), 'The Saviour'.

67. *The Monk of Farne: The Meditations of a Fourteenth-Century Monk* (trans. a Benedictine nun of Stanbrook; Baltimore: Helicon Press, 1961), p. 64.

68. The first documented case of stigmata, for example, was Francis of Assisi. See Wilson, *The Bleeding Mind*. Wilson lists cases of stigmata from the thirteenth century

framework of social and religious practice. However it undoubtedly gave bodily and female experience, within that framework, a far greater significance in religious terms.[69]

The point of this short digression into the mediaeval period is, in the broadest sense, to suggest that modern commentators of this biblical text may be being constrained by more than the availability of archaeological or documentary evidence relating to the period in which the Gospel was composed. Twentieth-century commentators find representations of Christ's body that conflate Eucharistic and maternal symbols[70] bizarre, while they clearly seemed both helpful and acceptable in the twelfth or thirteenth centuries.

The passage in John 6 which describes Jesus' flesh as life-sustaining (Jn 6.53) and in which he calls on his followers to eat it is absolutely in harmony with the piety of mediaeval women that saw Christ's body as food and those who denied that God became flesh and food in the Eucharist as the greatest heretics.[71] If Jn 6.53 might seem, to some commentators, an intrusion of theology quite foreign to the Gospel as a whole, it would nevertheless have made perfect sense to those who, like certain of the nuns at Töss during the fourteenth century, had visions of Christ as food on a platter[72] or to women such as Margaret of Cortona and Catherine of Genoa who consciously substituted the Eucharist for the food they denied themselves in the course of long fastings.[73] And of course, in terms of disputes about the 'real presence' of Christ in the Eucharistic elements, Jn 6.53-56 is grist to the dogmatic mill. Rudolf

to the twentieth. The majority of all these cases are women, although the list is, admittedly, not comprehensive. Adrienne von Speyr, for example, does not figure in the appendix (it is perhaps indicative, however, of differing attitudes to these issues in the twentieth century, that the best-known cases today—Francis himself and perhaps the modern figure, Padre Pio—are both men).

69. See Feher (ed.), *Fragments*, pp. 167-68. Here she refers particularly to the work of Peter Dronke, in, for example, *Women Writers of the Middle Ages: A Critical Study of Texts from Perpetua (d. 203) to Marguerite Porete (d. 1310)* (Cambridge: Cambridge University Press, 1984).

70. One particular symbol of Corpus Christi was, of course, that of the Pelican 'in her piety' (heraldically represented, for example, in the crest of Corpus Christi College, Cambridge). The Pelican pecks her breast and feeds her young with her own blood.

71. See Walker Bynum, *Holy Feast and Holy Fast*, p. 252.

72. See Walker Bynum, *Holy Feast and Holy Fast*, p. 131.

73. See Walker Bynum, *Holy Feast and Holy Fast*, p. 140.

Schnackenburg—a Roman Catholic scholar—for example, in summing up the discussion on the whole disputed passage (Jn 6.51c-58), writes:

> All this is a long way from the later dogmatic issues and controversies, but even so it is impossible to deny the existence of the idea of a real presence of the incarnate and glorified Christ.[74]

What is certainly true is that the text at Jn 1.13-14 and at Jn 6.53-63 continues to bear witness to two apparently contradictory assignations for the term 'flesh' within this Gospel. This reading might be said to present the contrast, unresolved as between the two readings, as its focus. Within the narrative in John 6, the hierarchical symbolism of Spirit over flesh is challenged to the point of offence (Jn 6.60-61) and then, almost directly, reaffirmed (Jn 6.63). Arguably, in spite of its relevance to mediaeval piety, the assumption of a Eucharistic context for this passage simply seeks to subsume the scandal of this 'somewhat animal banquet'[75] within a context of reflection that already belongs within a patriarchal dualistic spiritualized and spiritualizing tradition. I see this *contradiction*, then, as representation of the trace of the multiplicity which, within patriarchal culture, is symbolized in a framework of gendered hierarchies as woman and the feminine. Like Christ's flesh, it is necessary for life but eludes categorization within the existing symbolic framework.

6. *Feminist Suspicions*

Feminist theory that reads our Western culture as 'phallogocentric' will inevitably regard with suspicion these attempts to redeem the biblical text. The dynamic, radical shift that sympathetic or confessional interpretation claims for the New Testament as a whole is frequently categorized as that which has the potential to create a society in which women—among other groups of formerly disadvantaged people—are no longer enslaved or denied autonomy. But I believe that this is not to reckon sufficiently with the impact of the gender symbolism that pervades our thinking in the West. Forms of thinking that are phallogocentric cannot simply abandon that 'centricity'. It is definitive. It is

---

74. Schnackenburg, *The Gospel According to St John*, I, p. 69.

75. Julia Kristeva, *Strangers to Ourselves* (trans. Leon Roudiez; New York: Harvester Wheatsheaf, 1991), pp. 11-12. Could the Eucharist itself be about ritual feasting as the symbolic representation/repression of a violence involving blood?

expressed in symbolic terms that inevitably devalue the feminine. To exist as body, whether suffering or enjoying, is to take the value accorded to woman or the feminine in relation to a masculine God or a divine masculinity. And, in this sense, Jesus' sacramental or Eucharistic flesh will be seen to belong to the same persistent model. In a Eucharistic sense, Jesus' flesh (σάρξ, βρῶσις, ἄρτος) becomes precisely the means of satisfying the needs of others. Which effectively means, within such a context, satisfying needs determined by men. It becomes, as fleshly and feminine, a commodity like a loaf of bread or the body of a prostitute or, indeed, any possessed woman, a person/thing, dehumanized, body without life. Even more alarmingly, humanity is once again configured as that which is symbolically feminine, that is to say consumable, penetrable by violence, whether of the male organ or of the nails through the flesh, violently dismembered as a collection of parts, a means to life, but of itself inanimate.

Clearly, within the mediaeval context, readers worked more flexibly with this framework of gender symbolism so that it was possible to avoid always and only identifying the feminine with women. In consequence, the Word made flesh was sometimes seen as nurturative and maternal in relationship to the divine. Equally women could be, so to speak, clothed with masculine authority. However, evidence of this sort of flexibility is not always easy to find. And, certainly, women working in the field of biblical criticism and the analysis of documents contemporary with the New Testament texts have noted the pressures, already evident there, to devalue or obliterate the work of women within the early Christian Church.[76] Already, within the context of the New Testament period, there were forces frustrating the attempt to clothe women with masculine-identified authority.

And finally, it remains true that, while there may be some evidence here in John 1 and John 6 for hinting at the configuration of the Word/flesh in terms of the nurturative maternal, this is only one fairly slender

---

76. See for example, Elisabeth Schüssler Fiorenza, 'Missionaries, Apostles, Co-workers: Romans 16 and the Reconstruction of Women's Early Christian History', in Ann Loades (ed.), *Feminist Theology: A Reader* (London: SPCK, 1990), pp. 57-71; Elaine Pagels, *The Gnostic Gospels* (Harmondsworth: Penguin Books, 1979), on, for example, the figure of Mary Magdalene in the Gospel of Mary; Turid Karlsen Seim, *The Double Message: Patterns of Gender in Luke–Acts* (Edinburgh: T. & T. Clark, 1994), on Luke–Acts.

strand from the intertwining thread that makes up any adequate definition of woman and the feminine.

7. Conclusions

I have suggested, in the course of this chapter, that the Incarnation, described in summary in Jn 1.14, should be read with the disturbing contradictions of the word σάρξ very much in the forefront of the reader's
mind.

The word σάρξ functions well as the lower term in a hierarchy which
is controlled within a context of spiritual values (see, for example, Jn
3.4-7) and which has an overriding gender identification. As such, it
indicates, at Jn 1.14, a divine humiliation and descent, a compassionate
divine, masculine downreach towards a feminine humanity. It is assumed that it is only through God taking on this fleshly life that
humankind may be saved or redeemed. And as a result, of course, salvation or redemption bears the character of a removal from the 'fleshly'
order of being human into the realm of a divine and masculine, spiritual
singularity.

However, in order to maintain this sort of reading, commentators
must ignore the evident contradictions in the text where σάρξ does not
simply indicate a lower order within a divine/human hierarchy but
something altogether darker and more threatening, something regarded
as flawed and dangerous that has a clear relationship, within the Prologue (and in John 6), to an actual and necessary bodily existence. And
it is, I believe, the contradictions in the incarnational text which have
the potential to deconstruct the edifice of the masculine singularity of
the divine and reveal an unavoidable paradox of the flesh in the texts of
John 1 and 6.

The Prologue of John's Gospel offers a quite startling vision of radical
openness within the community of believers but, perhaps more significantly, by its double inscription of flesh as both essential for life and of
no avail, it suggests the possibility of dismantling the far stronger walls
constructed by the monolithic symbolic use of gender and its associations.

9

In the Beginning Was Love

> Every question, no matter how intellectual its content, reflects suffering.
> In our subject may lurk the suffering of religion as well as of rationalism,
> along with more strictly personal discomforts and anxieties. Let us try
> simply to be receptive to this suffering, and if possible to open our ears to
> meaning of another kind.[1]

1. *Introduction*

My final reading of the Prologue of John's Gospel will be, as I have
already indicated, more constructive than deconstructive. My aim is to
read this text as if it were the description of the human subject *'en
procès'*, employing, as theoretical support, the work of French semioti-
cian and theorist Julia Kristeva.

Margaret Davies is a modern biblical critic with feminist sympathies.[2]
She describes the Prologue as a 'theological introduction'[3] to a Gospel
that is a 'theological' work.[4] Her understanding of 'theological', interpreted in respect of the assumed intentionality[5] of the original author(s),
seems related to a view of God as singular, transcendent divinity, underpinning and, as it were, guaranteeing all creation including humankind.
I have been arguing that this characterization of the divine belongs to a
phallogocentric mindset which, seeking definition of *all* truth (including

---

1. Julia Kristeva, *In the Beginning Was Love: Psychoanalysis and Faith* (trans.
A. Golhamner; New York: Columbia University Press, 1987), p. xiii.

2. See Margaret Davies, *Rhetoric and Reference in the Fourth Gospel* (JSNTSup,
69; Sheffield: JSOT Press, 1992) p. 20: 'women cannot overlook that the Fourth
Gospel is one of many texts which has lent its authority to the subordination of
women in societies where it has been read'. Her solution is 'to deny the subservient
role that the Gospel tries to foist on her, and to include herself alongside the male
disciples as a fully responsible human agent'.

3. Davies, *Rhetoric and Reference*, p. 126.

4. Davies, *Rhetoric and Reference*, p. 119.

5. See Chapter 1, pp. 29-30.

value and identity) in terms of transcendent, masculine singularity, excludes a defining 'otherness' which it symbolizes in terms of a feared/
devalued feminine. I have also tried to argue, along the lines of feminist
analysis, that this commitment to singularity, while understandable, is
always really at odds with the multiplicity to which I believe gender—
masculinity and femininity and the difference between them—bears
witness.

Of course, Davies does not claim to share the view of the divine that
she describes in her analysis of the Prologue. However, interestingly, she
adopts a form of 'inclusive' language in reference to God so that God
sometimes figures as 'she' within her study of the Prologue. Davies
argues that the Prologue contains a vision of God. This is, she says, a
vision that is then elaborated within the Gospel of John. The God described within this Prologue is, first of all, transcendent. God exists
'before and independently of the world'[6] (Jn 1.1-2) and is 'other',
'beyond the powers of human comprehension ... mysteriously different
from anything encountered in the world'[7] (Jn 1.18). However, God is
also revealed in the form of λόγος made flesh. λόγος is not God in
herself but, nevertheless, God's expression of her purpose in creating
and sustaining the world. The word λόγος itself is 'the term that con-
notes God's plan in creation'[8]—a significance found in earlier biblical
texts, for example in Genesis and in the Psalms.[9] In becoming flesh (Jn
1.14)—an individual man—Davies suggests that the Gospel text reflects
a sense of completion. 'God's plan is instantiated'[10] for all to see and
fully revealed in Jesus. The whole significance of λόγος is concentrated
into that event:

> God has finally and fully communicated her purpose in the life, death and
> resurrection of Jesus, and ... the reader has no need to look elsewhere to
> find it.[11]

Lastly, this God is the Father (Jn 1.18) who is loving but also, in an
absolute sense, authoritative.[12]

---

6.   Davies, *Rhetoric and Reference*, p. 120.
7.   Davies, *Rhetoric and Reference*, p. 120.
8.   Davies, *Rhetoric and Reference*, p. 121.
9.   See, for example, in the Greek translation of the Septuagint, Gen. 1.3, 6, 9
etc., and particularly Ps. 33.6: 'By the word of the Lord, the heavens were made'.
10.   Davies, *Rhetoric and Reference*, p. 122.
11.   Davies, *Rhetoric and Reference*, p. 122.
12.   Davies elaborates the concept in respect to his only begotten son (*Rhetoric*

Davies's reading of the Prologue, in spite of the inclusive language, turns up little evidence of the sort of female presences or clues to a disturbing 'otherness' that I have been looking at throughout this study. She notes the arresting resemblances between λόγος (Word) and the female-identified σοφία (Wisdom) but also makes a clear distinction between them in this passage.[13] She argues, for example, that Jn 1.3-4 should be interpreted in terms that distinguish the Word Incarnate from the created cosmos and that exclude this as a means of divine illumination. This is in contrast to the interpretative direction taken by Hildegard of Bingen, for example, who understands the text to be laying a much greater emphasis on the light of the whole of creation[14] which she views in terms of the work of divine Wisdom or Love, the feminine figure of Sapientia or Caritas. Then again, Davies does not regard the absence of the mother of the Incarnate Word in this text, where only the presence of the Father (Jn 1.18) is made explicit, as significant. She does note, at Jn 1.14, that the reader is likely to be surprised. In other words, after the negative intimations concerning the flesh contained in Jn 1.9-13, she clearly thinks that there are grounds for being surprised that the Word should still become 'flesh'. But she does not question the reasons for that surprise. 'Flesh' in Jn 1.14 is still glossed as a reference to 'susceptibility, to injury, decay and death',[15] bringing it within what I have described as the devalued or excluded feminine sphere of a phallogocentric symbolism. But Davies makes no comment on this issue.

2. *Julia Kristeva and the* Sujet en Procès

Margaret Davies's unorthodox and even startling use of 'she' in order to describe the divine initiative narrated within the Prologue does not seem then, on closer examination, to be an integral part of her analysis of this text. Though I want to acknowledge its clarity and usefulness, her analysis is not really designed to grapple with the issue of gender, and particularly female gender, as it is operating in a contemporary reading context. And in order to do this, as I have already indicated in

and Reference, p. 131), but also in terms of Israel's sonship and contemporary cultural understandings of, for example, the *pater familias* in Roman society (*Rhetoric and Reference*, pp. 129-30).

13. Davies, *Rhetoric and Reference*, p. 82.
14. See Chapter 3.
15. Davies, *Rhetoric and Reference*, p. 127.

the forgoing two alternative readings, a more fundamental change of perspective is needed in which the Prologue has to be seen as more than a 'theological' introduction if 'theology' is only to be related to the absolute presence of a transcendent being.

The theoretical work of Julia Kristeva is concerned with literature, language, reading and writing and this would make her work of interest to anyone concerned with textual interpretation. Furthermore, she is concerned with issues of gender and its relationship to the speaking, reading and interpreting subject. Kristeva's work was influenced at an early stage by the intellectual movement called structuralism and she continues to defend the value of the structures she identifies as 'masculine'—and particularly the symbolic realm of language—as essential. In this sense her approach remains contentious within the field of feminist theory as a whole where she is sometimes regarded in the light of a collaborator with the phallogocentricity of all existing cultural structures including the currency of language.[16] However I believe that the structuralist impetus of her fundamental 'framework', which does imply some sort of closure or exclusion or singularity, is always complicated and problematized by its stress on an equally essential multiplicity, something she identifies as 'heterogeneity' and characterizes as fundamentally irrational, but not thereby either avoidable or of inferior value. What

16. She has been accused of being fundamentally conditioned by her debt to Jacques Lacan. Lacan provided feminists with a way of explaining the operations of a patriarchal society and its systematic oppression or devaluation of women which accounts for its characteristic persistence and resistance to change. For Lacan, this distinctive way of constituting and imagining the relationship of men and women belongs to the very processes whereby human identity is first formed in infancy and childhood, and is locked into levels of subjectivity beyond the conscious control of individuals. Lacan recast Freudian insights in terms of language and signification. Language is the key feature within the Lacanian 'Symbolic Order' to which social law and exchange also belong. For a child to function adequately within society, they must internalize this symbolic order through language. Within this symbolic order, Lacan uses the word 'phallus' to describe that which represents for him the internalized sense of difference between men and women. It is less a single word than a pattern of understanding. It characterizes men as those in possession (of a penis), and women as those who lack, or who are, that which men possess. Moreover it also symbolizes that which is the ultimate object of all desire. Some feminist theorists have strongly contested Lacanian analysis and its implication that women must either submit to the phallic symbolic order or lapse into feminine inarticulateness, seeing in his work a prescriptive rather than a descriptive impulse—Lacan's arguments always tending towards preservation of the patriarchal status quo.

Kristeva constructs in the body of her theoretical work is a description of 'subjects' who, as interpreters of their own lives as of the texts they read, are involved in an intertextuality which is characterized by multiplicity. This multiplicity—or heterogeneity—is not limited to multiple elements within the linguistic/symbolic realm but also involves the drives, needs and pleasures of the embodied, speaking subject itself.

What I want to suggest is that the Prologue is read alongside the drama Kristeva describes, in psychoanalytic terms, of a human journey towards a life made possible, particularly through the imaginative interpretation of lives conceived as texts. In this case, the Prologue becomes, so to speak, the baffling text of the analysand's experiences, lived and dreamed and expressed creatively in literary form. Imaginatively, I take on the psychoanalytical discussion. I attempt to create out of this difficult Johannine text a delimitation of the divine as multiply, heterogeneously, masculine-and-femininely human, in order to make it make sense for me as both a woman and, in Kristeva's terms, a *'sujet en procès'*.[17] I am, as it were, reading the narrative of the Prologue as it reflects my own journey as *sujet en procès*, thus filling out the theological notion of divine 'Incarnation'. Moreover, I see this text as a meditation upon an originating love, that is to say the sort of love by means of which the creation and sustaining of individual human subjects is made possible. The human subject rises—in Kristeva's view—at the source which contains its whole creative potential, that is in undifferentiated absorption with the maternal. From there or then, subjectivity breaks out into a recognition of division or separation. But it is, at once, part of the symbolic realm of language and culture and, at the same time, still motivated and driven by forces within a volatile, antithetical, semiotic realm—so to speak, returning to source. In a similar way, I suggest, the description of God in the Prologue begins in undifferentiated absorption

17. Diachronically, the narrative of the *sujet en procès* is a psychoanalytic drama, in which human individuals are released or pushed out of the realm of absorption with gratification and drives that are identified with the maternal, towards individual subjectivity—a sense of being a separate self—brought about through identification with the thetic, symbolic, paternal realm of language. Individual subjects, however, remain permanently unstable, permanently *en procès*, 'both biological organism *and* talking subject, both unconscious *and* conscious' (Kristeva, *In the Beginning*, p. 26). Synchronically, the *sujet en procès* is the representation of an intertextuality between a series of symbols, languages and social codes, and a series of powerful bodily energies or drives which, from the unconscious, perpetually threaten and challenge, or alternatively free up and lubricate, the order of language, code and law.

with God, the site of creative potential which waits for division into light and darkness, before realizing that potential as separated and differentiated, perpetually struggling and sometimes suffering, embodied Logos. In other words, I think Kristeva's theoretical body of work offers me, as reader, the possibility of seeing the theological concept of Incarnation as it is taken from this text as a description of the divine which integrates the symbolism of gender but manages not to copy into that symbolism the hierarchical framework that necessarily devalues the feminine term.

And in this way, as reader, I am also enabled to resolve something of my own dissociation as both human subject in process and also as a woman, seeking to see myself within a text that has been largely interpreted in terms of a gender hierarchy that suggests, powerfully, the debasing of my own gender and thus of my very identity.

I believe it will help to clarify what I am trying to do if, at this point, I give some more extended account of what I believe to be the relevant areas of Kristeva's work. Kristeva's earliest published works are particularly concerned with linguistics and semiotics. They certainly demonstrate a debt to structuralism but they are not uncritical of it. Structuralism, which began with Ferdinand Saussure (1857–1913)[18] introduced the perception—related initially to language—that signification occurs within structures or systems and that it is the relationship between the signs within the system that is important rather than the relationship between the signs and some external body, object or relationship. Kristeva's interest in the science of ideologies (semiology) follows on from Saussure's conclusions about language and Claude Lévi-Strauss's related work in structuralist anthropology, but challenges it in some important ways.

These earlier theorists drew attention to the sense in which the signifying practices, myths, rituals and moral codes belonging to a certain culture or society are related in a largely arbitrary sense to the motivations of that culture or society. However, Kristeva goes on to develop her own theory of 'semanalysis'. She is interested in the interior logic of such signifying practices, in other words, how one moves into signifying practice and, above all, in how such practices are the work of complex speaking subjects. She sees language as a product of speakers who naturally straddle a divide between bodily drives and the creation of

18. Saussure's lectures in linguistics were collected and completed for publication by colleagues after his death: *Course in General Linguistics* (Paris, 1915).

symbolic relationships or language. In this, she distances herself from earlier structuralists who focus on linguistic or cultural structures as homogeneous and static.[19]

Kristeva, as distinct from a number of other modern philosophers, still finds the concept of the 'subject' useful. However, it should be remembered that this subject is never simply a static, relatively unproblematic 'subject' of consciousness, related to basically Cartesian categories of body and soul but, rather, it incorporates what I have already called a functional irrationality, something unspeakable and unknowable which is only seen in the effect of its dialectic with rational consciousness, that is to say in its breakdowns or creative outbursts. This encompassing complexity which cannot eradicate its own irrationality Kristeva frequently refers to as 'heterogeneity'. This is a recognition of the role of that which escapes and then continually irritates the boundaries or defences of all our rational linguistic and symbolic projects. The concept of heterogeneity refers to the unavoidable presence of all that remains, in some sense, still in play beyond or outside rational discourse and capable of subverting or changing it. It represents what Kristeva calls the attempt to 'go beyond the theater of linguistic representations'.[20] In other words it represents multiplicity, contesting the logic of identity, and still investing significance in the materiality of a bodily, physical existence that evades the linguistic representations of rational structures. Kristeva's 'semiotic project' is centrally concerned with both texts and subjects because it is an analysis of how signifying practices, such as language, exert their fragile control over the human subject in process.

19. See Julia Kristeva, *Revolution in Poetic Language* (trans. Margaret Waller; New York: Columbia University Press, 1984), p. 13. Kristeva writes critically of earlier attempts to contain and schematize language: 'Our Philosophies of language, embodiments of the Idea [...*avatars de l'Idée*...], are nothing more than the thoughts of archivists, archaeologists, and necrophiliacs. Fascinated by the remains of a process which is partly discursive, they substitute this fetish for what actually produced it. Egypt, Babylon, Mycenae: we see their pyramids, their carved tablets, and fragmented codes in the discourse of our contemporaries, and think that by codifying them we can possess them.

These static thoughts, products of a leisurely cogitation removed from historical turmoil persist in seeking the truth of language by formalizing utterances that hang in midair, and the truth of the subject by listening to the narrative of a sleeping body—a body in repose, withdrawn from its socio-historical imbrication, removed from direct experience.'

20. Kristeva, *In the Beginning*, p. 5.

In terms of this project she proposes an important *gendered* distinction between the 'semiotic' and the 'symbolic'. She relates the semiotic to the nourishing 'chora'—a pre-verbal space which precedes *any* form of subjectivity. It is a concept derived from Plato's *Timaeus* where the expression refers to an unstable and unnameable receptacle or space existing before the nameable form of the One.[21] The semiotic is related to the *feminine*, to the archaic mother with whom the developing child is at first absorbed, without any sense of distinction or difference, simply in a preoccupation with primary motivations sometimes referred to as drives. The *masculine* symbolic is correspondingly associated with the 'father of individual pre-history', Freud's *'Vater der personlichen Vorzeit'*, which acts as the catalyst for developing an initial sense of difference and distinction and which persists as the representative of the currency of social organization and development that is, pre-eminently, language but also non-verbal forms of the symbolic—various codes or forms of behaviour. In developing this aspect of her theory, Kristeva has drawn on the work of the psychoanalyst Jacques Lacan (1901–81), who followed and then reinterpreted some of Sigmund Freud's key ideas. Thus Kristeva discusses human subjectivity in terms of a drama that involves, most significantly, the 'archaic' parents, mother and father. These parents are not the particular parents of any child but rather reflect the primary functions or parental roles vis à vis the developing subjectivity of all children.

What semanalysis does for Kristeva, in the development of the ideas of the semiotic and the symbolic, is to give her an analytical tool for constructing a view of human subjectivity—and of culture—that acknowledges, in a non-pathological, functional sense, the tensions and splits and irrationality of a postmodern speaking subject while continuing to affirm the validity of some form of rationality.

Kristeva's work as a whole is increasingly concerned with psychoanalysis. Psychoanalysis is, of course, a term coined by Sigmund Freud (1856–1939) to describe a fundamentally therapeutic process. The theoretical basis of this therapeutic process is, put at its simplest, that human behaviour is significantly determined by a collection of infantile drives repressed within self-conscious adults but still located within the 'unconscious'. They are not available to the conscious 'rational' mind but, nevertheless, find expression in, for example, dreams, jokes, verbal puns

---

21. See Pamela Sue Anderson, 'Introduction to Julia Kristeva's *In the Beginning Was Love*', in Graham Ward (ed.), *The Postmodern God: A Theological Reader* (Oxford: Basil Blackwell, 1998).

and slips as well as in a wide variety of symptoms, understood as pathological.

An important concept within Kristeva's work, belonging to her psychoanalytic discourse, is that of '*jouissance*'. Within her writing, it represents the point at which the drive/desire-related economy of the semiotic meets or, rather, breaks through into the order of language and the symbolic. Kristeva argues that the meeting of the two is continually accessible to developing subjectivity through art and literature and through moments of extreme pleasure, including sexual pleasure.[22]

That idea that the birth into the symbolic within each developing subjectivity must be related to a break and a rejection of the (m)other/child continuum is developed at length in Kristeva's concept of 'abjection' which complicates, explicates and darkens any easy conception of a simple, clean or once-and-for-all step into the symbolic order of language. In *Powers of Horror* in particular, Kristeva movingly and convincingly conjures up a vision of the horror of separation, 'the immemorial violence with which a body becomes separated from another body in order to be'.[23] She also describes the corresponding horror or repugnance which that separated, abjected, creates in 'me', like the gagging of food-loathing,[24] that is characteristically the response of a complex, developing and incorporated subjectivity:

> But when I *seek* (myself), *lose* (myself), or experience *jouissance*—then 'I' is *heterogeneous*. Discomfort, unease, dizziness stemming from an ambiguity that, through the violence of a revolt *against*, demarcates a space out of which signs and objects arise. Thus braided, woven ['*torsé, tissé ...*'] ambivalent, a heterogeneous flux marks out a territory that I can call my own because the Other, having dwelt in me as *alter ego* points it out to me through loathing.[25]

In terms of the psychoanalytic drama Kristeva describes, that which becomes abject is essentially identified with the mother. And herein lies the vital significance of the father. Again this is not any particular father but the Freudian 'father of individual pre-history':

---

22. In Julia Kristeva, *Strangers to Ourselves* (trans. Leon Roudiez; New York: Harvester Wheatsheaf, 1991), the drama of a necessary but painful separation and the subsequent possibilities of meetings or—perhaps—reunions is laid out in some detail.

23. Julia Kristeva, *Powers of Horror: An Essay on Abjection* (trans. Leon Roudiez; New York: Columbia University Press, 1982), p. 10.

24. Kristeva, *Powers of Horror*, p. 2.

25. Kristeva, *Powers of Horror*, p. 10.

In such close combat, the symbolic light that a third party, eventually the father, can contribute helps the future subject, the more so if it happens to be endowed with a robust supply of drive energy, in pursuing a reluctant struggle against what, having been the mother, will turn into an abject. Re-pelling, rejecting: repelling itself, rejecting itself. Ab-jecting.[26]

Kristeva expands the individual drama, in a synchronic sense, into something that is continually re-enacted. In *Powers of Horror* for example, she considers the food laws of Leviticus in terms of an abjection, whose purpose is closely tied to the process of maintaining the identity of the people of Israel as clean and proper, separated from the rest of humanity and particularly those contemporary pagan cults devoted to feminine deities. And yet, and at the same time, Leviticus is a text that speaks to the individual reader. In her most recent work, *New Maladies of the Soul* (1995), she writes:

The Book of Leviticus speaks to me by locating me at the point where I lose my 'clean self'. It takes back what I dislike and acknowledges my bodily discomfort, the ups and downs of my sexuality, and the compromises or harsh demands of my public life. It shapes the very borders of my defeats, for it has probed into the ambivalent desire for the other, for the mother as the first other, which is at the base, that is, on the other side of that which makes me into a speaking being (a separating, dividing, joining being). The Bible is a text that thrusts its words into my losses. By enabling me to speak about my disappointments, though, it lets me stand in full awareness of them.[27]

Some feminists are naturally suspicious of Kristeva's insistence on the necessity of fatherhood and law with a masculine index and of the identification she seems to make between woman, motherhood and aspects of the irrational and the heterogeneous. The irrationality, simplistically we can perhaps talk about the 'drive economy', that Kristeva believes incurs violent and creative effects in the subject's struggle to enter or stay within an order or rational framework of language and symbolism, is identified, within her work, with a feminine/maternal principle or relationship.

In one sense, however, it might be argued that her conclusions reflect a radically feminist analysis. It could be said, for example, that she shows how the feminine/maternal principle 'spooks' the system of language

---

26. Kristeva, *Powers of Horror*, p. 13.

27. Julia Kristeva, *New Maladies of the Soul* (trans. Ross Guberman; New York: Columbia University Press, 1995 [1993]), p. 119.

and symbolism, seen as phallogocentric or dominated by the presence of the male sign. However, Julia Kristeva differs from Mary Daly, who coined this expression[28] to denote the powers of women to combat male terrorism, not least in the extent to which she resists the mythic tendency of many feminists to identify the feminine exclusively with women, either as a group or as individuals. Within Kristeva's work, the ongoing discussion of *human* subjectivity presents gender as extraordinarily significant and problematic but no less so for men than for women.

Kristeva is no friend to sexist practice but she is also highly critical of feminists who suggest a prohibition on all dealings with men and, in her essay 'Women's Time', she attacks the kind of response that

> refusing homologation to any role of identification with existing power no matter what the power may be, makes of the second sex a *counter-society*.[29]

The criticism levelled at this counter-society is that it simply reiterates the logic of any society based on the expulsion of an excluded element, 'a scapegoat charged with the evil of which the community duly constituted can then purge itself'.[30]

Kristeva shares Lacan's view that the development of human subjectivity takes place within the dynamic of the individual's acquisition and experience of language as the key element of the social or cultural order. For this reason she believes that all women and men need to find their place within this order. But she rejects Lacan's claim that, within that order, women will find themselves silenced anyway and excluded from language except as symbolic concepts (either as representations of something else, for example Liberty or Beauty, or as objects of desire). She argues that women are themselves the space and possibility of any form of representation. What they represent is not simply a theoretical difference but a theoretical difference 'with an attitude'. This difference has a *specific and material* index. It represents a crossing over, a transgression into that symbolic order from a different 'order' that, precisely, cannot be represented as an 'order' at all and which, therefore, cannot

28. For a definition of 'spooking/speaking', see Mary Daly, *Gyn/Ecology: The Metaethics of Radical Feminism* (London: The Women's Press, 1991), p. 317.

29. Julia Kristeva, 'Women's Time', in Toril Moi (ed.), *The Kristeva Reader* (Oxford: Basil Blackwell, 1986), p. 202.

30. Moi (ed.), *The Kristeva Reader*, p. 202.

be adequately resisted. For Kristeva, the problem for individual women is determining how to participate in an existing socio-symbolic contract without continually being forced *personally* to represent or embody this difference.

3. *Reading the Prologue*

Superficially there seems little common ground between the awe-inspiring scope of the Evangelist(s)' claims in the Prologue and Kristeva's deliberate rejection of divine transcendence or the providential ordering of human lives within the 'whole black history of the Church'.[31] Kristeva presupposes that the nature of religious discourse is fundamentally concerned with illusion. Yet, of course, she does not believe that the creation of illusions is merely the practice of self-deception. She relates the illusions created within religious discourse to the work of the imagination which, in her work as a psychoanalyst, plays a literally 'vital' role in the process of practising to be human and of, so to speak, 'riding the surf' of our daily lives. As she notes,

> [i]n both religion and psychoanalysis a destabilized subject constantly searches for stabilization.[32]

Of course, this reading of scriptural and theological narratives differs from one that could be given by any religious believer defined as a believer *in* transcendent divinity and a believer *that* transcendent divinity became incarnate in the person of Jesus of Nazareth. But the points of confluence make suggestive, not to say challenging, reading. Does our theological understanding of Incarnation within the Christian tradition not come also from deeply rooted perceptions about human subjectivity and about what it means to be human? In other words, I suggest that the Word did not simply become incarnate, but that the myth of the Incarnation itself, quite apart from its 'political' ramifications within the early Christian Church's doctrine of the two natures,[33] is in some ways representative of the drama of becoming—and remaining—human.

31. Kristeva, *Powers of Horror*, p. 131.
32. Kristeva, *In the Beginning*, p. 19.
33. See, for example, Elisabeth Schüssler Fiorenza, *Jesus: Miriam's Child, Sophia's Prophet: Critical Issues in Feminist Christology* (London: SCM Press, 1995), p. 22. Fiorenza argues that the Chalcedonian doctrine of Christology was an attempt to reproduce within divine/human relations the imperial ordering of the contemporary

The narrative I intend to read within the Prologue is one of a pre-existent unity, emerging out of which the Word made flesh appears as a divided speaking subject, witnessing to a hope of revealing the Father—that is, becoming like him—which is poignant because it is never realized unambiguously. This narrative seems to me, in many suggestive ways, to parallel the experience of being human as described by Kristeva in psychoanalytical categories. In other words, she implies that being human entails the need to cope with a split between vital, drive energy and the necessity of curbing this in fragile and interrupted subjection to speech and symbolic codes. The split which continually impinges on the subject, in a sense of loss and unwarranted exclusion, nevertheless provides that developing subject with the very capacity and energy to hold together, to be creative and to love others. And it does this because it provides the impetus for distinguishing difference and thus, eventually, the basis for establishing a sense of subjectivity that is sufficient but never 'dead safe'.

To test the thesis that some of the theoretical tools of Kristeva's analysis might be illuminating in reading the text of the Prologue, let me begin with the strong echoes of Genesis 1 within this Johannine passage. Raymond Brown notes the likelihood that the Septuagint would have been available to the author or authors of the Gospel.[34] What more apposite quotation for the opening of a new Gospel, a new Scripture, than the opening words of the old book of the Law it was bound (Jn 1.17) to supersede: ἐν ἀρχῇ ἐποίησεν ὁ Θεὸς οὐρανὸν καὶ τὴν γῆν... (Gen. 1.1, 'In the beginning, God made the heaven and the earth...')? This is a description of 'before creation' or out of time. But although the spirit of God is there in the darkness, the descriptive terms are negative: ἀόρατος (form*less*/*un*seen/*in*visible/*un*sightly)[35] and ἀκατασκεύαστος (*un*furnished/*un*prepared/*un*ready/*void*) (Gen. 1.2). What begins, what happens in a positive and temporal sense (Gen. 1.4-5), is a separation, brought about by God's word: 'And God said, 'Let there be light...and God separated the light from the darkness' (Gen. 1.3-5).

---

political world. 'It shaped and was shaped by the imperial politics of meaning that legitimated kyriarchal domination and exploitation.'

34. Raymond E. Brown, *The Gospel According to John I–XII: A New Translation with Introduction and Commentary* (AB, 29; New York: Doubleday, 1966), p. 4.

35. See Sir Launcelot Lee Brenton (trans.), *The Septuagint Version of the Old Testament in Greek and English* (London: Samuel Bagster and Sons), p. 1.

In the Prologue, there is a similar pattern. The atemporal sphere is characterized by a duality that is, at the same time, inseparable and indistinguishable: 'the Word was with God, and the Word was God' (Jn 1.1). In terms of Kristeva's psychoanalytic discourse, what lies 'in the beginning' before time, a symbolic concept that is unavailable to the very young child, is the intimate absorption—without articulation or sense of distinction, form or separation—of the child with its maternal, nourishing environment. And yet this is an environment which contains the seeds of a separation, a separation as dramatic as that between light and darkness (Gen. 1.3-5; Jn 1.4-5). What I am suggesting here is that the pattern within both Gen. 1.1-5 and the Jn 1.1-5 is reflected also within the narrative of subjectivity which Kristeva constructs.

The Word that is the light (Jn 1.4-5) may refer to the advent of the Word made flesh or to the enlightening presence of the Word before the advent of Jesus.[36] But in either case, it shines in a darkness, a darkness (ἐν τῇ σκοτίᾳ, Jn 1.5), which is reminiscent of the darkness before creation: καὶ σκότος ἐπάνω τῆς ἀβύσσου ('and darkness was over the deep', Gen. 1.2). But although the darkness has never seized the light for itself, or taken possession (οὐ κατέλαβεν, Jn 1.5) of it, the text does not suggest, in any explicit sense, that the darkness is removed or, in its turn, seized and possessed.

Within the drama of developing subjectivity which Kristeva lays out for her readers, beyond the desire for and receiving of gratification, the child registers that there is not simply gratification but sometimes this is being withheld from her or him—that is, understood as enacted, but elsewhere. In terms of concrete experience, the mother wants something other than to gratify the child's wishes. This identification with maternal desire for something else is primary—the first step. But along with the possibility this gives of enacting a 'primary identification' with the maternal desire, of learning about *agape* as opposed simply to *eros*, comes the possibility of recognizing the maternal as other—as abject. Identification with maternal desire leads on to maternal abjection which

---

36. The ambiguity centres on whether in Jn 1.9 ἐρχόμενον (was coming) in ἐρχόμενον εἰς τὸν κόσμον (was coming into the world) agrees with φῶς (light) or ἄνθρωπον (hu/man). In other words, is this a light that enlightens every man coming into the world in a general and universal sense, or is it a specific reference to the incarnate Word about to become flesh? See C.K. Barrett, *The Gospel According to St John: An Introduction with Commentary and Notes on the Greek Text* (London: SPCK, 2nd edn, 1978), pp. 160-61.

might very appropriately be described as darkness within a narrative of enlightenment.

Abjection, as Kristeva describes it, is all that, in recognizing the sameness/otherness of the maternal, flings the human subject, what she calls the *sujet en procès* into fuller identification with what is represented solely by the father. It is characterized by

> a sudden emergence of uncanniness, which, familiar as it might have been in an opaque and forgotten life, now harries me as radically separate, loathsome. Not me. Not that. But not nothing either. A 'something' that I do not recognize as a thing. A weight of meaninglessness, about which there is nothing insignificant, and which crushes me.[37]

Such an emergence is, Kristeva argues, crucial to the establishment of any sense of identity, whether personal or cultural, because it so forcefully propels away from the primary maternal, semiotic realm where the subject in waiting, so to speak, is absorbed simply in the immediate gratification of its infantile desires or drives. Abjection comes to mark a borderline that is always under threat. In an important sense, the establishment of the borderline gives scope for the emergence of the new, the ecstatic, the revelatory or salvific,[38] into the realm of language and symbolism. But it should be noted that, for Kristeva, it defends a definition and, as it were, a shape of the greatest fragility. The boundaries of this shape or definition are constantly in need of reconstruction, like the walls of a child's sandcastle at the edge of an encroaching tide. She is not speaking of human tranquility.

Abjection, this non-object, this borderline is not there 'from the beginning', although it is a precondition for beginning of a recognizable subjectivity. Abjection is one step along the route of developing subjectivity but, once established, becomes an unavoidable and indeed necessary sensitivity. It is in this sense that I suggest Kristeva's analysis might shed some light upon the mysterious darkness of Jn 1.5, whose origins or provenance is not explained within this text.

The appearance of darkness (Jn 1.5), which does not come in the beginning of the text, is something of a mystery in its implication, after the comprehensive claims of Jn 1.3 that 'all things were made through him'. For then it suggests that either darkness has an independent existence or exteriority or that it was made through God. And for many

---

37. Kristeva, *Powers of Horror*, p. 2.
38. Kristeva, *Powers of Horror*, p. 8.

commentators, these conclusions are highly questionable. Thus, Raymond Brown assumes that this darkness is a reference to the 'sin' of Gen. 3.6, not God's responsibility but the woman's.[39] C.K. Barrett deals with the problem by assuming, in a similar though less explicit sense, that darkness here reflects the 'ethical' quality of all that is opposed to Jesus the light of the world and that darkness is, in a simple sense, the correlative of light.[40] Barnabas Lindars argues that neither this text, nor the Genesis text to which it makes reference, has to do with the *origin* of evil but interprets the darkness of Jn 1.5 as any present threat to the fulfilment of God's purpose in creation[41] such as the rejections of human unbelievers in Jn 1.10 and 11. It is, however, difficult to read the first five verses avoiding completely all cosmogonical reflection. The same inexplicable principle of evil or rather *exteriority to God* appears in the narrative of Genesis 3 in the shape of the serpent. In Kristeva's work, abjection is essentially the construction of an exteriority, a something out there, beyond—understood as abominable, a reversal of desire, what necessarily sickens or turns the stomach:

> When the eyes see or the lips touch that skin on the surface of milk—harmless, thin as a sheet of cigarette paper, pitiful as a nail paring—I experience a gagging sensation and, still farther down, spasms in the stomach, the belly; and all the organs shrivel up the body, provoke tears and bile, increase heartbeat, cause forehead and hands to perspire. Along with sight-clouding dizziness, *nausea* makes me balk at that milk cream, separates me from the mother and father who proffer it. 'I' want none of that element, sign of their desire; 'I' do not want to listen, 'I' do not assimilate it, 'I' expel it. But since the food is not an 'other' for 'me', who am only in their desire, I expel *myself*, I spit *myself* out, I abject *myself* within the same motion through which 'I' claim to establish myself.[42]

Kristeva argues that this abjection occurs as a result of a process of primary identification with the maternal desire for something other than satisfying the developing subjectivity. This desire is symbolized by the masculine sign—using the psychoanalytic terminology of Lacan—the phallus. And following Lacan, Kristeva sees this maternal desire for the phallus as that which initiates and strengthens the process of repression—

39. Brown, *The Gospel According to John*, p. 8.
40. Barrett, *The Gospel According to St John*, p. 158.
41. Barnabas Lindars, *The Gospel of John* (NCB Commentary; Grand Rapids: Eerdmans, 1972), p. 77.
42. Kristeva, *Powers of Horror*, pp. 2-3.

the law of the father—which in turn, allows the fragmented self[43] to constitute itself, albeit in extreme fragility, to function, to live, by going beyond the realm Kristeva calls the semiotic and which she identifies with the pre-linguistic realm of the feminine maternal figure, into the symbolic realm of language and symbolism, dominated by and identified with the father figure. And it is interesting to note, in this context, the close association between light, life and Torah, that makes, in the case of the Wisdom and rabbinic literature particularly, the study of Torah—Law—life-giving.[44] In other words, the psychoanalytic drama of the *sujet en procès* concurs, at this point, with the veneration of the Law attested within the culture of the Hebrew Bible and its interpretation.

To reiterate, abjection is an incident in a personal history, and yet it remains a fellow-traveller. And it is a darkness (Jn 1.5) in the sense that it shades or blinds, covering over the prehistory of a fusion with the gratifying mother with a series of more or less repulsive and repulsing associations or symptoms that help to prevent subjects imploding or reverting and yet porous enough to allow some of that drive energy to find expression in a creative zest for life.

But the process of becoming or being a unitary subject is very often a painful one. What we let through into conscious forms of expression is not simply a form of *jouissance*—joy, pleasure, energy—but very often a memory of loss, expressed in depression and loss of motivation. Whether we look at it in terms of a single progression from the early infancy of human children towards the emergence of language, or whether we consider the myth of the Prologue as related synchronically to 'the further trials set by the life process of the passions',[45] there is much loss here. In order to move or progress out of a pre-linguistic realm of repetitious sounds and recurring rhythms, before the abstraction of absence and time have been formed, into the world (Jn 1.9) of speech, symbolism and linear time, the *infans*, the developing subjectivity, must wait upon the emergence of a loathsomeness. There must be a darkness—abjection—before she or he can bear witness (Jn 1.6-8), speaking

---

43. For a Freudian understanding of fragmentation—life and death drives, the potential for controlling them and the necessity of dealing with the impact of external circumstances—see Sigmund Freud, 'The Ego and the Id', in Peter Gay (ed.), *The Freud Reader* (London: Vintage, 1995), pp. 656-58.

44. See Barrett, *The Gospel According to St John*, p. 157.

45. Kristeva, *In the Beginning*, p. 9.

in the light, to the symbolic, linguistic and the communicative realm of the father.

The text of the Prologue moves on beyond the point of the Baptist's announcement (Jn 1.6-8) to a passage that is expressive of alienation and disjointedness (Jn 1.10, 11). The creator is not always or everywhere welcomed by the creatures. This new world, created from and by Word, excludes the darkness but cannot eclipse it altogether. Even if those who accept the Word can become children of God (Jn 1.12-13), some will not accept the Word. Something lies beyond the Word. For Kristeva, the analyst, the 'unconscious' is a good word for this:

> After a lengthy process of remembering and self-discovery, the analysand learns to know himself, submerged though he is in the immanence of a significance that transcends him. That significance can be given a name: the *unconscious*. The analysand knows the unconscious, orders it, calculates with it, yet he also loses himself in it, plays with it, takes pleasure from it, lives it. Psychoanalysis is both objectification and immersion; it is both knowing and, through language, unfolding. It is an extraordinary effort to recast our whole intellectual tradition from its inception to its annihilation. On the one hand there is nothing (*nihil*) but the knowing subject; on the other hand I know that that subject derives from an alien significance that transcends and overwhelms it, that empties it of meaning.[46]

From Lacan, Kristeva has also taken and adapted the important concept of 'the mirror stage' in her theoretical work as a description of the moment at which the child first sees 'I', as in a mirror, and is able to fix on and imitate a specular structure as the basis for seeing herself as a subject. In other words it is the moment or stage in which she recognizes that the image in the mirror is both what she is and yet not her. It is complex perception. In Kristeva's terms, the mirror stage marks the threshold between the semiotic and the symbolic time. That is to say, it lies between a primary context oriented towards the mother and preoccupied by drive energies, where there is no articulation of absence or, thus, of the symbolic or the real, and the time dominated by Oedipal conflicts primarily directed towards the father.

What brings about this change? The site of this change is the presence of a third party beyond the child/(m)other dyad. It is the possibility for the pre-subject, the forming subjectivity, what Kristeva calls the *infans*,

---

46. Kristeva, *In the Beginning*, p. 61.

to exercise an ability, a capacity—akin in some ways to the identifi-
cations of those caught up hysterically with the emotions of a crowd—
to identify with a desire, not initially its own, for something beyond or
outside its own immediate gratification. This is a wanting not simply to
have, but to be like. Understood as akin to Freud's 'Father of individual
pre-history',[47] identification with a desire for this object is the precondition of any human capacity to love. Maternal care for the child is
always, Kristeva suggests, in danger of becoming a morbid form of self-
absorption. The child may become, for the mother, a substitute for the
ultimate object of desire which is symbolized by the phallus. The child
—to a greater or lesser extent—is unable, in this situation, to move
beyond gratification and the pull of drive energies, unable to make an
identification with this first pattern of love. However, the mother's
desire for an object of love *other* than the child, through what Kristeva
calls the maternal desire for the father's phallus,[48] is the possibility for an
enlightening lesson of love.

In the Prologue, in a narrative sense, what emerges out of fusion and
absorption between God and Word is light, associated both with God's
illuminating separation (Jn 1.5), through its references to the Genesis
passage (Gen. 1.4), and with life (Jn 1.4). This life-giving illumination is
further linked, within the Prologue, to a capacity to become the children of God (Jn 1.12-13). And to read this as a reflection of the desire
to gain an intimate relationship with God and even to imitate that God's
actions and become like that God, attaining in some sense that God's
power and immortality, does not seem to push interpretation unduly
into eccentricity at this point. What it does do, however, is to cut across
the sort of dualisms found so often in interpretation and exegeses of this
passage, relating to spiritual and physical birth to which Jn 1.13 is
commonly thought to refer.[49] In other words, if I use Kristeva's analytical categories, the significance of becoming God's child is simply trans-
ferred into the realm of the speaking subject which is *always and necessarily* at the intersection of conscious and unconscious motivations.

47. Kristeva does not resist the impetus towards a religious discourse in seeking
to explicate this concept/symbol. She speaks of it as a 'godsend' (Moi [ed.], *The
Kristeva Reader*, p. 257), and of 'the father who brings a people into being through
his love' (p. 261), as an appropriate definition.

48. Julia Kristeva, 'Freud and Love: Treatment and its Discontents', in Moi (ed.),
The Kristeva Reader, p. 256.

49. See, for example, Lindars, *The Gospel of John*, p. 92.

However, what the denials of Jn 1.13 'not of blood nor of the will of the flesh nor of the will of man' do reflect, perhaps, is a certain appropriate dissociation at this point. The process of identification that Kristeva describes in the developing human subject is directed away, here, from the drive-related semiotic realm of maternal care and gratification that, in cultural terms, has so often been associated with the flesh, with blood and with sexuality.

So, this is to suggest what, exactly? Kristeva's analysis can be illuminating, even given her clearly stated objections to orthodox interpretation, such as seeing the God of the biblical text as having a transcendent existence.[50] It opens up the text to an interpretation in terms of two interlinking narratives. First there is a common human process, a life-giving process of identification with a father, leading to the capacity for language and love beyond self—*agape*. And secondly there is the mythological progress of Word's divinely gracious coming-to among human believers. And within this second narrative, divine Word follows the same process of identification, of coming to love beyond initial fusion and self-absorption through identification, through a desire to mime, to be and act like the Father (Jn 1.18). It is an interpretation that has implications for the Gospel as a whole, in which the identification of Jesus with his Father is a strong if implicit theme:

> He who has seen me has seen the Father; how can you say, 'Show us the Father'? Do you not believe that I am in the Father and the Father in me? (Jn 14.9-10)

Within the Prologue, I believe that the sign of what unites Word with humanity and suggests, most clearly, the nature of a divine subjectivity is the transformation of Word becoming flesh (Jn 1.14). The divine Word appears to take on the necessary heterogeneity of subjectivity. That is to say, divine Word, associated so clearly within Christian ecclesiastical tradition with the realm of language, symbolism and cultural order—the realm of the Father—becomes implicated in the functional irrationality or heterogeneity of Kristeva's notion of subjectivity. And in this sense, the Word must also be involved in the maternal realm through abjection and also *jouissance*.

Kristeva argues that heterogeneity encompasses that within subjectivity which has the potential to be both threatening and nourishing. She believes that, within Christian theology, it has become largely attached

50. See, for example, Kristeva, *In the Beginning*, p. 27.

to a concept of sinning flesh[51] and to the devalued symbols of woman and the feminine, making the nourishing potential for *jouissance* invariably perverse. She attributes this identification to the generation, within Christian theology, of the concept of sin that is an internalizing of the notions of separation and impurity that, in the Judaic world of the Temple, were largely dealt with by external avoidance and purification. In other words, it is as if she were saying that Christian theology turned human subjectivity itself into the Temple, making it impossible ever to have the place clean and proper, since it was by its very nature divided in a way that was equally impossible for God to avoid. Even Christ must be regarded as the special case of body without sin,[52] whose 'heterogeneity' can still, so to speak, only be shared by subjecting oneself to spiritualizing remedies. The consequences were, she argues, unending guilt and a sense of self-defilement that cannot be dealt with since the only remedies offered are *linguistic* rituals—confession and Eucharistic *formulations*:

> abjection is no longer exterior. It is permanent and comes from within. Threatening, it is not cut off but is reabsorbed into speech. Unacceptable, it endures through the subjection to God of a speaking being who is innerly divided and, precisely through speech, does not cease purging himself of it.[53]

As if to support this reading, Jn 1.17 seems to suggest the failure of Moses. Moses was pre-eminently identified with the Law of the Temple, the external laws of purification, and yet he could not see God's face (Jn 1.18) and live (Exod. 33.20),[54] whereas Jesus Christ/Word made flesh brings grace and truth and reveals the Father and makes him known.

---

51. Kristeva, *Powers of Horror*, p. 115.
52. Kristeva, *Powers of Horror*, p. 120.
53. Kristeva, *Powers of Horror*, p. 111.
54. However, note that Raymond Brown argues that this does not have to be read as an implicit criticism of Moses: 'There is no suggestion in John that when the Law was given through Moses, it was not a magnificent act of God's love. A contrast similar in spirit to that of John i 17 is found in Heb i 1: "God spoke of old to our ancestors through the prophets, but in these last days He has spoken to us through His Son" ' (Brown, *The Gospel According to John*, p. 16). Note too that this v. 17 is regarded by Bultmann, Käsemann and Schnackenburg as a later editorial addition. Brown, *The Gospel According to John*, p. 16.

However, Kristeva must admit that this absorption of flesh into Word, which she believes abandons the 'inexorable carnal remainder'[55] by spiritualizing the Incarnation and attempting to disguise the sign of heterogeneity within a realm of linguistic representations—particularly Eucharistic liturgies and exegesis that stresses the metaphorical sense of nourishment as understanding—belongs to some extent *to the history of Christian interpretation*. In this Johannine text, Logos/Word may certainly take its place within the realm of language that separates light from darkness and sets up an order that sustains creatures and pleases the Father Creator. But I would argue that the text may be read against Kristeva's strictures, with Word settling for a truce with unformed darkness which it does not (cannot?) destroy (Jn 1.5). Moreover I believe that Word becoming flesh is still, in the Prologue, a powerful sign of the inexpressible heterogeneity which involves that Word with all the associations of the maternal body. And it is abundantly clear, for example, that this particular scriptural association of Word and flesh has very much continued to alarm and perplex commentators.[56] I believe that it remains possible then to read in this incarnational text the sort of transgressive, boundary-crossing tensions and irresolutions that appear to me so characteristic of heterogeneity as Kristeva defines it.

What I am suggesting is that within this narrative of the Word there is a reminiscence of the disquiet of human subjectivity, composed as it is, in terms of Kristeva's psychoanalytic drama, of conscious and unconscious, biological organism and talking subject. Kristeva proposes that it is necessary to live within this disquieting diversity, and possible, practically, to treat the sickness which it sometimes causes, through psychoanalysis, as a form of imaginative interpretation:

> Analysis gives me confidence that I can express all the parts of my being, and this confidence quells my narcissism and enables me to transfer my desire to others. I can then open myself up to the variety of experience that becomes possible with others who may be different from me or similar to me…the discovery of an other in me does not make me schizophrenic but enables me to confront the risk of psychosis, which is perhaps the only truly frightening hell.[57]

---

55. Kristeva, *Powers of Horror*, p. 120.
56. See Chapter 8, where I deal with this issue in greater detail.
57. Kristeva, *In the Beginning*, p. 56.

Theoretically then, one may perhaps read the rest of the Prologue as the celebration of this achievement—to live as heterogeneous subjectivity, so to speak, revealing the Father.

4. *Conclusions*

Julia Kristeva's theoretical work demonstrates the complexity of a working intertextuality. 'In the beginning was the Word' becomes for her a suitable echo or indeed a *summons* for an understanding of the whole analytical venture to which she is committed. It is echoed in the title of an essay, 'In the Beginning Was Love', that she wrote on psychoanalysis and faith. It evokes 'the mobilization of two people's minds and bodies by the sole agency of the words that pass between them'[58] that constitutes the healing of psychoanalysis, the growth and life-restoring work of the analyst and analysand together within the context of transferential love.

My analysis is an intertextuality along reverse lines, in which the narrative within the Johannine Prologue is illuminated or opened out by means of a reference to a narrative of developing human subjectivity which is all the more appropriate, I believe, in a text which has fuelled discussion about the divine Word becoming a human being. I think that to read the Prologue in the light of Kristeva's 'semananlysis' offers readers a view of Incarnation which takes into account the multiplicity or heterogeneity—symbolized in terms of gender—that I believe to be a key feature of what it means to be, as *any* human subjectivity, 'incarnate', that is to say 'human'.

Moreover, returning to Margaret Davies's description of the Prologue as a theological introduction, this reading of the Prologue preserves the status of the text as, in some sense, a theological narrative, in spite of the reader's abandonment of the categories of divine presence or transcendence. For example, it offers some explanation as to why there appears to be no cross within the Prologue since that could be said—in terms of the whole Gospel—to be contained within the revelation of Incarnation itself, as a part of the process of dealing with abjection, the dark suffering of living. One could also say that this reading places the reader in relation to the text of the Prologue, created by other speaking subjects, as the analysand in relation to the (sometimes deeply confusing) text of her or his own life. The analysand/reader must then imaginatively,

---

58. Kristeva, *In the Beginning*, p. 3.

construct a narrative for themselves, out of this textual confusion, that accounts for, and to that extent heals, the painful dissociations to (by) which they are subject(s). And making imaginative sense of the text is perhaps as good a way as any to understand the significance of divine communication.

10

Conclusion:
Wrestling with the Angel

1. *The Context: Phallogocentricity*

This study has been a study of texts rather than a text. That is to say it has not considered the Prologue of John's Gospel as a particular Greek version or English translation or as a document transfixed at a single point—the point at which it was first written or read, for example. What has interested and concerned me is the intertextuality of reading in a number of specific instances, notably within the exegetical or meditative readings of Augustine of Hippo, Hildegard of Bingen, Martin Luther, Rudolf Bultmann, Adrienne von Speyr and myself.

I believe readers 'put on' or interpret the garment of the text for their own particular and individual reasons and I have tried to show here how these interpretations are indeed formed at the intersection of biblical text and interpretative desire or need, by highlighting some of the similar and also some of the different themes and preoccupations displayed by readers.

However, in the case of the five historical readings of the Prologue that I consider in this study, I believe that individual reasons for producing a certain interpretation are all determined, to a considerable extent, by the phallogocentric context of reading. To characterize the context as 'phallogocentric' is to refer to a determination of singularity within the interpretative context, according to which, all meaning and value is determined in relation to a single transcendent notion of truth which is typically identified as masculine. Put briefly, this singular no-tion of transcendent truth—for example, a singular, masculine-identified divinity—guarantees an all-encompassing hierarchy of gendered values which can be seen to be operating within textual interpretations.

One classic feminist formulation of this analysis, drawn up by the French feminist writer Hélène Cixous, lists a series of pairs as:

Activity/passivity
Sun/Moon
Culture/Nature
Day/Night
Father/Mother
Head/Heart
Intelligible/Palpable
Logos/Pathos
Form, convex, step, advance, semen, progress.
Matter, concave, ground—where steps are taken, holding—and dump-
ing—ground.

Finally Man is placed over a line of division, and Woman underneath.
Cixous concludes:

> Always the same metaphor: we follow it, it carries us, beneath all its fig-
> ures, wherever discourse is organized. If we read or speak, the same
> thread or double braid is leading us throughout literature, philosophy,
> criticism, centuries of representation and reflection.[1]

As the double braid is harnessed to a fundamental drive towards masculine singularity, male identity, male autonomy and male comfort tend
to take priority. And one characteristic tendency of this analysis,
illustrated within all five historical readings of the Prologue of John's
Gospel, is the collapse of all references to woman and the feminine, and
particularly their cultural associations with sexuality and the human
body, into devalued terms or modalities.

But this feminist analysis also implies that phallogocentricity is caught
up by the implications of its own logic. To determine a singular truth—
of either identity or value—in masculine-identified terms, woman and
the feminine inevitably become symbols of difference, the defining
'otherness' and, moreover, the sign of a multiplicity that can hold no
singular value. That is to say, the realm which, by being different, defines a valorized (masculine-identified) singularity, is symbolized in the
devalued terms of woman and the feminine. However, feminist theory
also sees this realm of the excluded 'other' as potentially deconstructive
of the whole notion of singularity. In its defining relationship to the
valorized realm of masculine-identified singularity, it represents an unavoidable multiplicity. However much the difference or 'otherness', of

---

1. Susan Sellers (ed.), *The Hélène Cixous Reader* (London: Routledge, 1994),
p. 37. Reprinted from Cixous' essay, 'Sorties', published in Hélène Cixous and
Catherine Clément, *La jeune née* (Paris: Union Générale d'Editions, 1975).

which woman and the feminine are the symbols, is denied, disowned, avoided or anathematized and however much actual women are beaten, veiled, silenced or confined in response to anxiety about it, the multiplicity is unavoidable. And, in terms of my argument, this is because human living is not simply conceptual, linguistic, spiritually singular, or dependent upon men. Human living is essentially multiple, bodily and linguistic, desiring and needing to gain nourishment and satisfaction, as well as articulation and control, and thus also dependent upon the devalued roles and qualities that are symbolized by and culturally associated with women and the feminine.

In the particular context of the Prologue, I believe that the effort of maintaining a defining identity as singular/masculine/(-feminine) provokes a tremendous anxiety which can be shown to be controlling the direction of textual interpretation away from the recognition of any form of multiplicity, whether this is expressed in terms of confusion and mixing of divine and human or in terms of their mutual dependence. The general tenor of the argument is towards a separation by means of which that which is human is defined as feminine and either devalued or, symbolically, excluded.

2. *Five Historical Readings*

The text of the Johannine Prologue is an appropriate one to read, of course, since it is concerned thematically with the narrative of divine Incarnation in which divinity and humanity are drawn together in such intimacy that Christian tradition claims God became a human male individual. At the same time, this Christian tradition has continued to refer to the relationship between God and humankind in terms of a gendered hierarchy of value, implying the inevitable (feminine-identified) subjection of humankind to divine authority.

St Augustine, then, in reading this passage within John's Gospel, is always mindful of the feminine-identified carnality of the Word's human existence, relating it to the dust with which Christ the physician (Jn 9.6) mixed spittle and healed the bodily ills of the blind man. To this extent he appears to recognize the necessity of this carnality—this trace of otherness and defining difference. And yet, in the final analysis, he tries to make the Word's fleshly humanity both typical and representative, and, at the same time, a special case—untouched by the irrationality of desire in conception or the contamination of birth that characterize every other human being in a negative sense. In other words, though he appears to recognize his need for the element of carnality in order to interpret this passage, he shrinks from it. In other respects too, he appears to be skirting around the problem, trying to have his cake and eat it too. Thus, more positive references to the bodily, physical and material dimension of human living are subtly redrawn in this commentary within a spiritualized, metaphorical 'upgraded' context. Augustine draws attention to the bodily substances of spittle and to the physical conditions of blindness in a predominantly metaphorical sense, in order to make a point about spiritual blindness. Similarly, the image of Christ as nursing mother is compelling in its evocation of the divine maternal giving her children milk from her own body and yet, ultimately, it too is qualified as a reference to the needs of a *spiritual* infancy. And yet readers will be impressed and moved by the sense in which Augustine cannot entirely relinquish the carnality of the Word.

Hildegard of Bingen, writing about 700 years later and several thousands of miles further north into Europe, is still very much influenced by the theology of Augustine, as indeed were most of her contemporaries in the Christian world. Hildegard appears to have registered the presence of the divine in her own life in visions and communications which were not simply spiritualized metaphors of divine influence and inspiration but to some degree experienced physically, as if in some acknowledgment of the fact that she was desiring feminine-identified body as much as the speaking subject of spiritual sensibility. Nevertheless, these physical experiences appear to have been pleasurable in an ambivalent sense, that is to say often accompanied by such pain and incapacity that readers might interpret Hildegard's joy in them as perverse.

Nevertheless, and arguably because she was a woman, Hildegard appears to have been more open than was Augustine to the possibility that the bodily exuberance of sexual desire, for example, belonged within God's providential wisdom. Rather than concentrating narrowly upon the figure of Christ, she sees Incarnation in the broadest possible terms as divine Wisdom expressed in cosmic creation and every aspect of human existence as indicative of God's plan. And this clearly included desire for bodily satisfaction and nourishment, albeit controlled by a superior, if 'loving' spirituality. There is, too, abundant evidence of Hildegard's own enjoyment of other sensual pleasures in colour, music, the perfumes of flowers and the contemplation of the fine clothing and bright jewels of her symbolic and frequently female figures representing aspects of divinity or divine grace. But in the end, the fundamental Augustinian framework of gendered hierarchy as between the sphere of desire and the context of spiritualized articulation tends to restrict her vision of divine embodiment.

Within the work of Martin Luther, on the other hand, the reader may understand a passionate desire to banish the otherness against which his decidedly singular and masculine divinity is defined. Of course Luther was notably less misogynistic and more sympathetic to hetero-sexuality within Christian marriage than many earlier Christian Fathers. He was, after all, an ex-celibate priest who married an ex-celibate nun and had six children. In his personal relationship with his own wife, he appears a tolerant and loving husband who recognized his wife's value— at least to him and his children. However, objections to the cult of Marian devotion, to which he gives expression within his sermons on the Prologue, tell a possibly more revealing story. He rejects the many traditional roles of the Virgin Mary—and particularly her role as inter-cessor, or advocate—at once inserting her within his interpretation as the maternal sign of a woman's place within a patriarchal family and devaluing her as the feminine sign of human depravity within Christian patriarchy. It is possible, perhaps first of all then, to connect this absolute rejection of Mary's autonomous value to his rejection, in a cultural sense, of women's independence or autonomy—for example, as celibate nuns outside marriage. But his dislike of Marian pretensions is also related to his theological view of humanity as utterly without positive significance outside its undeserved and gracious relationship to God the Father, of which Christ's Incarnation was the key element. His efforts to define her in the most minimal sense as mother look like a bid abso-lutely to exclude the traces of any autonomous human 'otherness'.

Rudolf Bultmann's interpretation of the Prologue is, for me, in some ways the most intriguing case. None of the other commentators I have dealt with in detail appears to me to have had quite such an acute appreciation of the implications of Incarnation. And yet, ultimately, I believe that he still fails to evade the consequences of the phallogo-centric context with its drive towards singularity. In terms of the analysis presented by feminist theory, the 'otherness' of which woman and the feminine have been the most persistent symbols is located within the nexus of bodily materiality and desire and attempts to give this significance or meaning. Bultmann, I believe, to some extent appreciates this, recognizing that the Christian doctrine of Incarnation, whatever its Chalcedonian references to dual natures that are not confused, cannot be interpreted from this Johannine text in a sense that implies any reserve or differentiation between the humanity of humankind and the humanity of Jesus as a fully embodied, 'this worldly' creature. He thus resists the attempt to make Jesus different by sleight of hand, as some other commentators appear to me to do, using the expedient of virgin birth or the absence of original sin.

However, it seems to me that he still operates within the fundamentally phallogocentric context which devalues all it associates with woman and the feminine. For Bultmann, then, the Word's humanity consists in its subjection to all the feminine-identified, negative qualities—that is transitoriness, helplessness and vanity *(Nichtigkeit)*. Bultmann still regards human existence as ultimately problematic without reference to a singular transcendent truth, even if that truth is expressed in the Word's completely historical and material registration. If the Word has to become human, he has to be subject to the determination of humanity as a devalued form of existence. In other words, by abolishing the sense of the Word's divinity as a separated *form* of existence, Bultmann has not thereby abolished the differential between God and the Word's 'human' nature, which, in typically feminine mode, is still seen to be lacking. At the same time the possibility that the text of the Prologue might contain the sign of a categorical difference—outwith and challenging the gendered hierarchy of values—represented by the conundrum of Word become flesh, is completely swallowed up and lost.

Finally Adrienne von Speyr, within her commentary on the Prologue of John's Gospel, makes divine Incarnation burst out of the Trinitarian 'singularity' with all the bloody force of a human birth. And it is possible that von Speyr, as a doctor, had this particularly shattering and bodily event in her mind when she wrote of human heterosexual love and the birth of a child as analogous to divine Incarnation which represents the new direction of love beyond the previous absorption of God and Word in love for each other. However, von Speyr's own absolute insistence on the authority of the Roman Catholic Church seems to have trapped her, as a woman, within structures of silent and suffering, Marian obedience. In a curious sense, von Speyr's desire, expressed within her study of the Prologue, to be totally defined in relation to

God's unfathomable will is akin to the intensity of Luther's vision of human worthlessness in itself. Of course, von Speyr differs from Luther in her extreme asceticism and in her absolute conviction in the divine authority of the Roman Catholic Church to command her obedience. It is, perhaps, possible to see von Speyr's stigmatic experience as the way in which she both fulfilled and evaded that demand for obedience, ultimately giving expression to God's privileged Word through her own suffering flesh. However, her interpretations of the Prologue remain, I believe, clearly bound within the terms of perversity in which pleasure, satisfaction and nourishment can be achieved only through pain and deprivation.

3. Challenging the Direction of Traditional Interpretation: Three Readings

Feminist critics hoping to make the garment of the biblical text fit or reflect the shape of its women readers better may be encouraged by the inability of commentators altogether to eradicate the trace of an unsettling 'otherness' that is, I believe, symbolized by woman and the feminine and located within a nexus of desire and materiality and the means of giving this significance. From Augustine's vision of desire that evades reason's control, through Luther's absent virgin mother, to von Speyr's reaffirmation of Marian obedience, the traces of this 'otherness', symbolized by feminine-identified presences or absence, persist. But, within the historical context, these are all still caught up within the phallogocentric reading context in which the process of finding significance for whatever woman and the feminine symbolize is dislocated and reappears in disguises such as loving obedience or pleasure through pain and deprivation. The conclusions drawn by historical readers of this text do not seem to me to allow a clear reflection of my face as an autonomous human, feminine subject. I am defined within these interpretative texts as a negative symbol, or even not represented at all.

Therefore, in the second part of this study, I have tried (and the emphasis must be upon the word tried!), to produce an interpretation of the same Johannine text in which some attempt is made to disrupt the phallogocentric direction of historical reading contexts. In my first reading, I deconstruct this text as, ironically, the source of a counter-mythology. While no female figures are referred to overtly, God is situated, by my interpretation, within the context of inarticulate desire.

The feminine-identified humanity of John the Baptist, as friend and witness, represents the articulation God needs. In other words, the divine Word is shown to be dependent upon this human being. In this interpretation, I attempt through a close reading of the text to challenge the 'rhetorical mythology' of divine (masculine) self-sufficiency that I believe is constantly struggling, within traditional interpretations, to reimpose its limiting parameters on readers.

In my second reading, I interpret the double definition of 'flesh' at Jn 1.13 and 14 in terms of a multiplicity that contests any drive towards singularity. In particular I read the doubly defined word 'flesh' within this text against interpretations that reduce the sense of 'Word become flesh' to a mere spiritualized divine (masculine) condescension to a depraved (feminine) humanity. In a spiritualized scheme of this nature, the raw, nourishing, bloody and satisfying body is typically replaced by the suitably debased and dismal condition of (feminine) humanity. The spiritualized 'condition of humanity', because it does not incorporate any suggestion of transgression—that is any crossing through the margins into the realm of the material, physical, bodily and non-linguistic—evades the heterogeneity and the positive trace of the feminine to which I believe Jn 1.14 may itself be read as witness.

In my third reading I relate the Prologue of John's Gospel, in which divine Word becomes fully human, to the narrative of human subjectivity, described by philosopher and theorist Julia Kristeva. Kristeva's theoretical construction of human subjectivity '*en procès*' begins with an initial and painful separation from what she calls the pre-linguistic 'semiotic' realm, preoccupied with desires and drives, and associated with the feminine/maternal. However, while Kristeva's description of this separation in terms of the maternal abject suggests that this feminine-identified realm has to be resisted if living is to be bearable, she does not, thereby, automatically devalue this realm. The semiotic/maternal realm remains the locus of all our creative drives and energies and, in both an individual and a cultural sense, these energies constantly challenge the monolithic, singular and totalitarian impetus of the masculine/paternal identified context of the symbolic—that is, of language and law. In other words, masculine and feminine function together in terms of a necessary multiplicity. Using her theoretical framework, then, I read the text of the Prologue alongside Kristeva's psychoanalytic drama of a human journey towards life made possible. Just as the human subject begins in undifferentiated absorption with the maternal in the semiotic realm, God begins in undifferentiated absorption with Word, although the potential for separation and for the creativity of that separation is already present. And just as human life is made possible in the tension between the symbolic realm of culture and language and the motivations of desire rooted in the semiotic realm of the maternal, so embodied Logos, so to speak, represents a vision of Incarnation that manages to avoid the usual devaluation of the feminine term that accompanies most traditional interpretation. In other words, whereas in traditional forms of biblical interpretation, the Word becoming flesh (Jn 1.14) is a descent or a humiliation or a mark of divine condescension, Kristeva's theoretical framework of human subjectivity challenges the hierarchical sense of the division between symbolic (Word) and semiotic (flesh), while retaining the sense of separation. I believe that it is illuminating then, to see the Prologue as a mythic reflection of the difficult but necessary journey of all human subjects from initial fusion/confusion into a recognition of identity based upon difference and separation which does not have to be elaborated in terms of a hierarchy of values.

4. Should Women Read the Prologue?

I believe that, in the past, the *authority* of the biblical text has been strongly associated with the sort of institutional power that demands interpretative conformity and punishes alternatives as deviant or heretical. And this is why my first reason for wanting to re-read this text has to do with challenging the singular, exclusive tendency of existing biblical interpretations by trying to create what Mieke Bal calls 'counter-coherences', in which close reading reveals multiple or deconstructive interpretations.[2]

But I have said that I want, if possible, to be able to see the feminine face reflected within the biblical text. This could be viewed as a thinly disguised wish to retain something of the perceived authority of the biblical text in order to justify either my own position or the text itself as still charged with 'Good News'. And, of course, this would be a questionable move from a feminist perspective. However, I believe that, beyond illustrating a series of basically hostile assumptions, I have still been able to find this text *significant*.

---

2. See Chapter 1, p. 18, for a description of what Mieke Bal means more precisely by this term.

In order to sum up the sense in which I understand *significant* here, let me refer briefly to two recent examples of biblical interpretation in poetic—that is to say non-scholarly but not thereby non-critical—form. First of all, the the poet Alicia Ostriker is well aware that there is a tradition of reading the Hebrew Bible that encourages a series of widely different conclusions. As she looks to her own Jewish traditions of interpretation, she is not unhopeful, for

> the rabbis have long told us, 'there is always another interpretation'. If biblical interpretation until the present moment has been virtually exclusively the prerogative of males, so much the more reason for women to make a beginning. 'Turn it and turn it,' the rabbis say of Torah 'for everything is in it'.[3]

In both her critical and poetic work Ostriker expresses the belief that women do approach what could be called 'male texts' in a particular and different way, a way that recognizes the potential of such texts or their interpretation for damaging women in both the past and the present, but which also recognizes that women may take, from both the richness and the indeterminacy of canonical Scripture, resources for what might be described as *jouissance*: intense pleasure, vitality and a sense of empowerment. And this liveliness that speaks to a very female desire is all the more empowering because it is the result of engagement with rather than evasion of the other, the oppressor. That is to say, Ostriker sees it as a form of, as it were, wrestling with the angel,[4] a biblical contest in which, you will remember, Jacob, in spite of a painful dislocation, forced God into giving him a blessing (Gen. 32.26).

Modern historical or scientific biblical criticism tells us that there are two stories about the creation of humankind in the book of Genesis. They are very often attributed to two different sources, or writers: the first, in Genesis 1 (Gen 1.27), to the so-called 'Priestly Writer' (P), who is thought to have been writing during the exilic period—the sixth century BCE; and the second, longer account (Gen 2.18-25) to the Elohist source (E), who, it is said, was the earlier writer of the two—working

---

3. Alicia Suskin Ostriker, *Feminist Revision and the Bible* (Oxford: Basil Blackwell, 1993), p. 31.

4. See on wrestling as an image of spiritual growth in William H. Becker, 'Celie as Spiritual Wrestler', in Jacquelyn Grant (ed.), *Perspectives on Womanist Theology* (Black Church Scholars Series, 7; Atlanta, GA: ITC Press, 1995), pp. 147-81. See also Ostriker, *Feminist Revision*, p. 58.

during the ninth or eighth century BCE and coming from the Northern or Israelite kingdom.

This theory presents us with one form of 'coherence' in reading the text but, of course, it leaves the reader with another puzzle to solve. Why should two accounts be preserved and not simply one? On the other hand Jewish legendary reflection and midrash make from this, so to speak, embarrassment of women, a story of two wives. Lilith is the first wife—the female created alongside the male in Gen. 1.27—a troublesome and even dangerous woman who is subsequently replaced by Eve. In the legend, Lilith and Adam begin quarrelling very soon after creation because she refuses to accept his lordship over her. She takes badly to his demands and finally leaves. Adam complains to God who sends angels to get her back but she has found more congenial company frolicking in the Red Sea and obdurately refuses to return with them.

> When she would not go with them she was cursed; she would have to give birth to a hundred demons every day, and they would die by nightfall. It is said that Lilith attempts to seduce men, and that she slips between a man and his wife to steal drops of his semen and make demons from it to plague mankind. Traditional households protected themselves from Lilith with amulets and spells.[5]

Ostriker, writing from a distinctively Jewish background, has written a collection of poems called 'The Lilith Poems', in which she explores this story. From a feminist perspective, she shows that the legend of Lilith is resonant. Lilith does not feature in the Hebrew Bible but is the product of reflection and interpretation. And yet she fits so naturally within the fabric of the Genesis narrative that she is hard to forget once conjured up. She seems not so much absent as 'covered up' and 'silenced'. And, in this sense, she aptly symbolizes Ostriker's conclusion that the Hebrew biblical narrative is fundamentally a cover-up, an obsessive retelling of erased female power, or of 'repeated acts of literal murder and oppression'.[6] Lilith sums up the oppressive narrative of biblical patriarchy that turns the anonymity of the first human female creation within the text into a determinate, exiled or demonized being, either by equating her with Eve or elaborating her in terms of Lilith. In a modern discourse of 'objective' or 'scientific' biblical criticism, she is similarly removed, although this time even more radically, from the

---

5.   Ostriker, *Feminist Revision*, p. 99.
6.   Ostriker, *Feminist Revision*, p. 31.

authoritative text, since the existence of two different creation narratives undercuts any sense of narrative continuity in which there might be space for an independent, pleasure-seeking woman or a 'failed' marriage. Although they approach the text from widely differing perspectives, neither reading really comes to terms with a wild woman inhabiting the world without a male partner to whom she is subject. But with Ostriker's guidance we see that there is no clear indication, at Gen. 1.27, that female has been created to help or to be ruled by male:

> Girl, that man of yours
> Was one pathetic creature
> Puffing his chest, thinking the world of himself,
> Standing there saying *Lie down* and *hold still*,
> Waving his sceptre at the jacaranda,
> The bougainvillea, like the boss of something,
> Though wasn't he only taking orders
> From a bigger boss[7]

The midrashic legend of Lilith—as recorded by Ostriker—ultimately falls back into demonizing its female anti-heroine. It constructs Lilith as a figure who apparently threatens all men, wanting to steal their seed or semen, a substance that comes disturbingly out of the intimacy of sexual pleasure and touching but which may be sanctified once it becomes fixed within properly constituted connubial responsibility as a religious duty, a '*mitzvah*'. Lilith is, then, representative of both unsubmissive wife and the seductive temptation to dissent, to rebel and turn aside from duty, a temptation that faithful God-fearing men must resist at all costs. She becomes another Eve. But the text is polyvalent, indeterminate, and open to interpretation. In Ostriker's poetic rendering of the legend, Lilith squeezes back into the text rupturing carefully constructed coherences that exclude her and refusing to be quiet. The text retains its indeterminacy and the poet is able to take from the interpretative legend of Lilith, in dialogue with the biblical text, the liveliest pleasure, vitality and blessing, notwithstanding her continuing sense of dislocation as a woman within patriarchy.

But the reference to Jacob's wrestling with the angel is surely also a reminder that men need to figure in any reading of the biblical text, so to speak, 'for the siginificance of the feminine'. The feminine face, so frequently associated symbolically and culturally with actual women, is

---

7.   Ostriker, *Feminist Revision*, p. 94, 'Lilith Jumps the Fence', The Lilith Poems number 2.

maintained as their exclusive property only, I would argue, at great risk. To fear and distrust men as always and only the villains of the piece, however understandable on one level, is simply to encourage the sort of scapegoating behaviour and attitudes that have already wrecked and impoverished the lives of so many women. And in so far as the feminine represents a dimension of the world in which all humankind partake, both women and men need to confront and wrestle with it, equally resolute in their desire for a blessing.

Irish poet and singer Christy Moore tells a story of creation that is related to the creation story/stories in Genesis, except that God is 'She'. The story implicitly challenges the account of creation in Genesis for its bias towards a masculine God. And from the perspective of his own background as an Irish Roman Catholic, he taps into a rich vein of associations. His invocation of a female Creator reminds us of Mary giving birth to Jesus, of Eve as 'spare rib', of Roman Catholic iconography of the sacred heart of Mary, linking Mary's feminine/maternal suffering with Eucharistic feeding and, of course, of all the pre-Christian traditions surrounding Brigit, the Celtic goddess of fertility, healing and divination. But Christy Moore's 'God Woman'[8] is neither Mary nor the God of Genesis nor Brigit. The writer makes her act and commission, like the Creator of Genesis, rather than submit like the woman of Lk. 2.38. Not at all a remodelled male rib, she draws out of her own divine female body a male creature and then sends him away with tasks to complete. But, at the same time, her creating is an embodied creating. She does not fashion her male creature out of words and symbols but draws him from her own feminine body.

Of course, the mother/son relationship that, within Mariology, has sometimes been seen to exclude, as significant, mother/daughter relationships remains largely intact in this song. But arguably, like Ostriker, Christy Moore shows himself alive to the continuing significance of the biblical text as well as to its dangerous and damaging potential. He, like Ostriker, is able to weave a gendered reading into the fashion of a work which is, in his case moreover, also a performance, addressed as much to the senses as to the intellect.

I conclude, finally, that it is perfectly possible to read the text of the Prologue from a woman-centred perspective. It is perfectly possible, that is, to subject it to feminist critical analysis. But I also believe that I have

---

8. Christy Moore, 'God Woman', *Graffiti Tongue* (London: CNR Music, 1996).

been able, to some extent, to weave a critical interpretation of the Prologue into the fashion of a creative dialogue, in a way, moreover, that does some justice to the multiplicity or heterogeneity of the reader. I believe, for example, that in its statement of the central mystery of Christian Incarnation—'The Word became flesh'—is contained a potential for destabilizing the phallogocentric context of so many readings of this passage in the past which have compounded the identification of human depravity and vulnerability with women and the feminine in general. And I believe that it is also possible to find readings of the text that emphasize both the bodily and the inter-relational significance of human living as a means to understanding a divinely creative initiative.

BIBLIOGRAPHY

Andersen, K., 'Mimetic Reflections when Reading a Text in the Image of Gender', in A.E. Jasper and A.G. Hunter (eds.), *Talking It Over: Perspectives on Women and Religion 1993–5* (Glasgow: Trinity St Mungo Press, 1996), pp. 1-21.

Anderson, P.S., 'After Theology: End or Transformation?', *Literature & Theology* 7.1 (1993), pp. 66-78.

—'Wrestling with Strangers: Julia Kristeva and Paul Ricoeur on the Other', in A.E. Jasper and A.G. Hunter (eds.), *Talking It Over: Perspectives on Women and Religion 1993–5* (Glasgow: Trinity St Mungo Press, 1996), pp. 129-49.

Ashton, J., 'The Transformation of Wisdom: A Study of the Prologue of John's Gospel', *NTS* 32 (1986), pp. 161-86.

—*Understanding the Fourth Gospel* (Oxford: Oxford University Press, 1991).

Auerbach, E., *Mimesis: The Representation of Reality in Western Literature* (Princeton: Princeton University Press, 1953).

Bal, M., *Narratology: Introduction to the Theory of Narrative* (Toronto: University of Toronto Press, 1985).

—*Lethal Love: Feminist Literary Readings of Biblical Love Stories* (Bloomington: Indiana University Press, 1987).

—*Death and Dissymmetry: The Politics of Coherence in the Book of Judges* (Chicago: University of Chicago Press, 1988).

—*Murder and Difference: Gender, Genre and Scholarship on Sisera's Death* (Bloomington: Indiana University Press, 1988).

Balthasar, H.U. von, *First Glance at Adrienne von Speyr* (San Francisco: Ignatius Press, 1981).

—*Unser Auftrag: Bericht und Entwurf* (Einsiedeln: Johannes Verlag, 1984).

Barrett, C.K., *The Gospel According to St John: An Introduction with Commentary and Notes on the Greek Text* (London: SPCK, 2nd edn, 1978 [1955]).

Beckwith, S., *Christ's Body: Identity, Culture and Society in Late Medieval Writings* (London: Routledge, 1993).

Booth, W.C., *A Rhetoric of Irony* (Chicago: University of Chicago Press, 1974).

Boyarin, D., *A Radical Jew: Paul and the Politics of Identity* (Berkeley: University of California Press, 1994).

Bronfen, E., 'From Omphalos to Phallus: Cultural Representations of Femininity and Death', *Women: A Cultural Review* 13.2 (1992), pp. 145-58.

Brown, P., *Augustine of Hippo: A Biography* (London: Faber & Faber, 1967).

Brown, R.E., *The Gospel According to John I–XII: A New Translation with Introduction and Commentary* (AB, 29; New York: Doubleday, 1966).

—*The Community of the Beloved Disciple* (New York: Paulist Press, 1979).

Bultmann, R., *Essays, Philosophical and Theological* (London: SCM Press, 1955).

—*Theology of the New Testament*, II (London: SCM Press, 1955).

—*Jesus Christ and Mythology* (New York: Charles Scribner's Son's, 1958).

—*Jesus and the Word* (New York: Charles Scribner's Son's, 1958).

—'Bultmann Replies to his Critics', in H.W. Bartsch and R.H. Fuller (eds.), *Kerygma and Myth: A Theological Debate* (2 vols.; London: SPCK, 2nd edn, 1964).

—*The Gospel of John: A Commentary* (trans. R.W.N. Hoare and J.K. Riches; Philadelphia: Westminster Press, 1971).

—'New Testament and Mythology', in S.M. Ogden (ed.), *New Testament and Mythology and Other Basic Writings* (London: SCM Press, 1985).

Bynum, C.W., *Holy Feast and Holy Fast: The Religious Significance of Food to Medieval Women* (Berkeley: University of California Press, 1987).

—'The Female Body and Religious Practice in the Later Middle Ages', in M. Feher (ed.), *Fragments for a History of the Human Body* (New York: Zone Books, 1989).

—*Fragmentation and Redemption: Essays on Gender and the Human Body in Medieval Religion* (New York: Zone Books, 1991).

Chadwick, H., *Augustine* (Oxford: Oxford University Press, 1986).

Collins, A.Y., 'New Testament Perspectives: The Gospel of John', *JSOT* 22 (1982), pp. 47-53.

Connolly, W.E., *The Augustinian Imperative: A Reflection on the Politics of Morality* (Newberry Park, CA: Sage Publications, 1993). Newberry

Cross, F.L. (ed.), *The Oxford Dictionary of the Christian Church* (London: Oxford University Press, 1958).

Crossan, J.D., 'It Is Written: A Structuralist Analysis of John 6', in M.W.G. Stibbe (ed.), *The Gospel of John as Literature: An Anthology of Twentieth Century Perspectives* (Leiden: E.J. Brill, 1993).

Culpepper, R.A., *Anatomy of the Fourth Gospel: A Study in Literary Design* (Philadelphia: Fortress Press, 1983).

Daly, M., *Beyond God the Father: Towards a Philosophy of Women's Liberation* (London: The Women's Press, 1986).

—*Gyn/Ecology: The Metaethics of Radical Feminism* (London: The Women's Press, 1991).

Davies, M., *Rhetoric and Reference in the Fourth Gospel* (JSNTSup, 69; Sheffield: JSOT Press, 1992).

Dronke, P., *Women Writers of the Middle Ages: A Critical Study of Texts from Perpetua (d. 203) to Marguerite Porete (d. 1310)* (Cambridge: Cambridge University Press, 1984).

Duke, P.D., *Irony in the Fourth Gospel* (Atlanta, GA: John Knox Press, 1985).

Evans, G.R., *Augustine on Evil* (Cambridge: Cambridge University Press, 2nd edn, 1990).

Exum, J.C., 'Murder They Wrote: Ideology and the Manipulation of Female Presence in Biblical Narrative', in A. Bach (ed.), *The Pleasure of her Text* (Philadelphia: Trinity Press International, 1990).

—*Tragedy and Biblical Narrative* (Cambridge: Cambridge University Press, 1992).

Faludi, S., *Backlash: The Undeclared War against Women* (London: Vintage, 1992).

Fiorenza, E.S., *In Memory of Her: A Feminist Theological Reconstruction of Christian Origins* (London: SCM Press, 1983).

—*The Book of Revelation: Justice and Judgement* (Philadelphia: Fortress Press, 1984).

—*Bread not Stone: The Challenge of Feminist Biblical Interpretation* (Boston: Beacon Press, 1985).

—'Remembering the Past in Creating the Future: Historical-critical Scholarship and Feminist Biblical Interpretation', in A.Y. Collins (ed.), *Feminist Perspectives on Biblical Scholarship* (Chico, CA: Scholars Press, 1985), pp. 36-63.

—'Missionaries, Apostles, Co-workers: Romans 16 and the Reconstruction of Women's Early Christian History', in A. Loades (ed.), *Feminist Theology: A Reader* (London: SPCK, 1990), pp. 57-71.

—*But She Said: Feminist Practices of Biblical Interpretation* (Boston: Beacon Press, 1992).

—*Jesus: Miriam's Child, Sophia's Prophet: Critical Issues in Feminist Christology* (London: SCM Press, 1994).

Flanagan, S., *Hildegard of Bingen, 1098–1179: A Visionary Life* (London: Routledge, 1989).

Fox, M. (ed.), *Illuminations of Hildegard of Bingen* (Santa Fe, NM: Bear and Company, 1985).

—*Hildegard of Bingen's Book of Divine Works with Letters and Songs* (trans. R. Cunningham; Santa Fe, NM: Bear and Company, 1987).

Fuchs, E., 'Who Is Hiding the Truth? Deceptive Women and Biblical Androcentrism', in A.Y. Collins (ed.), *Feminist Perspectives on Biblical Scholarship* (Chico, CA: Scholars Press, 1985).

Fulkerson, M.M., 'Sexism as Original Sin: Developing a Theacentric Discourse', *JAAR* 49.4, pp. 653-75.

—*Changing the Subject: Women's Discourses and Feminist Theology* (Philadelphia: Fortress Press, 1994).

Gay, P. (ed.), *The Freud Reader* (London: Vintage, 1995).

Graef, H., *Mary: A History of Doctrine and Devotion*. I. *From the Beginnings to the Eve of the Reformation* (London: Sheed & Ward, 1963).

—*Mary: A History of Doctrine and Devotion*. II. *From the Reformation to the Present Day* (London: Sheed & Ward, 1965).

Griffiths, M., and A. Sellar, 'The Politics of Identity: The Politics of the Self', *Women: A Cultural Review* 3.2 (1992), pp. 133-44.

Grosz, E., 'Contemporary Theories of Power and Subjectivity', in Sneja Gunew (ed.), *Feminist Knowledge: Critique and Construct* (London: Routledge, 1990).

Haenchen, E., *John: A Commentary on the Gospel of John* (2 vols.; eds. Robert W. Funk and Ulrich Basse; trans. Robert W. Funk; Philadelphia: Fortress Press, 1984).

Hampson, D., 'Luther on the Self: A Feminist Critique', in Ann Loades (ed.), *Feminist Theology: A Reader* (London: SPCK, 1990).

Heine, S., *Women and Early Christianity: Are the Feminist Scholars Right?* (trans. John Bowden; London: SCM Press, 1987).

Hengel, M., *The Johannine Question* (trans. John Bowden; London: SCM Press, 1989).

Holl, K., 'Martin Luther on Luther', in Jaroslav Pelikan (ed.), *Interpreters of Luther: Essays in Honor of Wilhelm Pauck* (Philadelphia: Fortress Press, 1968), pp. 9-35.

Horrocks, R., 'The Divine Woman in Christianity', in A. Pirani (ed.), *The Absent Mother: Restoring the Goddess to Judaism and Christianity* (London: Mandala, 1991).

Humm, M. (ed.), *Feminisms: A Reader* (New York: Harvester Wheatsheaf, 1992).

—*The Dictionary of Feminist Theory* (New York: Harvester Wheatsheaf, 2nd edn, 1995).

Ihde, D. (ed.), *Paul Ricoeur: The Conflict of Interpretations. Essays in Hermeneutics* (Evanston, IL: Northwestern University Press, 1974).

Irigaray, L., *Speculum de l'autre femme* (Paris: Minuit, 1974; ET *Speculum of the Other Woman* [trans. G.C. Gill; New York: Cornell University Press, 1985]).

—*Marine Lover of Friedrich Nietzsche* (New York: Columbia University Press, 1991).

—*Je, tu, nous: Toward a Culture of Difference* (New York: Routledge, 1993).

—*Sexes and Genealogies* (trans. G.C. Gill; London: Routledge, 1993).

Jasper, A, 'Interpretative Approaches to John 20: 1-18: Mary at the Tomb of Jesus', *ST* 47 (1993), pp. 107-18.

Jasper, A.E., and A.G. Hunter (eds.), *Talking It Over: Perspectives on Women and Religion 1993–5* (Glasgow: Trinity St Mungo Press, 1996).

Jasper, D., *Rhetoric, Power and Community* (London: Macmillan, 1993).

Jobling, D., and S.D. Moore (eds.), 'Poststructuralism as Exegesis', *Semeia* 54.

Käsemann, E., *The Testament of Jesus: A Study of the Gospel of John in the Light of Chapter 17* (London: SCM Press, 1968).

Kim, C.W.M., S.M. St. Ville and S.M. Simonaitis (eds.), *Transfigurations: Theology and the French Feminists* (Minneapolis: Fortress Press, 1993).

Knowles, D. (ed.), *Augustine: City of God* (trans. H. Bettenson; Harmondsworth: Penguin Books, 1972).

Kristeva, J., *Powers of Horror: An Essay on Abjection* (trans. L. Roudiez; New York: Columbia University Press, 1982).

—*Desire in Language: A Semiotic Approach to Literature and Art* (Oxford: Basil Blackwell, 1984).

—*Revolution in Poetic Language* (trans. Margaret Waller; New York: Columbia University Press, 1984), pp. 59-60 (first published as *La révolution du langage poétique: L'avant-garde à la fin du XIX* siècle: Lautréamont et mallarmé* [Paris: Seuil, 1974]).

—*In the Beginning Was Love: Psychoanalysis and Faith* (trans. A. Golhammer; New York: Columbia University Press, 1987).

—*Black Sun: Depression and Melancholia* (trans. L. Roudiez; New York: Columbia University Press, 1989).

—*New Maladies of the Soul* (trans. R. Guberman; New York: Columbia University Press, 1995).

Le Doeuff, M., *Hipparchia's Choice: An Essay Concerning Women, Philosophy, etc.* (Oxford: Basil Blackwell, 1991).

Lechte, J., *Fifty Key Contemporary Thinkers: From Structuralism to Postmodernity* (London: Routledge, 1994).

Lienhard, M., *Luther: Witness to Jesus Christ* (trans. E.H. Robertson; Minneapolis: Augsburg, 1982).

Lindars, B., *The Gospel of John* (NCB Commentary; Grand Rapids: Eerdmans, 1972).

Lloyd, G., 'Augustine and Aquinas', in *The Man of Reason: 'Male and Female' in Western Philosophy* (Minneapolis: University of Minnesota Press, 1984), pp. 28-37; repr. in Ann Loades (ed.), *Feminist Theology: A Reader* (London: SPCK, 1990), pp. 90-99.

Lodge, D. (ed.), *Modern Criticism and Theory: A Reader* (London: Longmans, 1988).

Long, A., 'The Goddess in Judaism: An Historical Perspective', in Alix Pirani (ed.), *The Absent Mother: Restoring the Goddess to Judaism and Christianity* (London: Mandala, 1991).

Lorde, A., *Sister Outsider: Essays and Speeches by Audre Lorde* (Freedom, CA: The Crossing Press, 1984).

—*Undersong: Chosen Poems Old and New* (London: Virago Press, 1993), pp. 100-101.

Luther, M., *Table Talk* (trans. W. Hazlitt; London: Fount Paperbacks, 1995).

Macrae, G.W., 'Theology and Irony in the Fourth Gospel', in M.W.G. Stibbe (ed.), *The Gospel of John as Literature: An Anthology of Twentieth Century Perspectives* (Leiden: E.J. Brill, 1993), pp. 103-14.

Martyn, J.L., *History and Theology in the Fourth Gospel* (New York: Harper & Row, 1968).

McKinlay, J., *Gendering Wisdom the Host: Biblical Invitations to Eat and Drink* (JSOTSup, 216; Gender, Culture, Theory, 4; Sheffield: Sheffield Academic Press, 1996).

McLaughlin, E., 'Women, Power and the Pursuit of Holiness in Medieval Christianity', in R.R. Ruether and E. Mclaughlin (eds.), *Women of Spirit: Female Leadership in the Jewish and Christian Traditions* (New York: Simon and Schuster, 1979), pp. 93-130.

Moi, T., *Sexual/Textual Politics: Feminist Literary Theory* (London: Routledge, 1988).

—(ed.), *The Kristeva Reader* (Oxford: Basil Blackwell, 1986).

Moore, S.D., *Literary Criticism and the Gospels: The Theoretical Challenge* (New Haven: Yale University Press, 1989).

—*Poststructuralism in the New Testament: Derrida and Foucault at the Foot of the Cross* (Minneapolis: Fortress Press, 1994).

Newman, B., *Sister of Wisdom: St. Hildegard's Theology of the Feminine* (Aldershot: Scolar, 1987).

Nye, A., *Feminist Theory and the Philosophies of Man* (London: Routledge, 1989).

O'Carroll, M., *Theotokos: A Theological Encyclopedia of the Blessed Virgin Mary* (Wilmington, DE: Michael Glazier, rev. edn, 1983).

O'Day, G., *Revelation in the Fourth Gospel: Narrative Mode and Theological Claim* (Philadelphia: Fortress Press, 1986).

Oakes, E.T., *Pattern of Redemption: The Theology of Hans Urs von Balthasar* (New York: Continuum, 1994).

Oberman, H.A., *Luther: Man between God and the Devil* (trans. E. Walliser-Schwarzbart; London: Fontana Press, 1993).

Ogden, S. (ed.), *Existence and Faith: Shorter Writings of Rudolf Bultmann* (New York: The World Publishing Company, 1961).

Ostriker, A.S., *Feminist Revision and the Bible* (Oxford: Basil Blackwell, 1993).

Pelikan, J. (ed.), *Luther's Works. XXII. Sermons on the Gospel of St. John, Chapters 1–4* (trans. Martin H. Bertram; 55 vols.; St Louis, MO: Concordia, 1957).

—(ed.), *Luther's Works. I. Lectures on Genesis Chapters 1–5* (St Louis, MO: Concordia, 1958), p. 147.

Pine-Coffin, R.S. (ed. and trans.), *St. Augustine: Confessions* (Harmondsworth: Penguin Books, 1961).

Portefaix, L., *Sisters Rejoice: Paul's Letter to the Philippians and Luke–Acts as Received by First Century Philippian Women* (Uppsala: Almqvist & Wiksell, 1988).

Rad, G. von, *Wisdom in Israel* (London: SCM Press, 1972).

Reinhartz, A., *The Word in the World: The Cosmological Tale in the Fourth Gospel* (Atlanta, GA: Scholars Press, 1992).

Rettig, J.W. (ed. and trans.), *St. Augustine: Tractates on the Gospel of John 1–10* (Washington: Catholic University of America Press, 1988).

—*St. Augustine: Tractates on the Gospel of John 28–54* (Washington: Catholic University of America Press, 1993).

Richardson, A., and J. Bowden (eds.), *A New Dictionary of Christian Theology* (London: SCM Press, 1983).

Riches, J.K., *A Century of New Testament Study* (Cambridge: Lutterworth, 1993).

Ricoeur, R., *The Symbolism of Evil* (Boston: Beacon Press, 1969).

—'Preface to Bultmann', in D. Ihde (ed.), *Paul Ricoeur: The Conflict of Interpretation. Essays in Hermeneutics* (Evanston, IL: Northwestern University Press, 1974).

—*The Rule of Metaphor* (Toronto: University of Toronto Press, 1977).

Roberts, R.C., *Rudolf Bultmann's Theology: A Critical Interpretation* (London: SPCK, 1977).

Ross, E.M., 'Human Persons as Images of the Divine', in A. Bach (ed.), *The Pleasure of her Text* (Philadelphia: Trinity Press International, 1990).

Ruether, R.R., *Sexism and God-Talk* (London: SCM Press, 1983).

—'The Liberation of Christology from Patriarchy', *New Blackfriars* 66 (1985), pp. 324-35; 67 (1986), pp. 92-93.

—*Gaia and God: An Ecofeminist Theology of Earth Healing* (New York: HarperSanFrancisco, 1992).

Russell, L. (ed.), *Feminist Interpretation of the Bible* (Oxford: Basil Blackwell, 1985).

Saiving, V., 'The Human Situation: A Feminine View', in C. Christ and J. Plaskow (eds.), *Womanspirit Rising: A Feminist Reader in Religion* (New York: Harper & Row, 1979).

Schnackenburg, R., *The Gospel According to St. John* (trans. K. Smyth; 3 vols.; New York: Herder & Herder, 1968).

Schneiders, S., *The Revelatory Text: Interpreting the New Testament as Sacred Scripture* (New York: HarperSanFrancisco, 1991).

—'Women in the Fourth Gospel and the Role of Women in the Contemporary Church', in M.W.G. Stibbe (ed.), *The Gospel of John as Literature: An Anthology of Twentieth Century Perspectives* (Leiden: E.J. Brill, 1993).

Scott, M., *Sophia and the Johannine Jesus* (JSNTSup, 71; Sheffield: JSOT Press, 1992).

Seim, T.K., *The Double Message: Patterns of Gender in Luke–Acts* (Edinburgh: T. & T. Clark, 1994).

Sellers, S. (ed.), *The Hélène Cixous Reader* (London: Routledge, 1994).

Speyr, A. von, *The Word: A Meditation on the Prologue to St. John's Gospel* (trans. A. Dru; London: Collins, 1953).

—*Meditations on the Gospel of St. John* (London: Collins, 1959).

—*Confession* (San Francisco: Ignatius Press, 1985).

—*Handmaid of the Lord* (San Francisco: Ignatius Press, 1985).

—*The World of Prayer* (San Francisco: Ignatius Press, 1985).

—*The Christian State of Life* (San Francisco: Ignatius Press, 1986).

Staley, J.L., *The Print's First Kiss: A Rhetorical Investigation of the Implied Reader in the Fourth Gospel* (Atlanta, GA: Scholars Press, 1986).

Stanton, Elizabeth Cady, *The Woman's Bible* (New York: European Publishing Company, 1895).

Stead, G.C., 'The Valentinian Myth of Sophia', *JTS* NS 20 (1969), pp. 75-104.

Steinmetz, D.C., *Luther in Context* (Bloomington: Indiana University Press, 1986).

Stibbe, M.W.G., *John as Storyteller: Narrative Criticism and the Fourth Gospel* (Cambridge: Cambridge University Press, 1992).

—*John* (Sheffield: Sheffield Academic Press, 1993).

Tilborg, S. van, *Imaginative Love in John* (Leiden: E.J. Brill, 1993).

Tolbert, M.A., 'Defining the Problem: The Bible and Feminist Hermeneutics', *Semeia* 28 (1983), pp. 113-26.

—'Protestant Feminists and the Bible: On the Horns of a Dilemma', in Alice Bach (ed.), *The Pleasure of her Test: Feminist Readings of Biblical and Historical Texts* (Philadelphia: Trinity Press International, 1990).

Tong, R., *Feminist Thought: A Comprehensive Introduction* (London: Routledge, 1989).

Trible, P., *God and the Rhetoric of Sexuality* (Philadelphia: Fortress Press, 1978).

—'Feminist Hermeneutics and Biblical Studies', *The Christian Century* 3.10 (1982), pp. 116-18.

—*Texts of Terror: Literary-Feminist Readings of Biblical Narratives* (London: SCM Press, 1992).

Warner, M., *Alone of All her Sex: The Myth and the Cult of the Virgin Mary* (London: Pan Books, 1990).

Wiesner, M., 'Luther and Women: The Death of Two Marys', in A. Loades (ed.), *Feminist Theology: A Reader* (London: SPCK, 1990).

Wigram, G.V., *The Englishman's Greek Concordance of the New Testament* (London: Samuel Bagster and Sons, 9th edn, 1903).

Wilson, I., *The Bleeding Mind: An Investigation into the Mysterious Phenomenon of Stigmata* (London: Paladin, 1991).

Yarom, N., *Body, Blood and Sexuality: A Psychoanalytic Study of St. Francis' Stigmata and their Historical Context* (New York: Peter Lang, 1992).

Young, R., *Analytical Concordance to the Holy Bible* (Guildford and London: The Lutterworth Press, 8th edn, 1939).

INDEXES

INDEX OF REFERENCES

OLD TESTAMENT

Genesis		Exodus		Proverbs	
1	243	33.20	230	8	70
1.1-5	223			8.22-31	38
1.1	170, 171,	Deuteronomy		9	39
	222	18.18	176	9.1-5	40
1.2	222, 223			9.1	40
1.3-5	222	Judges			
1.3	211	13–16	181	Isaiah	
1.4-5	222	19	14	31.3	192
1.4	228			40.3	176
1.6	211	2 Samuel		55	199
1.9	211	13.1-22	14	55.2-3	199
1.27	243–45				
1.28	172	Psalms		Wisdom of Solomon	
2–3	74	18.11	205	7–9	70
2.15-17	172	33.6	211	9	38
2.18-25	243	104.24	38		
3	225			Sirach	
3.6	225			24	38, 70
				24.8	40

NEW TESTAMENT

Matthew		2.38	246	1.1-14	63, 64, 73,
13.55	102	2.41-51	102		81, 162
		2.51	102	1.1-12	145
Mark		12.21	173	1.1-5	38, 223
6.3	102			1.1-2	211
		John		1.1	142, 171,
Luke		1–4	87		172, 223
1.35	102	1	73, 208	1.2	145
1.38	180	1.1-18	9, 19, 73, 87,	1.3-18	145
1.39-45	102		97, 103, 166,	1.3-14	212
1.42	102		169, 174,	1.3-4	40, 67
2.34-35	102		181, 193	1.3	152, 170,

171, 183, 224

1.4-5   223
1.4   67, 68, 138, 195
1.5   70, 157, 158, 176, 177, 223-26, 228, 231
1.6-24   44
1.6-8   146, 226, 227
1.6   171, 174-77, 179, 194
1.7-8   178
1.7   73, 175, 176, 195
1.8   175
1.9-14   177
1.9-13   176, 212
1.9   147, 195, 223, 226
1.10-13   187
1.10-11   110
1.10   70, 177, 225, 227
1.11   177, 225, 227
1.12-14   183, 190, 197, 200
1.12-13   74, 111, 191, 192, 195, 196, 227, 228
1.12   73, 177, 178, 195
1.13-14   207
1.13   153, 155, 164, 177, 183, 187, 189-92, 195, 196, 199, 228, 229, 241
1.14-15   177
1.14   19, 23, 45, 78, 80, 111, 123, 125-27,

1.15-36   175
1.15-18   73, 177
1.15   176-78
1.16   187
1.17   46, 49, 51, 187, 222, 230
1.18   177, 211, 212, 229, 230
1.19   177
1.20-21   176
1.20   176, 177
1.21   176, 177
1.23   176, 177
1.26   177
1.27   177, 178
1.29-34   176, 177
1.29   179
1.31   176
1.35   179
1.45   51, 123, 124, 179
2.5   179
2.8   39
2.11   172
3.1-21   190
3.4-7   208
3.4   190
3.6   125, 126
3.14   51, 187
3.22-36   175
4.10   39
4.39   194
5.46   51, 187
6   197-201, 206, 208
6.11-14   39
6.22-27   200
6.26-58   198, 155, 164, 174, 176-78, 183, 187, 189-91, 193, 196-98, 208, 211, 212, 229, 241, 242

6.27   199
6.31-51   200
6.35   39, 199
6.42   123, 124
6.49-50   199
6.51-59   200, 201
6.51-58   200, 207
6.51   200
6.53-63   207
6.53-58   198
6.53-56   206
6.53   126, 198, 202-204, 206
6.58   200
6.60-61   207
6.63   125, 126, 199, 202, 207
6.64   172
6.68   179
7.27   123, 124
7.28   123
8.2   172
8.40   123
8.44   172
9   46
9.1-2   46
9.6   236
9.18-22   46
10.33   123
11.27   179, 180, 194
12.19   126
13.37   67
14.9-10   229
15.13   67
15.27   172
16.4   172
20.17-18   194
20.28   179

Romans
5.20   49
16   16

1 Corinthians
3   186

3.1–2	41	*Galatians*		*Hebrews*	
3.17–18	186	3.13	109	1.1	230
7.9	186			5.12	41
11.1–16	194	*Ephesians*		5.13	41
11.5	186	5.25–33	20		
				1 Peter	
2 Corinthians		*1 Timothy*		2.2	41
5.21	109	4.12	186		
13.35	20			*Revelation*	
				22.4–5	151

OTHER ANCIENT REFERENCES

Philo		12.8	43	3.4.2–3	91
Quaest. in Gen.		2.7.18	53	3.4.3	51
46.53	185			3.6.2	46
		Tractate		3.6.3	46
Christian Authors		1–3	42	3.11.1	49
Augustine		1.1.1	36	3.12.1	43, 56
City of God		1.7.2	41	3.12.2	49
12.7	50	1.9.3	35	3.14.1	46
		1.11.1	35	3.14.2	36
Confessions		1.12.2	41	3.16.1	49
2.2	49, 52	1.14.2	35	3.18.1	36
2.4	50	1.16.1	38	3.19.1	34, 36, 56
2.5	49	1.16.3	38	3.19.3	56
5.7	42	1.17.3	41	3.21.1	56
5.8	42	2.2.4	36	44	46
5.9	42	2.4.1	35, 36	44.2.1	47
6.13	56	2.5.1	36	44.2.2	47
6.15	56	2.7.1	36		
8	53	2.7.2	36	Eusebius	
9.9	56	2.10.1	35	*Historia Ecclesiastica*	
9.10	56	2.14.3	43	6.14.7	202
		2.15.1	44		
Contra Julianum Pelagianum		2.15.2	36, 44	Tertullian	
4.7	55	2.16.1	45	*De cultu feminarum*	
		2.16.2	45	1.1	37, 185
De Trinitate		3.3.1	36		
12.7	38	3.4	57		

INDEX OF AUTHORS

Albrecht, B. 137
Andersen, H. 13, 17
Andersen, K. 27
Anderson, P.S. 167, 217
Ashton, J. 29, 194
Atwood, M. 55

Bakhtin, M. 27, 28
Bal, M. 18, 19, 24, 27, 169, 181, 242
Balthasar, H.U. von 135-37, 140, 141,
    143, 147-52, 160
Barrett, C.K. 67, 191-93, 199, 223, 225,
    226
Bartsch, H.W. 116
Beardsley, M.C. 29
Beauvoir, S. de 25, 190
Becker, W.H. 243
Berrouard, M.-F. 35
Bois, B. du 21
Booth, W.C. 174
Bowles, G. 21
Boyarin, D. 187, 189, 193, 194
Brown, R.E. 51, 67, 73, 167, 168, 170,
    171, 173, 174, 188, 190, 198, 200,
    222, 225, 230
Bultmann, R. 23, 29, 113-34, 163-64,
    200, 230, 234, 238, 239
Bynum, C.W. 60, 72, 79, 80, 96, 105,
    128, 160, 203-207

Caputo, J.D. 114
Chadwick, H. 37, 53, 55
Chatman, S. 31
Chodorow, N. 25
Cixous, H. 13, 21, 25, 26, 234, 235
Collins, A.Y. 15, 39, 40
Connolly, W.E. 48, 52

Culpepper, R.A. 30
Daly, M. 16, 17, 32, 138, 139, 220
Davies, M. 191, 210-12, 232
Derrida, J. 13, 21
Dronke, P. 59-62, 76, 206
Duke, P.D. 173, 174

Evans, G.R. 53

Feher, M. 203, 205, 206
Fiorenza, E.S. 15, 16, 26, 111, 112, 130,
    179, 208, 221
Flanagan, S. 58, 60-62, 64
Fox, M. 58, 59, 64
Freud, S. 26, 133, 148, 155, 213, 217,
    218, 226, 228
Fuller, R.H. 116
Funk, R.W. 192

Genette, G. 28
Gilligan, C. 25
Graef, H. 99, 101
Grant, J. 243
Grosz, E. 166
Gunew, S. 166

Haenchen, E. 192, 195, 197, 200, 203
Haering, T. 131
Haley, A. 15
Hampson, D. 111
Harnack, A. 131
Haskins, S. 194
Heine, S. 186
Herrmann, W. 131
Humm, M. 138
Hunter, A.G. 27, 167

Ihde, D. 113, 133
Irigaray, L. 20, 25, 27, 32, 184
Iser, W. 30

Jasper, A.E. 27, 167
Jasper, D. 173

Kaftan, J. 131
Kant, E. 133
Käsemann, E. 24, 162, 166-69, 181, 230
Klein, R.D. 21
Knowles, D. 35
Kristeva, J. 10, 17, 25, 27-30, 79, 80, 83,
     84, 85, 165, 167, 207, 210, 213-16,
     218-24, 226-29, 231, 232, 241, 242

La Bonnardière, A.-M. 35
Lacan, J. 13, 32, 166, 213, 217, 219,
     220, 225, 227
Lamphere, L. 185
Laplanche, J. 148
Lee Benton, L. 222
Lehmann, M.E. 111
Lévi-Strauus, C. 215
Lienhard, M. 90, 102
Lindars, B. 170, 171, 173, 191, 192, 202,
     225, 228, 230
Lloyd, G. 37
Loades, A. 16, 111, 186, 208
Lorde, A. 25, 141, 142, 156-59

Macquarie, J. 131
Macrae, G.W. 173, 174, 177
Marx, K. 26, 133
McKinlay, J. 39
Migne, J.-P. 59, 64
Moi, T. 28, 30, 84, 125, 220, 228
Moore, C. 246

Neumann, E. 16
Newman, B. 59, 61-65, 78, 80
Nickell, J. 204
Nietzsche, F. 26, 133

O'Carroll, M. 95, 96, 103
Oakes, E.T. 135, 136, 140, 146
Oberman, H.A. 105, 109
Ogden, S.M. 118, 119, 122, 132
Ortner, S. 185

Ostriker, A.S. 243-46

Pagels, E. 208
Pelikan, J. 87, 88, 90-94, 97-104, 107,
     109, 110
Pine-Coffin, R.S. 35
Pontalis, J.-B. 148
Przywara, E. 143, 146

Rettig, J.W. 34, 45, 46
Rich, A. 25
Riches, J. 11, 132
Ricoeur, P. 25-27, 113-15, 120, 122,
     132, 133, 167
Roberts, R.C. 113-16, 130, 131
Rosaldo, M. 185
Ruether, R.R. 16, 17, 184

Saussure, F. 215
Schipperge, H. 58
Schnackenburg, R. 170, 171, 176, 191,
     192, 195, 196, 198, 200, 204, 207,
     230
Schweizer, E. 200, 204
Scott, M. 40
Sellers, S. 13, 21, 235
Seim, T.K. 208
Singer, C. 61
Speyr, A. von 23, 25, 135-60, 163, 206,
     234, 239
Stanton, E.C. 14
Steinmetz, D. 94, 109
Stibbe, M.W.G. 171, 173

Tilborg, S. van 73, 175-78
Trible, P. 14, 17
Turner, V. 128

Warner, M. 19, 63, 96, 97, 106
Werneke, A. 64
West, A. 186
Wilson, I. 136, 137, 204, 205
Wimsatt, W.K. Jr 29
Woolf, V. 32

Yarom, N. 148
Yates, F.A. 68

Zarb. S. 35

GENERAL INDEX

Abelard, Peter 62
abjection, the abject 218, 223, 225, 226,
    227, 229, 232, 241
Abraham 65, 73
Adam 49, 63, 66, 76, 80, 92, 140, 185,
    205, 244
address 114, 116, 117, 119, 122, 132,
    163-64
agape 223, 229
Alaric 35
Albertus Magnus 68
Alcuin 63
Ammonius 198
analogical thinking 146
Anastasius IV, Pope 61
Anfechtungen 94
angel, angels 35, 108, 243, 244, 246
Angstbereitschaft 116
Annunciation, the 81, 103
Anselm of Canterbury 62, 66
Apocrypha 38, 39, 70, 71
Aquinas, St Thomas 62, 68, 83
Arians 35
Aristotle 175
Arius 88, 89
artificial memory 68, 69
asceticism 79, 100, 106, 110, 240
Augustine of Hippo 22, 34-57, 63, 77,
    79, 163, 234, 236-37
—view of reason and rationality 37-38,
    68
Augustinian tradition 22, 74, 75, 81, 82,
    101, 107, 123, 153, 162, 238, 240

baptism 47, 74, 155, 177, 191, 194
Bernard of Clairvaux 20, 63, 96, 97

Bingen, Hildegard von 22, 25, 58-86,
    94, 103, 162, 163, 204, 234, 237
birth 19, 42, 43, 44, 46, 54, 56, 75, 82,
    100, 120, 122, 125, 143-45, 153-
    55, 158, 159, 179, 184, 188, 190,
    191, 228, 236, 239, 246
—in Christ 56
blind man 236
blindness 44-47, 130, 157, 237
blood 99, 101, 110, 126, 190, 195, 198,
    205, 229
body 22, 28, 52, 63, 64, 65, 75-78, 85,
    93, 100, 110, 144, 150-52, 160,
    162, 163, 165, 166, 168, 185, 187,
    189, 194, 197, 198, 202-205, 208,
    209, 216, 218, 230-32, 235-38,
    241, 246
Boethius 62
Bonaventure 83
bread 197, 199, 200, 208
bride 150
Brigit 246

canon, canonical 181, 183, 196, 243
Cathars, the 78, 204
Catherine of Bora 105
Catherine of Genoa 206
celibacy 107
Chalcedon, Council of 19, 184, 239
Charlemagne 63
child, children 75, 93, 105, 106, 111,
    130, 144, 145, 153-55, 180, 188,
    189, 192, 195, 196, 217, 218, 223,
    224, 226-29, 237
chora 217
Christ
—as mother 237

—divinity of 19, 20, 107, 112, 163
—the physician 36, 45, 46
—son of Mary 99, 100
Christology 88, 90, 101, 112, 168, 221
church 26, 34, 37, 49, 53, 81, 89, 94,
        95, 104, 105, 108, 121, 122, 141,
        142, 147, 154, 155, 157, 158, 169,
        186, 205, 205, 207, 208, 221, 239
Cicero 68
Clement of Alexandria 198, 202
community 15, 112, 119, 154, 155,
        167, 194, 196, 209
—of St John 135
conception 143, 144
concupiscence 22, 43, 49, 56, 68, 75
confession 147, 151, 157, 230
Conrad III, King 62
Constantine, Emperor 34
conversion hysteria 148
Cornelisz, Jacob 205
Corpus Christi 204, 206
cosmos 63, 64, 66, 68, 78, 94, 170, 178,
        212
counter-coherences 18, 24
creation 63, 65, 67, 70, 78, 81, 83, 85,
        141, 162, 210, 223, 227, 237, 244,
        245
creation stories 20, 243, 246, 247
cross 16, 109, 232
crucifixion 16, 17, 23, 132, 136, 143,
        144, 146, 147, 149, 150, 152, 158,
        167, 204

death 73, 74, 80, 82, 95, 101, 107, 108,
        153, 166, 185, 197, 212
deconstruction 26, 164, 180
demythologization 23, 113, 114, 116,
        117, 121, 132
desire 52, 55, 73, 76, 163, 165, 166, 177,
        179, 181, 184, 185, 192, 195, 218,
        219, 223-25, 228, 234, 236, 237-43
dialogism 28, 152
difference 25, 185, 194, 211, 221, 222,
        236
Disibodenburg, Monastery of 59, 60, 62
divine gaze, the 139
divine Mother of all souls 81
divine, divinity 24, 78, 80, 85, 110, 118,

        119, 121, 126-29, 143, 147, 150,
        162, 164, 171, 179, 181, 182, 191,
        192, 209, 214, 221, 236, 237
Doceticism 166-69, 201, 204
Donatists 35, 37
Dormition 96
dualism 34, 73, 77, 78, 95, 127, 129,
        153, 180, 186-89, 194, 197, 201,
        228, 229
Dürr, E. 135

Ebion 88
Ecclesia 63
écriture féminine 21, 27
Eleanor of Aquitaine 62
Elizabeth, cousin to Mary 102, 103, 111
Erasmus 97
Erfurt, University of 88, 89
Erigena 66
eros 223
erotic, the 156, 157, 160
eschatology 132
Eucharist, Eucharistic practice and
        theology 79, 80, 90, 110, 111,
        147, 198-201, 203, 204, 206-208,
        230, 231, 246
Eugenius III, Pope 62
Eutychus 184
Eve 20, 42, 65, 76, 81, 92, 140, 185,
        205, 244, 245
evil 21, 37, 49, 50, 51, 53, 54, 66, 74,
        78, 185, 187, 192, 193, 220, 225
existential encounter 112, 117, 121
existentialist philosophy 113, 131, 201

faith 65, 72, 93, 109, 114, 118, 232
father, fatherhood 100, 123, 125, 145,
        147, 167, 177, 211, 217, 219,
        224-29, 231, 232, 238
female deities 219
feminine divine 71, 72, 82, 238, 246
feminine, the 14, 20, 23-25, 32, 37, 38,
        48, 56, 76, 78, 79, 85, 91, 95, 108,
        111, 118, 124, 126, 127, 129, 141,
        146, 150, 162-65, 179, 181, 183,
        184, 186, 188, 193, 196, 197, 202,
        208, 209, 217, 219, 230, 235, 236,
        238-42, 245-47

flesh (σάρξ) 2, 22-24, 31, 32, 42-45, 47,
48, 57, 68, 71, 75, 76, 78, 80, 85,
91, 92, 95, 96, 99, 106, 108, 109,
123-28, 149, 151, 155, 163, 164,
178, 183-90, 192, 193, 196-99,
201-203, 206, 208, 209, 211, 212,
222, 229-31, 239-41, 247
—born of the 41, 44, 56, 188, 189
—eyes of the 37
—of Mary 101
—will of the 36, 56
focalization 24, 169
Francis of Assisi 20, 89, 98, 136, 148,
205
Frederick Barbarossa 62

garment 68, 78, 84, 234, 240
gender hierarchy 21, 42
gender symbolism 24, 48, 129, 140, 189,
196, 201, 209, 215
Genesis 37, 65, 74, 169, 170, 172, 185,
211, 225, 243, 244, 246
Germanus of Constantinople 96
Gnosticism 120, 128, 202
God 24, 35, 36, 55, 65, 68, 70, 90, 91,
109, 119, 125, 129, 138, 142, 144,
152-56, 166, 167, 170, 171, 175,
180, 184, 187, 192, 195, 210, 211,
225, 227-30, 236, 238, 239, 240,
243, 246
—born of 44, 154
—creator 57, 69, 152, 169, 174, 211
—made in image of 37, 51
—word of 68, 69, 82, 88, 91, 102, 121,
142, 153, 223
God's glory 73, 167
God's wrath 107
Godfrey of Disibodenburg 59
good 53, 70, 74, 94, 154, 184
Gospel of Luke 98, 103, 120, 122, 172
Gospel of Matthew 98, 120, 122
grace 35, 36, 46, 49, 52, 98, 109, 110,
187, 230
greenness 85

Hadrian IV, Pope 61
handmaid, the 146
Hebrew Bible 20, 26, 226, 243

Heidegger, Martin 23, 113, 120, 131,
133
Henry II of England 62
Heracleon 202
hermeneutic circle 113, 122
hermeneutic of suspicion 25, 134
hermeneutics 115, 116, 119, 121
heterogeneity 25, 27, 44, 52, 80, 213,
216, 218-20, 229-32, 241
hiddenness 110, 111, 128, 144, 152, 153
hierarchy, hierarchical relationships 21,
42, 47, 55, 73, 77, 85, 124, 130,
140, 141, 149-51, 160, 163, 167,
180, 187, 189, 190, 196, 198, 201,
205, 207, 209, 215, 234, 236, 238,
242
Hippolytus 194
History of Religions school of
interpretation 131
Holy Spirit/Ghost 61, 62, 72, 74, 75, 81,
82, 103, 120, 121, 145, 158, 188,
192, 223
Honorius of Regensberg 66
human form 64, 65, 67, 69, 75
human, the 80, 126, 147, 164, 181, 214,
220, 221, 222, 232, 236, 237
humanity 23, 24, 64, 73, 77, 78, 93, 94,
97, 99, 101, 104, 109, 117, 118,
123, 130, 141, 150, 164, 166, 167,
170, 179, 180, 190, 191, 196, 208,
209, 219, 229, 236, 238, 239, 241
—of Jesus/Christ/Word 19, 20, 22, 54,
73, 74, 82, 88, 99-101, 111, 112,
163, 176, 178, 184, 232, 236, 239
humankind 76, 102, 103, 105, 127, 130,
141, 151, 166, 178, 180, 188, 191,
210, 236, 239, 243

imagination 177, 178, 221, 231-33
Immaculate Conception 95, 101
implied reader 30
Incarnation 19, 23, 24, 44-48, 54, 55,
63, 64, 66-68, 71, 73, 77, 80, 83,
85, 93, 94, 96, 102, 111, 126, 128,
130, 147, 149, 150, 155, 158, 163,
184, 192, 204, 209, 214, 215, 221,
222, 231, 236-39, 247
indulgences 108

inedia 80, 203, 204-205
infans 226, 227
intentionality 29-31, 172, 210
Intercession of Christ and the Virgin, the
    205
intertextuality 17, 22, 27, 28, 65, 140,
    147, 148, 152, 160, 232, 234
Irene, Empress 62
irony 24, 173-175, 177, 178, 180, 181
Israelites 56

Jacob 243, 245
Jerome 19, 107
Jesus 67, 129-31, 164, 176, 177-79, 190,
    211, 221, 223, 225, 229, 239, 246
Jesus Christ 187
Jesus of History school of theology 131
Jesus-Sophia 40
John the Baptist 36, 69, 70, 93, 98, 146,
    164, 174-77, 179, 180, 227, 241
John the Evangelist 36, 41, 58, 91, 97-
    99, 109
John, the beloved disciple 144
jouissance 21, 77, 84, 218, 229, 243
Jovinian 54
judgment 122, 162
Julian of Eclanum 52, 53
Juliana of Liége 204
justice 63, 72
Jutta of Disibodenburg 60

Kaegi, W. 135
kerygma 168, 169
kinship 121, 124
kiss 72, 73, 97

labour (childbirth) 143, 145, 151
language 25, 28, 121, 214, 219, 220,
    224, 226, 227, 229, 231, 241, 242
law 49, 51, 109, 165, 185, 187, 188,
    214, 219, 222, 226, 230
Leo X, Pope 109
Leviticus 219
light 36, 70, 89, 93, 98, 138, 140, 147,
    157-59, 223, 225-27, 231
Lilith 244, 245
liminality 128, 129
logic of identity 13, 21, 23, 216

love 62, 63, 65, 71, 81, 90, 109, 110,
    118, 129, 144, 145, 147, 149, 150,
    153, 156-58, 167, 203, 214, 222,
    228, 229, 232, 239
Lucifer 74
Luther, Martin 22, 87-112, 114, 122,
    163, 234, 238, 240

man (generic) ἄνθρωπος 174, 179, 180,
    193, 195, 196, 231, 232, 239, 241
man (not woman) ἀνήρ 179
Manes 88
Manichaean philosophy 22, 34, 48, 52,
    53, 94
Manichaeans 35, 88
Mansi, Giovanni Domenico 59
Marcion 202
Margaret of Cortona 206
marginalization, marginality 20-22, 85,
    124, 184, 189, 201
Marian traditions 20, 22, 104
marriage 42, 43, 53-55, 105, 107, 143,
    149, 150, 153, 155, 181, 238, 244,
    245
Martha of Bethany 180, 194
Mary 65, 82, 93, 97-99, 101-104, 106,
    108, 111, 146, 205, 246
Mary Magdalene 194
Mary of Nazareth 102
Mary
—her consent 95, 104, 141, 146, 147,
    162
—mediatrix 96, 97
—mother 42, 63, 77, 95, 97, 103, 104,
    136
—the new Eve 19, 20
—the Virgin 73, 81, 99, 238
masculine, the 48, 78, 164, 174, 179,
    181, 217, 219, 225, 242
masculinity,
—of God 48, 54, 141, 208
—of Jesus 40
Mass of St Gregory, the 205
materiality 73, 80, 166, 178, 189, 197,
    237, 238, 240
maternal, the 73, 111, 203, 228, 229,
    241, 242
midrash 244, 245

migraine attacks 61
milk 41, 42, 47, 63, 106, 198, 225, 237
mind 43, 232
mirror stage 227, 228
mirrors 32
misogynism 37, 38, 83, 91, 188
mitzvah 245
Mohammed 88
Monica 48
Monk of Farne, the 205
Montanus 202, 202
Moses 49, 51, 91, 93, 188, 230
mother 41, 46, 47, 73, 106, 108, 110,
　　　122-24, 155, 165, 180, 217-19,
　　　223, 224, 225, 226, 227-28, 238,
　　　240
Mother Church 63, 77, 106
Mother of God 81, 141, 143, 147
mother of Jesus 44, 146
motherhood 85, 146
multiplicity 18, 23, 24, 27, 110, 164,
　　　184, 185, 203, 207, 211, 214, 216,
　　　217, 232, 236
mysticism 137, 138
myth, mythology 114, 115, 122-24, 132,
　　　133, 141, 142, 165, 167, 172, 178,
　　　179, 182, 185, 215, 226, 241
mythology, Christian 17, 120, 123, 131
—Gnostic 128
—pagan 16

nakedness, exposure 17, 18, 139-41, 147
narcissism 119
Neoplatonism 34, 35, 66, 89
New Testament 15, 16, 26, 36, 119,
　　　131, 187, 189, 207, 208
Nichtigkeit 124, 239
Nicodemus 190, 191
nominalism 89
normative masculinity 38, 75, 118, 179,
　　　196
Novatus 88
nursing mother 41, 42, 47, 58, 63, 72,
　　　97, 104, 106, 205, 237

obedience 81, 82, 85, 118, 119, 129,
　　　141, 143, 146, 151, 157, 162, 240
Occam, William of 89, 90

Oedipal conflict 227
offence 127-29
Old Testament 20, 38
orthodoxy, 22, 24, 35, 77, 83, 87, 95,
　　　117, 168, 169, 170, 178, 186, 202
otherness, the other 21, 23, 44, 48, 55,
　　　56, 101, 125, 127, 129, 130, 164,
　　　167, 180, 181, 183, 189, 212, 219,
　　　225, 228, 234-36, 238, 240, 243

Padre Pio 137, 206
parent(s), parenthood 123, 143
patriarchy 25, 115, 117, 129, 151, 155,
　　　165, 166, 172, 178, 179, 181, 183,
　　　195, 196, 207, 238, 244, 245
Paul, the apostle 41, 49, 62, 114
Pauline literature 186-88, 194
Pelagianism 52, 53
Pelagius 34, 53, 88
perverse, the 24, 160, 230, 237, 238, 240
Abelard, Peter 62
phallocentric, the 20, 25-27, 128, 141,
　　　164, 166, 169, 184, 186, 188, 193,
　　　197, 201, 207, 210, 212, 220, 234,
　　　235, 238-41, 247
phallocracy 16, 17
Philo 37, 198
Pilate 174
Platonic thought 34, 53, 62
pleasure 25, 27, 49, 83, 84, 153, 214,
　　　218, 240, 243, 245
Plotinus 34
poetry 156, 158-59, 243-247
Eugenius III, Pope 61
Porphyry 34
postmodernism, literary theory 18
postmodernism, philosophy and
　　　philosophers 18
power, empowerment 24, 30, 49, 65,
　　　105, 129, 138, 150, 154, 155, 156,
　　　157, 178, 182, 189, 195, 220, 228,
　　　242, 243, 244
pre-existence 40, 89, 115, 120, 180, 222
priesthood 96, 144
Psalms 211
psychoanalysis 18, 148, 165, 214, 217,
　　　218, 221, 223, 226, 231, 232, 242

Quintillian 68
Quirizio of Murano 205

reason, rationality 21, 37, 38, 51, 65, 74,
    78, 83, 88, 91, 93, 108, 137, 138,
    217, 220, 240
Richard of St Victor 61
Rumpelstiltskin 108
Rupertsberg, Convent at 61

sacrament 110, 142, 144, 145, 147, 155,
    157, 204
sado-masochism 17
Santa Sophia, Cathedral of 63
sapiential themes 22, 70-72, 85
scholasticism 89
Scotus, Duns 95
semananalysis 29, 215, 217, 232
semen 55, 244, 245
semiotic, the 27, 28, 129, 148, 165, 215-
    17, 224, 226, 227, 229, 241, 242
Septuagint 222
sexual intercourse 51, 54, 55, 74, 76
sexuality 51, 52, 54, 55, 73, 75, 76, 94,
    107, 121, 124, 143, 144, 162, 185,
    186, 191, 192, 195, 197, 219, 229,
    235
significance 30, 243
sin 36, 49, 66, 73, 74, 80-82, 93, 95,
    102, 108, 110, 147, 183, 191, 225,
    230, 239
singularity 22, 52, 110, 119, 125, 185,
    209, 211, 234-236, 238, 239, 241
Society of Jesus 135
Solomon 39
Son 125, 145
Son of David 121
Son of God 40, 73, 100, 120, 185
Son of Man 126
Son of Mary 121
soul 43, 48, 51, 59, 64, 65, 68, 72, 75,
    77, 78, 81, 85, 93, 185, 203, 216
spirit (πνεῦμα) 125, 189
spirit, spiritual 42, 43, 45, 46, 144, 149,
    150, 155, 160, 187-89, 191, 192,
    197, 202, 203, 207
stigmata 23, 136, 137, 147, 147-52, 155,
    203, 205, 240

structuralism 164, 165, 213, 215
subjectivity 24, 29, 167, 214, 216-18,
    220-23, 227-32, 241
suffering 23, 25, 48, 79, 136, 141-43,
    147, 150-53, 160, 162, 163, 208,
    210, 215, 233, 240, 246
sujet en procès 24, 29, 211, 214, 217, 224,
    226, 241
suttee 138
synergetic theology 81, 108
Synoptic Gospels 102, 119, 202

Tamar, sister of Amnon 14
Temple, the 230
text 29-31, 108, 114, 119, 164, 202,
    210, 214, 233, 234, 243, 245, 247
—biblical 13, 14, 17, 18, 20-22, 24, 26,
    30, 116, 131, 140, 162, 164, 172,
    219, 229, 240, 242, 243, 245
—Johannine 19, 23, 24, 44, 73, 87, 123,
    133, 144, 171, 201,
Theodoric of Echternach 59
Theotokos 96
Torah 40, 187, 226, 243
Trent, Council of 100
Trier, Synod of 61
Trinity, Trinitarian 80, 87, 88, 145, 146,
    149, 162, 239
truth 49, 211, 230, 234, 235, 239
two natures of Christ 19, 90, 184, 239
tyranny 18, 48

unconscious, the 217, 227, 231
Urban IV, Pope 204

Valentius 202
Vater der personlichen Vorzeit (father of
    individual pre-history) 217, 219,
    228
victim 144, 150
virgin 44, 63, 74, 75, 82, 85, 105, 108,
    240
virginity 44, 54, 96, 100, 107, 141, 163
visions, visionary experience 58, 59, 61,
    203, 204
voyeurism 140

William of Conches 62

Wisdom literature 38-40, 70, 122
Wisdom, figure of 20, 38-40, 42, 62, 63,
      66, 70-72, 77, 80, 83, 162, 212,
      237
Wittenberg 87
woman 14, 20, 23, 24, 37, 38, 56, 76,
      85, 91, 95, 106, 119, 124, 125,
      129-31, 140, 141, 144, 150, 163,
      166, 183, 186, 188, 193, 208, 209,
      219, 225, 235, 239, 240, 247
—clothed with the sun 143
—centred 25, 26, 247

womb 102, 190
word (λόγος) 19, 23, 24, 35, 39, 47, 63,
      65, 67, 68, 73, 74, 78, 80, 82, 91-
      94, 106, 108, 113, 121, 123, 125,
      129, 130, 145, 149, 150, 151, 152,
      162-64, 168, 170, 171, 177, 183-
      86, 188, 192, 193, 197-99, 201,
      203, 211, 215, 221-23, 227-29,
      231, 232, 237, 239, 241, 247
world 35, 131, 192

JOURNAL FOR THE STUDY OF THE NEW TESTAMENT
SUPPLEMENT SERIES

1   William R. Telford, *The Barren Temple and the Withered Tree: A Redaction-Critical Analysis of the Cursing of the Fig-Tree Pericope in Mark's Gospel and its Relation to the Cleansing of the Temple Tradition*

2   E.A. Livingstone (ed.), *Studia Biblica 1978, II: Papers on the Gospels (Sixth International Congress on Biblical Studies, Oxford, 1978)*

3   E.A. Livingstone (ed.), *Studia Biblica 1978, III: Papers on Paul and Other New Testament Authors (Sixth International Congress on Biblical Studies, Oxford, 1978)*

4   Ernest Best, *Following Jesus: Discipleship in the Gospel of Mark*

5   Markus Barth, *The People of God*

6   John S. Pobee, *Persecution and Martyrdom in the Theology of Paul*

7   Christopher M. Tuckett (ed.), *Synoptic Studies: The Ampleforth Conferences of 1982 and 1983*

8   Terence L. Donaldson, *Jesus on the Mountain: A Study in Matthean Theology*

9   Stephen Farris, *The Hymns of Luke's Infancy Narratives: Their Origin, Meaning and Significance*

10   R. Badenas, *Christ the End of the Law: Romans 10.4 in Pauline Perspective*

11   Colin J. Hemer, *The Letters to the Seven Churches of Asia in their Local Setting*

12   Darrell L. Bock, *Proclamation from Prophecy and Pattern: Lucan Old Testament Christology*

13   Roger P. Booth, *Jesus and the Laws of Purity: Tradition History and Legal History in Mark 7*

14   Marion L. Soards, *The Passion According to Luke: The Special Material of Luke 22*

15   Thomas E. Schmidt, *Hostility to Wealth in the Synoptic Gospels*

16   Stephenson H. Brooks, *Matthew's Community: The Evidence of his Special Sayings Material*

17   Anthony Tyrrell Hanson, *The Paradox of the Cross in the Thought of St Paul*

18   Celia Deutsch, *Hidden Wisdom and the Easy Yoke: Wisdom, Torah and Discipleship in Matthew 11.25-30*

19   Larry J. Kreitzer, *Jesus and God in Paul's Eschatology*

20   Michael D. Goulder, *Luke: A New Paradigm*

21   Mikeal C. Parsons, *The Departure of Jesus in Luke–Acts: The Ascension Narratives in Context*

22   Martinus C. de Boer, *The Defeat of Death: Apocalyptic Eschatology in 1 Corinthians 15 and Romans 5*

23   Michael Prior, *Paul the Letter-Writer and the Second Letter to Timothy*

24   Joel Marcus & Marion L. Soards (eds.), *Apocalyptic and the New Testament: Essays in Honor of J. Louis Martyn*

25   David E. Orton, *The Understanding Scribe: Matthew and the Apocalyptic Ideal*

26   Timothy J. Geddert, *Watchwords: Mark 13 in Markan Eschatology*

27   Clifton C. Black, *The Disciples According to Mark: Markan Redaction in Current Debate*

28   David Seeley, *The Noble Death: Graeco-Roman Martyrology and Paul's Concept of Salvation*

29   G. Walter Hansen, *Abraham in Galatians: Epistolary and Rhetorical Contexts*

30   Frank Witt Hughes, *Early Christian Rhetoric and 2 Thessalonians*

31   David R. Bauer, *The Structure of Matthew's Gospel: A Study in Literary Design*

32   Kevin Quast, *Peter and the Beloved Disciple: Figures for a Community in Crisis*

33   Mary Ann Beavis, *Mark's Audience: The Literary and Social Setting of Mark 4.11-12*

34   Philip H. Towner, *The Goal of our Instruction: The Structure of Theology and Ethics in the Pastoral Epistles*

35   Alan P. Winton, *The Proverbs of Jesus: Issues of History and Rhetoric*

36   Stephen E. Fowl, *The Story of Christ in the Ethics of Paul: An Analysis of the Function of the Hymnic Material in the Pauline Corpus*

37   A.J.M. Wedderburn (ed.), *Paul and Jesus: Collected Essays*

38   Dorothy Jean Weaver, *Matthew's Missionary Discourse: A Literary Critical Analysis*

39   Glenn N. Davies, *Faith and Obedience in Romans: A Study in Romans 1–4*

40   Jerry L. Sumney, *Identifying Paul's Opponents: The Question of Method in 2 Corinthians*

41   Mary E. Mills, *Human Agents of Cosmic Power in Hellenistic Judaism and the Synoptic Tradition*

42   David B. Howell, *Matthew's Inclusive Story: A Study in the Narrative Rhetoric of the First Gospel*

43   Heikki Räisänen, *Jesus, Paul and Torah: Collected Essays* (trans. D.E. Orton)

44   Susanne Lehne, *The New Covenant in Hebrews*

45   Neil Elliott, *The Rhetoric of Romans: Argumentative Constraint and Strategy and Paul's Dialogue with Judaism*

46   John O. York, *The Last Shall Be First: The Rhetoric of Reversal in Luke*

47   Patrick J. Hartin, *James and the Q Sayings of Jesus*

48   William Horbury (ed.), *Templum Amicitiae: Essays on the Second Temple Presented to Ernst Bammel*

49   John M. Scholer, *Proleptic Priests: Priesthood in the Epistle to the Hebrews*

50   Duane F. Watson (ed.), *Persuasive Artistry: Studies in New Testament Rhetoric in Honor of George A. Kennedy*

51   Jeffrey A. Crafton, *The Agency of the Apostle: A Dramatistic Analysis of Paul's Responses to Conflict in 2 Corinthians*

52   Linda L. Belleville, *Reflections of Glory: Paul's Polemical Use of the Moses–Doxa Tradition in 2 Corinthians 3.1-18*

53   Thomas J. Sappington, *Revelation and Redemption at Colossae*

54   Robert P. Menzies, *The Development of Early Christian Pneumatology, with Special Reference to Luke–Acts*

55   L. Ann Jervis, *The Purpose of Romans: A Comparative Letter Structure Investigation*

56   Delbert Burkett, *The Son of the Man in the Gospel of John*

57   Bruce W. Longenecker, *Eschatology and the Covenant: A Comparison of 4 Ezra and Romans 1–11*

58   David A. Neale, *None but the Sinners: Religious Categories in the Gospel of Luke*

59   Michael Thompson, *Clothed with Christ: The Example and Teaching of Jesus in Romans 12.1–15.13*

60   Stanley E. Porter (ed.), *The Language of the New Testament: Classic Essays*

61   John Christopher Thomas, *Footwashing in John 13 and the Johannine Community*

62   Robert L. Webb, *John the Baptizer and Prophet: A Socio-Historical Study*

63   James S. McLaren, *Power and Politics in Palestine: The Jews and the Governing of their Land, 100 BC–AD 70*

64   Henry Wansborough (ed.), *Jesus and the Oral Gospel Tradition*

65   Douglas A. Campbell, *The Rhetoric of Righteousness in Romans 3.21-26*

66   Nicholas Taylor, *Paul, Antioch and Jerusalem: A Study in Relationships and Authority in Earliest Christianity*

67   F. Scott Spencer, *The Portrait of Philip in Acts: A Study of Roles and Relations*

68   Michael Knowles, *Jeremiah in Matthew's Gospel: The Rejected-Prophet Motif in Matthaean Redaction*

69   Margaret Davies, *Rhetoric and Reference in the Fourth Gospel*

70   J. Webb Mealy, *After the Thousand Years: Resurrection and Judgment in Revelation 20*

71   Martin Scott, *Sophia and the Johannine Jesus*

72   Steven M. Sheeley, *Narrative Asides in Luke–Acts*

73   Marie E. Isaacs, *Sacred Space: An Approach to the Theology of the Epistle to the Hebrews*

74   Edwin K. Broadhead, *Teaching with Authority: Miracles and Christology in the Gospel of Mark*

75   John K. Chow, *Patronage and Power: A Study of Social Networks in Corinth*

76   Robert W. Wall & Eugene E. Lemcio, *The New Testament as Canon: A Reader in Canonical Criticism*

77   Roman Garrison, *Redemptive Almsgiving in Early Christianity*

78   L. Gregory Bloomquist, *The Function of Suffering in Philippians*

79   Blaine Charette, *The Theme of Recompense in Matthew's Gospel*

80   Stanley E. Porter & D.A. Carson (eds.), *Biblical Greek Language and Linguistics: Open Questions in Current Research*

81   In-Gyu Hong, *The Law in Galatians*

82   Barry W. Henaut, *Oral Tradition and the Gospels: The Problem of Mark 4*

83   Craig A. Evans & James A. Sanders (eds.), *Paul and the Scriptures of Israel*

84   Martinus C. de Boer (ed.), *From Jesus to John: Essays on Jesus and New Testament Christology in Honour of Marinus de Jonge*

85   William J. Webb, *Returning Home: New Covenant and Second Exodus as the Context for 2 Corinthians 6.14–7.1*

86   B.H. McLean (ed.), *Origins of Method: Towards a New Understanding of Judaism and Christianity—Essays in Honour of John C. Hurd*

87   Michael J. Wilkins & T. Paige (eds.), *Worship, Theology and Ministry in the Early Church: Essays in Honour of Ralph P. Martin*

88   Mark Coleridge, *The Birth of the Lukan Narrative: Narrative as Christology in Luke 1–2*

89   Craig A. Evans, *Word and Glory: On the Exegetical and Theological Background of John's Prologue*

90   Stanley E. Porter & Thomas H. Olbricht (eds.), *Rhetoric and the New Testament: Essays from the 1992 Heidelberg Conference*

91   Janice Capel Anderson, *Matthew's Narrative Web: Over, and Over, and Over Again*

92   Eric Franklin, *Luke: Interpreter of Paul, Critic of Matthew*

93   Jan Fekkes III, *Isaiah and Prophetic Traditions in the Book of Revelation: Visionary Antecedents and their Development*

94   Charles A. Kimball, *Jesus' Exposition of the Old Testament in Luke's Gospel*

95   Dorothy A. Lee, *The Symbolic Narratives of the Fourth Gospel: The Interplay of Form and Meaning*

96   Richard E. DeMaris, *The Colossian Controversy: Wisdom in Dispute at Colossae*

97   Edwin K. Broadhead, *Prophet, Son, Messiah: Narrative Form and Function in Mark 14–16*

98   Carol J. Schlueter, *Filling up the Measure: Polemical Hyperbole in 1 Thessalonians 2.14-16*

99   Neil Richardson, *Paul's Language about God*

100   Thomas E. Schmidt & M. Silva (eds.), *To Tell the Mystery: Essays on New Testament Eschatology in Honor of Robert H. Gundry*

101   Jeffrey A.D. Weima, *Neglected Endings: The Significance of the Pauline Letter Closings*

102   Joel F. Williams, *Other Followers of Jesus: Minor Characters as Major Figures in Mark's Gospel*

103   Warren Carter, *Households and Discipleship: A Study of Matthew 19–20*

104   Craig A. Evans & W. Richard Stegner (eds.), *The Gospels and the Scriptures of Israel*

105   W.P. Stephens (ed.), *The Bible, the Reformation and the Church: Essays in Honour of James Atkinson*

106   Jon A. Weatherly, *Jewish Responsibility for the Death of Jesus in Luke–Acts*

107   Elizabeth Harris, *Prologue and Gospel: The Theology of the Fourth Evangelist*

108   L. Ann Jervis & Peter Richardson (eds.), *Gospel in Paul: Studies on Corinthians, Galatians and Romans for R.N. Longenecker*

109   Elizabeth Struthers Malbon & Edgar V. McKnight (eds.), *The New Literary Criticism and the New Testament*

110   Mark L. Strauss, *The Davidic Messiah in Luke–Acts: The Promise and its Fulfillment in Lukan Christology*

111   Ian H. Thomson, *Chiasmus in the Pauline Letters*

112   Jeffrey B. Gibson, *The Temptations of Jesus in Early Christianity*
113   Stanley E. Porter & D.A. Carson (eds.), *Discourse Analysis and Other Topics in Biblical Greek*
114   Lauri Thurén, *Argument and Theology in 1 Peter: The Origins of Christian Paraenesis*
115   Steve Moyise, *The Old Testament in the Book of Revelation*
116   Christopher M. Tuckett (ed.), *Luke's Literary Achievement: Collected Essays*
117   Kenneth G.C. Newport, *The Sources and Sitz im Leben of Matthew 23*
118   Troy W. Martin, *By Philosophy and Empty Deceit: Colossians as Response to a Cynic Critique*
119   David Ravens, *Luke and the Restoration of Israel*
120   Stanley E. Porter & David Tombs (eds.), *Approaches to New Testament Study*
121   Todd C. Penner, *The Epistle of James and Eschatology: Re-reading an Ancient Christian Letter*
122   A.D.A. Moses, *Matthew's Transfiguration Story in Jewish-Christian Controversy*
123   David Lertis Matson, *Household Conversion Narratives in Acts: Pattern and Interpretation*
124   David Mark Ball, *'I Am' in John's Gospel: Literary Function, Background and Theological Implications*
125   Robert Gordon Maccini, *Her Testimony is True: Women as Witnesses According to John*
126   B. Hudson Mclean, *The Cursed Christ: Mediterranean Expulsion Rituals and Pauline Soteriology*
127   R. Barry Matlock, *Unveiling the Apocalyptic Paul: Paul's Interpreters and the Rhetoric of Criticism*
128   Timothy Dwyer, *The Motif of Wonder in the Gospel of Mark*
129   Carl Judson Davis, *The Names and Way of the Lord: Old Testament Themes, New Testament Christology*
130   Craig S. Wansink, *Chained in Christ: The Experience and Rhetoric of Paul's Imprisonments*
131   Stanley E. Porter & Thomas H. Olbricht (eds.), *Rhetoric, Scripture and Theology: Essays from the 1994 Pretoria Conference*
132   J. Nelson Kraybill, *Imperial Cult and Commerce in John's Apocalypse*
133   Mark S. Goodacre, *Goulder and the Gospels: An Examination of a New Paradigm*
134   Larry J. Kreitzer, *Striking New Images: Roman Imperial Coinage and the New Testament World*
135   Charles Landon, *A Text-Critical Study of the Epistle of Jude*
136   Jeffrey T. Reed, *A Discourse Analysis of Philippians: Method and Rhetoric in the Debate over Lierary Integrity*
137   Roman Garrison, *The Graeco-Roman Contexts of Early Christian Literature*
138   Kent D. Clarke, *Textual Optimism: The United Bible Societies' Greek New Testament and its Evaluation of Evidence Letter-Ratings*
139   Yong-Eui Yang, *Jesus and the Sabbath in Matthew's Gospel*

140 Tom Yoder Neufeld, *Put on the Armour of God: The Divine Warrior from Isaiah to Ephesians*

141 Rebecca I. Denova, *The Things Accomplished Among Us: Prophetic Tradition in the Structural Pattern of Luke–Acts*

142 Scott Cunningham, *'Through Many Tribulations': The Theology of Persecution in Luke–Acts*

143 Raymond Pickett, *The Cross in Corinth: The Social Significance of the Death of Jesus*

144 S. John Roth, *The Blind, the Lame and the Poor: Character Types in Luke–Acts*

145 Larry Paul Jones, *The Symbol of Water in the Gospel of John*

146 Stanley E. Porter & T.H. Olbricht (eds.), *Rhetorical Analysis of Scripture: Essays from the 1995 London Conference*

147 Kim Paffenroth, *The Story of Jesus According to L*

148 Craig A. Evans and James A. Sanders (eds.), *Early Christian Interpretation of the Scriptures of Israel: Investigations and Proposals*

149 J. Dorcas Gordon, *Sister or Wife?: 1 Corinthians 7 and Cultural Anthropology*

150 J. Daryl Charles, *Virtue Amidst Vice: The Function of the Catalog of Virtues in 2 Peter 1.5-7*

151 Derek Tovey, *Narrative Art and Act in the Fourth Gospel*

152 Evert-Jan Vledder, *Conflict in the Miracle Stories*

153 Christopher Rowland & Crispin H.T. Fletcher-Louis (eds.), *Understanding, Studying and Reading: New Testament Essays in Honour of John Ashton*

154 Craig A. Evans and James A. Sanders (eds.), *The Function of Scripture in Early Jewish and Christian Tradition*

155 Kyoung-Jin Kim, *Stewardship and Almsgiving in Luke's Theology*

156 I.A.H. Combes, *The Metaphor of Slavery in the Writings of the Early Church: From the New Testament to the Begining of the Fifth Century*

158 Jey. J. Kanagaraj, *'Mysticism' in the Gospel of John: An Inquiry into its Background*

159 Brenda Deen Schildgen, *Crisis and Continuity: Time in the Gospel of Mark*

160 Johan Ferreira, *Johannine Ecclesiology*

161 Helen C. Orchard, *Courting Betrayal: Jesus as Victim in the Gospel of John*

162 Jeffrey T. Tucker, *Example Stories: Perspectives on Four Parables in the Gospel of Luke*

163 John A. Darr, *Herod the Fox: Audience Criticism and Lukan Characterization*

164 Bas M.F. Van Iersel, *Mark: A Reader-Response Commentary*

165 Alison Jasper, *The Shining Garmant of the Text: Gendered Readings of John's Prologue*